PLAYBOY'S
COMPLETE BOOK OF
PARTY
JOKES

PLAYBOY'S
COMPLETE BOOK OF
PARTY JOKES

SELECTED BY THE EDITORS OF PLAYBOY
Femlin illustrations by LeRoy Neiman

CASTLE BOOKS

Published simultaneously in the United States and Canada by Playboy Press, Chicago, Illinois. Printed in the United States of America. Library of Congress Catalog Card Number 70–167611. Eleventh Printing.

Designed by Bob Antler

Arrangement has been made to publish this edition by Castle Books, a division of Book Sales Inc. of Secaucus, New Jersey

AUGUST-1981

ISBN No.: 0-89009-405-5

CONTENTS

PLAYBOY'S
COMPLETE BOOK OF
PARTY JOKES

1
THE
YOUNGER
GENERATION

A father was shopping in a department store with his small daughter, when the little girl suddenly pulled on his coat sleeve and said, "Daddy, I gotta go."

"In a few minutes, dear," the father replied.

"I gotta go *now*," the little girl insisted in a very loud voice.

To avoid a scene, a saleslady stepped forward and said, "That's alright, sir, I'll take her."

The saleslady and the little girl hurried off hand in hand. When they returned, the father asked his daughter, "Did you thank the nice lady for being so kind?"

"Why should I thank her?" retorted the little girl, as loud as before, "She had to go too."

The farmer had borrowed a bull from a neighbor to service his two cows. He put the beast in the pasture and instructed his son to keep an eye on them. "As soon as the bull has finished, you come up to the house and tell me," he said.

When the farmer got back to the house, he found the Reverend there paying a social call. They were seated in the front room sipping tea when the boy burst in the door.

"Dad, Dad," he exclaimed, "the bull just————the brown cow!"

Greatly embarrassed, the farmer took his son outside. "Is that any way to talk in front of the Reverend?" he demanded. "Why couldn't you have said the bull *'surprised'* the brown cow? I would've understood. Now go back down to the pasture and come tell me when the bull is finished."

A few minutes later the boy again burst into the room.

"Dad, Dad—" he exclaimed.

Fearing another breach of verbal etiquette, the father interrupted. "I know, I know," he said. "The bull has *surprised* the white cow."

"He sure has," exclaimed the excited boy. "He———the brown cow again!"

A little girl answered the knock on the door of the farmhouse. The caller, a rather troubled looking, middle-aged man, asked to see her father.

"If you've come about the bull," she said, "he's fifty dollars. We have the papers and everything and he's guaranteed."

"Young lady," the man said, "I want to see your father."

"If that's too much," the little girl replied, "we got another bull for twenty-five dollars, and he's guaranteed, too, but he doesn't have any papers."

"Young lady," the man repeated, "I want to see your father!"

"If that's too much," said the little girl, "we got another bull for only ten dollars, but he's not guaranteed."

"I'm not here for a bull," said the man angrily. "I want to talk about your brother, Elmer. He's gotten my daughter in trouble!"

"Oh, I'm sorry," said the little girl. "You'll have to see Pa about that, 'cause I don't know what he charges for Elmer."

The little girl walked into the drugstore and asked the clerk, "Do you fit men for trusses here?" Bewildered but obliging, he replied, "Why, yes, we do."

"Well, wash your hands," said the little girl, "I want a chocolate soda."

"Why don't you smile?" the teacher asked young Johnny.

"I didn't have no breakfast," Johnny replied.

"You poor dear," said the teacher. "But to return to our geography lesson, Johnny: Where is the Polish border?"

"In bed with Mama—that's why I didn't have no breakfast."

The young mother skeptically examined a new educational toy. "Isn't it rather complicated for a small boy?" she asked the salesclerk.

"It's designed to adjust the tot to live in today's world, madam," the shop assistant replied. "Any way he tries to put it together is wrong."

The attractive governess, with her small charge in tow, left the park to visit her boyfriend in his hotel room. They embraced warmly and each longed for intimacy, but there seemed to be little they could do with the child watching. Then the governess hit on an idea.

"Bobby," she said to her small charge, "go look out that window and I will give you a dime for every red hat you see."

Delighted with the new game, Bobby ran to the window and stared intently at the passersby below.

Almost a minute passed before Bobby's voice popped up with, "I see a red hat!"

"That's nice," came the governess' muffled reply.

"There's another one," said the boy a short time later.

"Keep counting," the woman managed to say.

"Oh, governess," Bobby exclaimed suddenly.

"What now?" she asked, breathing heavily.

"I just wanted to tell you that this is going to be the most expensive roll in the hay you've ever had, 'cause here comes a Shriners Parade!"

One evening at dinner the small boy asked how he had been brought into the world. His father, a rather straightlaced gentleman, tried to dismiss the question with a reference to the stork. Unsatisfied, the youngster asked where the father had come from.

"The stork brought me, too, son," the father replied.

The boy sat quietly for a few moments. Then: "What about Grandfather?" he asked.

"Yes, the stork brought your Grandfather, too," father snapped, about to lose patience with his son for posing questions that were obviously none of a small boy's business.

"Gee, dad," the child exclaimed, "do you mean this family has gone through three generations without any sexual intercourse?"

A middle-aged woman stood watching a little boy on the curb, smoking a cigarette and drinking from a bottle of Scotch. Finally, unable to bear it any longer, she stalked up to the lad and demanded, "Why aren't you in school at this time of day?"

"Hell, lady," said the boy, gulping again from the bottle, "I'm only four years old."

The kindly old gentleman was visiting the home of his daughter. He entered the room of his two grandsons and found them busy studying at their desks. The first boy was reading a book on aviation.

"What do you want to be when you grow up?" asked the grandfather.

"A pilot, sir," said the boy.

"And what do you want to be when you grow up?" the old gentleman asked the second lad.

The boy looked up from the latest issue of PLAYBOY. "Nothing, sir," he said wistfully, "just growed up."

We were enjoying one of the more sensational Italian films the other evening, and during a torrid love scene we heard a small voice near us in the darkened theater say, "Mommy, is this where he puts the pollen on her?"

A spinster schoolteacher took her fifth-grade charges on a field trip to a country fair. There was a race track on the grounds and she asked them whether they would enjoy seeing the horses. The children enthusiastically exclaimed they would, but as soon as she got them inside the gate, they all requested to be taken to the lavatory. She accompanied the little girls, but sent the boys to the men's room alone. They trooped out almost immediately and announced that the facilities were too high for them to reach.

The situation was an awkward one, but after looking about to make sure she was unobserved, the teacher ushered the boys back in. She lined them up before the plumbing and moved methodically down the line. After lifting several, she came to one who was unusually heavy.

"Goodness," she exclaimed, "are you in the fifth?"

"Hell no, lady," came the startled reply. "I'm riding Blue Grass in the third."

A middle-aged friend of ours says he can't understand all the excitement over the movie version of *Lolita*. "I didn't see anything in it that could be considered even vaguely sensational," he told us, "and neither did my twelve-year-old wife."

George was describing his new secretary enthusiastically to the family at dinner: "She's efficient, personable, clever, punctual, and darned attractive, to boot. In short, she's a real doll!"

"A doll?" said his wife.

"A doll!" re-emphasized George.

At which point, their five-year-old daughter, who knew about dolls, looked up from her broccoli to ask: "And does she close her eyes when you lay her down, Daddy?"

Wee Willie was walking with Wanda, his new girlfriend, carrying her books home from grammar school. Both were eight years old.

"Wanda," said Wee Willie with worshiping gaze, "you are the first girl I have ever loved."

"Dammit," said Wanda, "I've drawn another beginner!"

Two little boys were engaging in the traditional verbal battle of little boys everywhere:

"My father is better than your father!"

"No, he's not!"

"My brother is better than your brother!"

"No, he's not!"

"My mother is better than your mother!"

A pause.

"Well, I guess you've got me there. My father says the same thing."

Bobby's mother had been away for a few weeks and was questioning her small son about events during her absence.

"Well," said the boy, "one night we had an awful thunderstorm. It was so bad that I got scared, and so Daddy and me slept together."

"Bobby," said Babette, the boy's pretty French nursemaid, "you mean 'Daddy and I.' "

"No, I don't," exclaimed Bobby. "That was last Thursday. I'm talking about Monday night."

One day in school young Johnny wrote on the blackboard, "Johnny is a passionate devil." The teacher reprimanded him for this act, and made him stay after school for one hour. When he finally left the school that evening, all his friends crowded about him, eager to hear what punishment he had received. "What did she do to you?" asked one little tyke.

"I ain't sayin' nothin'," Johnny replied, "except that it pays to advertise."

The grade-school principal dropped into the new third-grade teacher's room to see how she was adjusting to her first day of school. "There *is* one problem," she said. "That little boy in the first row belongs in second grade, but insists on remaining here, and he's so smart I hate to send him back."

"He can't be *that* smart," said the principal. "Ask him something."

The teacher called the boy forward and inquired, "What does a dog do on three legs that a man does on two legs that I do sitting down?"

"Shakes hands," said the boy.

"What has a cow got four of that I have only two of?" she went on.

"Legs," the boy replied.

"What is a four-letter word meaning intercourse?" she continued.

"Talk," he answered.

The teacher turned to the principal. "Well, what should I do?"

He drew her aside and whispered, "Better promote him to the *fourth* grade. *I* missed all *three* questions."

A stern father was taking his little son Johnny for a walk in the park when suddenly a honeybee settled on a rock in front of them. Just for spite, the boy smashed it with a rock, whereupon his father said, "That was cruel, and for being cruel you'll get no honey for a whole year."

Later, Johnny deliberately stepped on a butterfly. "And for that, young man," said the father, "you'll get no butter for a year."

When they returned home, Johnny's mother was busy fixing dinner. Just as they entered the kitchen, she spied a cockroach and immediately crushed it. The little boy looked at his father impishly, and said: "Shall I tell her, Dad, or will you?"

The pretty young schoolteacher was concerned about one of her eleven-year-old students. Taking him aside after class one day, she asked, "Victor, why has your schoolwork been so poor lately?"

"I can't concentrate," replied the lad. "I'm afraid I've fallen in love."

"Is that so?" said the teacher, holding back an urge to smile. "And with whom?"

"With you," he answered.

"But Victor," exclaimed the secretly pleased young lady, "don't you see how silly that is? It's true that I would like a husband of my own someday; but I don't want a child."

"Oh, don't worry," said Victor reassuringly. "I'll be careful."

A newspaperman, in Atlantic City for the Miss America Pageant, was seated in a boardwalk bistro when a lovely young blonde sat down beside him. They began to chat and, after a number of drinks, he proposed that they buy a bottle and finish it in his room. She was agreeable—so much so, in fact, that before the bottle was half finished, she began to undress. Before she got into bed, the newspaperman casually asked her how old she was.

"Thirteen," she replied.

"Thirteen? Good Lord!" he exclaimed. "Put your clothes on and get out of here!"

"What's the matter?" asked the girl, pouting. "Superstitious?"

The young kindergarten teacher had just instructed her charges to come forward as their names were called and be prepared to draw something on the blackboard that had been the cause of excitement in their homes during the previous week. One by one the pupils came forward and sketched such items as report cards, television sets, mothers' new hats, and the like. When it came time for Johnny, the class cutup, to comply with the assignment, however, he walked to the board and simply made two white dots before returning to his seat. Suspecting that he was up to one of his usual pranks, the teacher advised Johnny that he had better be able to explain why those two dots were exciting if he didn't want to be kept after school.

"Well," said Johnny, "the other day you told us that those dots are also called periods—"

"That's correct," the teacher interrupted. "But what could possibly be exciting about two periods?"

"Beats me," replied Johnny. "But that's how many my sister in high school says she's missed, and they're causing an awful lot of excitement around our house!"

"Tell me, Tommy," the elderly schoolmarm inquired of one of her fifth-grade students, "if you started with twenty dollars and gave seven of them to Nancy, five to Mary and eight to Judy, what would you then have?"

"A ball!" answered Tommy.

The Sunday-school teacher asked her class of youngsters if they could name any of the Ten Commandments and one kindergarten-aged boy stood up and announced proudly: "Thou shalt not omit adultery."

The expectant mother was in her seventh month when she decided to break the news to her small son.

"Darling," she said, "if you could have your choice, which would you like to have—a little brother or a little sister?"

"Well," said the child, "if it wouldn't put you too much out of shape, I'd really prefer a pony."

The precocious six year old, who had just completed his first day in the second grade at a progressive school, suddenly asked his parents, "What is sex?"

After an embarrassed pause, they finally managed to stammer out an explanation of the birds and the bees.

Puzzled, the tot pulled a school questionnaire from his pocket and asked, "How am I going to put all that information in this little space marked 'sex'?"

A little girl stared with fascination at the pregnant woman walking alongside her in the park. "What's that?" she asked, pointing to the woman's blossoming stomach.

"That's my own sweet baby," said the mother-to-be.

"Do you love him?" asked the child.

"Of course I do," the woman said, "I love him very much."

Whereupon the little girl exclaimed accusingly, "Then how come you ate him?"

The policeman was walking his beat when he saw two men fighting and a little boy standing alongside them crying, "Daddy, Daddy!"

The officer pulled the two men apart and, turning to the boy asked, "Which one is your father, lad?"

"I don't know," the boy said, rubbing the tears from his eyes. "That's what they're fighting about!"

Dressed as a pirate for Halloween, the small boy knocked on a door and was greeted by a matronly woman. "Aren't you a cute little pirate," she said. "But where are your buccaneers?"

To which the little boy replied: "Under my buccan hat."

As the two little girls walked hand in hand to kindergarten, one confided: "I found a contraceptive on the patio yesterday."

Asked her friend: "What's a patio?"

Her precocious six-year-old daughter came tugging at the mother's skirt, asking, "Mommy, can I have a baby?"

"Of course not, dear," the mother replied, without missing a stroke in her ironing.

"Are you sure?" the little girl persisted.

"Certainly," said the mother.

As she ran to rejoin her playmates in the yard, the child called out, "OK, fellas, same game!"

"I know how babies are made," boasted one small fry to another.

"That's nothing," the second small fry replied, "I know how they're not."

While lecturing the Sunday schoolers on the nature of sin and damnation, the rural minister asked one lad: "Do you know where little boys and girls go when they do bad things?"

"Yes, sir," replied the boy. "Back of Fogarty's barn."

Asked by his teacher to spell "straight," the third-grade boy did so without error. "Now," said the teacher, "what does it mean?"

"Without water."

"Gimme a double whiskey!" the little boy yelled to the barmaid as he entered the saloon.

"Do you want to get me in trouble?" she asked.

The lad replied: "Maybe later; but right now, I just want a drink."

The little boy pointed to two dogs in the park and asked his father what they were doing. "They're making puppies, son," the father said. That night, the boy wandered into his parents' room while they were making love. Asked what they were doing, the father replied, "Making you a baby brother."

"Gee, Pop," the boy pleaded, "turn her over—I'd rather have a puppy."

"Would you boys like to play house with us?" asked the bravest of several little girls.

"Sure," replied one lad. "Which one of you is going to be the madam?"

On a picnic with his parents, Tommy got lost. He wandered aimlessly through the forest and then fell to his knees to pray. "Dear Lord," he implored, "please help me find my way out of here."

As he was praying, a bird flew overhead and dropped an answer squarely in the palm of his outstretched hand. "Please, Lord," the boy begged, "don't hand me that stuff. I'm *really* lost."

The father was distressed by his thirteen-year-old son's preoccupation with breasts. The boy would repeatedly point to attractive girls and whisper: "Hey, Dad, look at the knockers on that one!"

The father finally took the boy to a psychiatrist, who assured him that just one day's intensive therapy could cure the boy. When the session was over, father and son walked several blocks to a bus stop. The boy remained silent as they passed a number of pretty girls. As they boarded the bus, the father was inwardly complimenting the psychiatrist. Then his son tugged at his sleeve and whispered: "Hey, Dad, look at the ass on that bus driver!"

Little Herbie was instructed by his mother to avoid any of the popular synonyms for urination and to substitute the verb "whisper."

That night, the boy approached his father, who had not yet been apprised of the new code. "Daddy," he said, "I want to whisper."

"All right, son," answered his father, "do it in my ear."

"All right, you bastards, fall in—on the double!" barked the sergeant as he strode into the barracks. Each soldier grabbed his hat and jumped to his feet, except one—a private who lay in his bunk reading a book. "Well?" roared the sergeant.

"Well," observed the private, "there certainly were a lot of them, weren't there?"

After going through the line at a crowded cafeteria, the three rambunctious teen-age boys found they were forced to share a table with a kindly looking old lady. One of the lads decided to have a bit of fun at the woman's expense and, nudging one of his buddies under the table, suddenly remarked, "Did your folks ever get married?"

"Nope," replied his tablemate, picking up the put-on. "How about yours?"

"They never bothered," answered the first young man.

"That's nothing," interrupted the third, "my mother doesn't even know who my father is."

The elderly woman looked up from her coffee and said sweetly, "Excuse me, but would one of you little bastards please pass the sugar?"

Trying to sell his new and totally omniscient computer to the youthful businessman, the inventor invited his skeptical client to ask it a question—any question. The executive sat down and typed out his query: "WHERE IS MY FATHER?"

The machine rapidly printed the reply: " YOUR FATHER IS FISHING IN MICHIGAN."

"This contraption doesn't know what it's talking about," bellowed the prospective customer. "My father's been dead for twenty years."

Certain that his creation was infallible, the scientist suggested, "Why don't you ask the same question in a different form?"

The chap then confidently typed: "WHERE IS MY MOTHER'S HUS-BAND?"—to which the mechanical brain answered: "YOUR MOTHER'S HUSBAND HAS BEEN DEAD FOR TWENTY YEARS. YOUR FATHER HAS JUST LANDED A THREE-POUND TROUT."

The wealthy old gentleman and his wife were celebrating their thirty-fifth wedding anniversary and their three grown sons joined them for dinner. The old man was rather irritated when he discovered that none of the boys had bothered to bring a gift, and after the meal, he drew them aside.

"You're all grown men," he said, "and old enough to hear this. Your mother and I have never been legally married."

"What?" gasped one of the sons. "Do you mean to say we're all bastards?"

"Yes," snapped the old man, "and cheap ones, too."

After watching an extremely attractive maternity-ward patient earnestly thumb through a telephone directory for several minutes, a hospital orderly finally asked if he could be of some help.

"No thanks," said the young mother, "I'm just looking for a name for my baby."

"But the hospital supplies a special booklet that lists every first name and its meaning," said the orderly.

"That won't help," said the girl, "my baby already has a first name."

"Darling," said the young bride, "tell me what's bothering you. We promised to share all our joys and all our sorrows, remember?"

"But this is different," protested her husband.

"Together, darling," she insisted, "we will bear the burden. Now tell me what our problem is."

"Well," said the husband, "we've just become the father of a bastard child."

A woman giving birth to an illegitimate child could be said to be laboring under a misconception.

> *Little Johnny, with a grin,*
> *Drank up all of pappy's gin.*
> *Mother said, when he was plastered,*
> *"Go to bed, you little love-child."*

Two farmers were discussing their sons' progress in the big city university. Ezra said, "I don't rightly understand them *degrees* the boys are workin' fer. Do you, Cy?"

"Reckon so," replied Cy, modestly. "First one they get is called a B. S. And you know what that means."

Being a man of the world, Ezra knew.

Cy went on: "Well, sir, they work a little harder and they get this here M. S. That means More of the Same."

Ezra nodded.

"Then comes the hard part. They study night and day, put in years of readin', write all kinds of papers and then, if they're lucky, they get the highest one of 'em all. The Ph.D."

"And what does that stand fer?" asked Ezra.

"Piled Higher and Deeper."

The Dean of Women at an exclusive girls' college was lecturing her students on sexual morality.

"In moments of temptation," said the speaker to the class, "ask yourself just one question: Is an hour of pleasure worth a lifetime of shame?"

A sweet young thing in the back of the room rose to ask a question of her own: "How do you make it last an hour?"

The farm had been mortgaged, and gladly, to give daughter a college education. Now, driving home from the station after meeting her at the train, farmer Johnson was greatly disturbed when his daughter whispered confidentially, "I have a confession to make, Paw—I ain't a virgin no more."

The old man shook his head sadly. "After all the sacrifices your Maw and I made to give you a good education, you still say 'ain't'!"

The curvy little coed in the tight-fitting cashmere sweater wiggled up to the professor after class and murmured in a honeyed voice, "I'm afraid I didn't do very well on that quiz today, professor. But I'll do anything to pass this course. Just *anything.*"

The professor raised an eyebrow. "Anything?"

"Uh-huh," she cooed. "Anything you ask."

"Then study," he said dryly.

The Dean of Women at a large Midwestern university recently began a speech to the student body with these memorable words: "The president of the university and I have decided to stop petting on campus."

The announcements of the professor's new book on astrophysics and his wife's new baby appeared almost simultaneously in the newspaper. Upon being congratulated on "this proud event in the family," the professor naturally thought of the achievement that had cost him the greater effort.

"Thank you," he replied modestly, "but I couldn't have done it without the help of two graduate students."

The two sorority sisters were babbling gaily over a doublemalted. "How did you like the bridge party that the Sigs threw last night?" asked one.

"Fine," answered the other, "until the campus cops came and looked under the bridge."

"Oh, I had a wonderful time," cooed the coed to her sorority sister. "Everybody said that Tommy and I were the cutest couple on the floor."

"I thought you said you weren't going to the Senior Dance," puzzled her friend.

"We didn't," said she, smiling. "Tommy took me to a pajama party."

An undergraduate acquaintance of ours discovered a way to cut classes at the correspondence school he's attending. He sends in empty envelopes.

Our Research Department has just come up with a stack of statistics proving that a considerable number of college students do *not* make love in parked cars. In fact, the report continues, the woods are full of them.

"Hey, Sally," said the college man, "how come you're not wearing my fraternity pin?"

"But, Bob, it was such a nuisance," the pretty coed pouted playfully. "All the fellows were complaining that it scratched their hands."

The current re-emphasis on education in our colleges is typified by one Midwestern university which has ruled that no athlete be awarded a letter unless he can tell at a glance which letter it is.

We know a progressive college professor who claims that you'll always have a student body where you find a faculty for making love.

An old fraternity brother told us about a gag an undergrad girlfriend of his pulled off last semester: She disguised herself as a boy, joined TKE and the authorities never found out about it.

"Wait a minute," we objected. "If this girl joined a fraternity, she would have had to dress with the guys and shower with them."

"Sure."

"Well then, someone must have discovered she was a girl!"

"Probably," said our friend, downing his drink. "But who'd tell?"

Once upon a time there were three coeds—a big coed, a medium-sized coed and a little tiny coed. One night they came home from a dance, and the big coed said, "Someone's been sleeping in my bed!"

The medium-sized coed looked in her room and said, "Someone's been sleeping in my bed!"

And the little tiny coed said, ". . . Well, nighty-night, girls!"

Annoyed by the professor of anatomy who told racy stories during class, a group of coeds decided that the next time he started to tell one they would all rise and leave the room in protest. The professor, however, got wind of their scheme just before class the following day, so he bided his time; then, halfway through the lecture, he began, "They say there is quite a shortage of prostitutes in France—"

The girls looked at one another, arose and started for the door. "Young ladies," said the professor, "the next plane doesn't leave until tomorrow afternoon."

A luscious coed majoring in sociology decided to write her thesis on campus sex behavior and ended up working under some of the greatest minds in the school.

The entire class sat spellbound as the professor announced: "That concludes my examination of the human sexual response. However, there's one more point I'd like to make before I get off the subject . . ."

Two young Atlanta engineers were reminiscing about their college days when one of them remarked, "I sure wish I could have gone to Georgia Tech."

Said his friend, "Oh, hell, you wouldn't have liked Tech too much. The only graduates they have are football players and whores."

"It just so happens that my wife graduated from Georgia Tech," the first snapped.

"Oh, really?" answered the friend, realizing his faux pas. "Tell me, what position did she play?"

The college dean phoned a student's father at home and told him that he had some good and some bad news about his son. "Tell me the bad news first," said the father.

"Your son's a hopeless homosexual," replied the dean.

"How awful," said the dismayed father. "But what's the good news?"

The dean confided, "He has just been elected Queen of the May."

Then there was the coed who passed biology by giving her body to science.

Lecturing a class of coeds on the anatomical intricacies of the male reproductive organ, the exasperated professor finally declared: "I don't know why you girls can't grasp this subject. You've had it pounded into you all semester."

Then there was the aging alumnus who lamented that when he went to college, it was only a lot of fun, but now it's a riot.

"Your housemother tells me that you smoke pot, take LSD and have made love to almost every boy on campus," exclaimed the angry dean of women. "Don't you know what good clean fun is?"
"No," replied the coed, "what good is it?"

"I sent my boy to college to get an education," complained one father to another, "but all he seems to do is shack up with coeds, smoke pot and have a good time."
"Most college students do that today," replied his friend.
"That's the trouble," snapped the first chap. "I should have kept him home and gone to college myself."

And, of course, you've heard about the bright young student who was awarded a full scholarship to the college of his choice—it paid for tuition, books and bail money.

A plain-looking coed home from school on summer vacation calmly confessed to her mother that she lost her virginity last semester. "How did it happen?" gasped the parent.

"Well, it wasn't easy," the girl admitted, "but three of my sorority sisters helped hold him down."

The fifty-five-year-old woman went to her doctor and asked for a prescription for birth-control pills. "But you don't need them at your age," he said. She went on to explain that she had tried some recently and now found that she couldn't sleep without them. "But birth-control pills have no tranquilizing agent in them," the doctor informed her.

"Well, I don't know what they have or what they don't have in them, but I give them to my daughter before she goes out each night, and I'm telling you, doctor, I sleep much, much better."

Late Friday afternoon, a college senior dropped by the campus drugstore and purchased three dozen prophylactics. On Monday morning, he returned to the drugstore and in a loud voice complained, "Last Friday, I came in here and ordered three dozen prophylactics, and you only gave me twenty-four."

"I'm very sorry, sir," said the pharmacist. "I do hope we didn't spoil your weekend."

Her bountiful bosom heaving in chagrin, Susan confessed her tearful tidings to her mother.

"Mom," she said, "I'm pregnant."

"Ye Gods!" screamed her mother. "Who is the father?"

She lifted her weeping face. "How should I know?" she wailed. "You never would let me go steady."

The young college physician was bewildered by the procession of unhappy coeds regularly visiting his office for a pregnancy test. "There seems to be something in the air this time of year that causes young girls to get pregnant," he commented to an older colleague. "What is it, I wonder?"

"Their legs," replied his friend.

Mrs. Brown pulled Mrs. Green out of earshot of the porch, where Mrs. Green's lovely young daughter Carol sat.

"It's really none of my business," whispered Mrs. Brown, "but have you noticed what your daughter is doing?"

"Carol?" Mrs. Green responded apprehensively. "Why, no. What's she up to?"

Mrs. Brown leaned closer. "She's knitting tiny garments," she hissed.

Mrs. Green's troubled brow cleared. "Well, thank goodness," she said, smiling. "I'm glad to see she's taken an interest in something besides running around with boys."

"**Y**oung lady," the football coach asked, "what are you doing with that varsity letter on your sweater? Don't you know that it's against campus rules to wear a letter unless you've made the team?"

"Yes, sir," she said.

Calling on an attractive coed, the theology professor asked, "Who was the first man?"

"If it's all the same to you, sir," replied the embarrassed coed, "I'd rather not tell."

Three young women were attending the same logic class given at one of the better universities. During a lecture the professor stated that he was going to test their ability at situation reasoning.

"Let us assume," said the professor, "that you are aboard a small craft alone in the Pacific, and you spot a vessel approaching you with several thousand sex-starved sailors on board. What would you do in this situation to avoid any problem?"

"I would attempt to turn my craft in the opposite direction," stated the redhead.

"I would pass them, trusting my knife to keep me safe," responded the brunette.

"Frankly," murmured the blonde, "I understand the situation, but I fail to see the problem."

Deciding to investigate rumors of immoral amusements among college students, a young professor arranged to have himself invited to a weekend party. After the party had been going for several hours without a single incident, the much-relieved prof said goodnight and went up to bed. He had hardly gotten beneath the covers when his door opened and a shapely coed in a flimsy nightgown entered. "Did you want me?" he asked in surprise.

"Not especially," the petite lass replied. "I just drew you."

A young college student appeared at his draft board one morning wrapped in the Stars and Stripes. As he entered, he proclaimed at the top of his lungs. "No matter what happens, don't hold up my induction! Let me start now and you can complete my papers later! I don't need a physical! I don't need a uniform, basic training, guns or anything! Just lemme at the enemy! I'll kill them with my bare hands! If they shoot me, I'll get up and keep on going! I'll rip their barbed wire . . . I'll—"

The draft-board examiner looked at him and said, "You're crazy."

To which the student replied, "Write that down! Write that down!"

"Gee, Mom," the young man complained, "none of the other guys are wearing lipstick."

"Be quiet, stupid," his mother replied. "We're almost to the draft board."

One summer night, as the elderly couple sat on their front porch looking at the cemetery across the street, the woman remarked: "You know, dear, every time I think of our wonderful daughter lying over there, it makes me want to cry."

"I know," the man agreed, "it saddens me, too. Sometimes I even wish she were dead."

And, of course, you've heard about the fellow who was hired to coach an all-girl softball team but spent the season in the batter's box.

"What do you give a man who has everything?" the pretty teen-ager asked her mother.

"Encouragement, dear," she replied.

"I suppose," snarled the leathery sergeant to the private, "that when you're discharged from the Army, you'll wait for me to die, just so you can spit on my grave."

"Not me," observed the private. "When I get out of the Army, I never want to stand in line again."

"You should be ashamed of yourself," the reproachful mother told her daughter. "All your girlfriends are divorced already and you're not even married."

Three decrepit, gray-haired gentlemen were seated together in the park discussing their personal philosophies for achieving a ripe old age.

"I'm eighty-six," said the first, "and I wouldn't be here today if I hadn't scorned tobacco and alcohol in every form, avoided late hours and the sinful enticements of the opposite sex."

"I owe my ninety-three years to a strict diet of blackstrap molasses, wheat germ bread and mother's milk," said the second old man.

"When I was eighteen," the third man said, "my father told me that if I wanted to enjoy life as much as he had, I should smoke black cigars, drink nothing but hard liquor and carouse with a different woman every night. And that's exactly that I've done."

"Incredible," said the first old man.

"Amazing," said the second, for their friend was obviously the grayest, most elderly appearing of the three. "Just how old are you?"

"Twenty-two."

Sylvester was a sprightly ninety years of age when he married Elizabeth, who was a resoundingly ripe eighteen-year-old. As they prepared for bed on their wedding night, he asked her:

"Tell me, sweet child, did your mother tell you the facts of life?"

She blushed furiously from her hairline to the tips of her toes.

"No," she shyly murmured.

"That's a great pity," he said, "because I'm afraid I've forgotten them."

Two ragged hippies were sitting on a small pier in the Florida Everglades, dangling their feet in the stagnant water. Suddenly an alligator swam up and snapped a leg off one of them.

"Hey, man," the unfortunate fellow said to his buddy, "like an alligator just bit off my leg."

"Which one?" asked the cool friend.

"I dunno," said the first cat. "You see one alligator, you seen 'em all."

Shed a tear for the beatnik who committed suicide, leaving this note: "Good-bye, cool world."

Two hipsters crossing the Atlantic by steamship were out on deck looking at the ocean. The first cat said, "Man, look at all that water out there!"

"Yeah, man," the second, even further-out cat replied. "And just think, like that's only the top of it."

Then there was the little old lady who walked up to the hippie in Greenwich Village and asked, "Cross-town buses run all night?" Whereupon the young bohemian snapped his fingers and replied, "Doo-dah, Doo-dah."

Two hipsters were sight-seeing in the Everglades when one suddenly stepped into quicksand and began sinking, while his fellow traveler calmly looked on.

"Hey, man," shouted the sinking swinger, "how about giving me a hand?"

"Sure thing, dad," replied the other hipster, as he began clapping.

"Hey, man," one hippie said to another, "turn on the radio."

"OK," the second hippie answered, and then leaning over very close to the radio, he whispered: "I love you."

"Hey, lover," said the hippie to a pretty flower child he'd just met, "have you ever been picked up by the fuzz?"

"No," she answered, "but I bet it really hurts."

A hippie newsdealer was questioned by one of New York's finest for peddling dirty pictures.

"But you're mistaken," said the hippie. "These pictures aren't dirty."

Selecting one, the policeman said: "Do you mean to tell me this isn't a dirty picture?"

The hippie shrugged. "Don't be square, officer. Haven't you ever seen five people in love?"

A youthful friend of ours in San Francisco describes hippiness as a warm poppy.

2
DATING

This is old, but it has always been one of our favorites.

The young playboy took a blind date to an amusement park. They went for a ride on the Ferris wheel. The ride completed, she seemed rather bored.

"What would you like to do next?" he asked.

"I wanna be weighed," she said. So the young man took her over to the weight guesser. "One-twelve," said the man at the scale, and he was absolutely right.

Next they rode the roller coaster. After that, he bought her some popcorn and cotton candy, then he asked what else she would like to do.

"I wanna be weighed," she said.

I really latched onto a square one tonight, thought the young man, and using the excuse that he had developed a headache, he took the girl home.

The girl's mother was surprised to see her home so early, and asked, "What's wrong, dear, didn't you have a nice time tonight?"

"Wousy," said the girl.

"I notice your daughter didn't get home until three o'clock this morning," said Mrs. Tyson to Mrs. Frisbee across the back-yard fence. "*My* daughter was in the house before midnight."

"I know," answered Mrs. Frisbee coolly. "But, you see, my daughter walked home."

"I told my boyfriend I didn't want to see him any more," said the pony-tailed model to her friend, over lunch.

"What did he say?" the friend asked.

"Nothing. He just pulled the covers over his head."

The none too bright young fellow had been dating the same girl for more than a year and, one evening, the girl's father confronted him and wanted to know whether the lad's intentions towards his daughter were honorable or dishonorable.

"Gee," said the young man, swallowing hard, "I didn't know I had a choice!"

"Why did you spend so much time parked in that fellow's automobile last night?" demanded the irate mother. "I could hear the giggling and squealing for a good half-hour."

"But, Mom," answered her daughter, "if a fellow takes you to the movies you ought to at *least* kiss him good night."

"I thought you went to the Stork Club?" countered the mother.

"We did."

We just heard about the unlucky fellow who phoned his girl to see if she was doing anything that evening. She said she wasn't, so he took her out. And sure enough, she wasn't.

"We're going to have a wonderful time tonight, dearest," said the young man to his date as he greeted her in the living room of her parents' home. "I have three tickets to the theater."

"But why do we need *three* tickets?" asked the truly voluptuous young lady.

"Simple," said he. "They're for your mother, father and brother."

"I understand you took out the gorgeous new receptionist last night," said one ad exec to another. "How was she?"

"Not so good," was the reply.

"Yeah," said the first exec, "you always were lucky."

A staff researcher has come up with proof that most girls wouldn't stay out late if fellows didn't make them.

The lights in the apartment were low and so was the music. "You say you can read my mind?" the handsome young bachelor demanded.

"Yes," replied his bountifully proportioned and beautiful date.

"OK," he challenged, "go ahead."

"No," she said. "*You* go ahead."

Carol had been dating one man steadily for almost a year, and her mother was growing concerned.

"Exactly what are his intentions?" she demanded.

"Well, Mom, I'm really not sure," Carol said. "He's been keeping me pretty much in the dark."

When Cleo's parents threatened to forbid her to see her boy-friend unless she told them why he'd been there so late the night before, she finally began to talk.

"Well," she said, "I took him into the loving room, and—"

"That's 'living,' dear," her mother interrupted.

Said the happy girl, "You're telling me!"

One thing that can be said in favor of going steady is that it gets the youngsters home and in bed at an early hour.

The girl who will go to a man's apartment to see his etchings may not know anything about art, but she knows what she likes.

Anxious to be on time for his date, Carl nevertheless dropped into a drugstore to make a hasty purchase. The druggist gave him a knowing smile, so Carl gave him a run-down on the expectations he had for the evening.

"I met this girl at a party last week," he explained. "A real hot number. Her folks are going to the opera tonight and it will be just the two of us with the whole apartment to ourselves."

Carl was greeted with a warm hug at the door by Nancy, his date. They settled on the couch and turned on the TV. Her folks would be leaving in a few minutes, she explained. Her father wasn't home from work yet and as soon as he arrived, the parents would be departing for dinner and the opera.

Nancy's father arrived soon after and she introduced both parents to Carl.

"Say, why don't Nancy and I join you this evening?" Carl suggested.

"Oh, you children don't want to be spending your evening with us old folks," said Nancy's mother.

"Sure we do," said Carl, before the flabbergasted Nancy could say a word.

"I didn't know you liked opera," said the bewildered Nancy to her date as he helped her on with her coat.

"No," said Carl, "and I didn't know your father was a druggist either."

Mist circled sluggishly in the air of the steam room as George and Charlie attempted to melt from their bodies the excesses of the night before.

"How was your date last night?" George asked.

"Awful," Charlie responded. "Beautiful, but awful. I was disgusted. The minute we got to her apartment, the phone started ringing—every big operator in town wanted a date with her. We didn't have a moment's peace. Man, was I fed up!"

"Come on, Charlie," George twitted his friend, "don't you expect a beautiful girl to have her number in the phone book?"

"Yeah," growled Charlie, "but not in the Yellow Pages."

A really promiscuous girl is one you can have a good time with even if you play your cards *wrong*.

A girl can be poor on history but great on dates.

Sipping her second alexander, the green-eyed secretary demanded of her girlfriend, "You've been dating Harold since you were both kids, and the relationship doesn't seem to be going anywhere. Hasn't he any ambitions?"

"Oh, yes," smiled her sexy companion, "ever since he's been knee-high."

The wondrously stacked blonde appeared at her door in a strapless evening gown that defied gravity. "Terrific!" said her admiring escort. "I don't see what holds that dress up!"

"Play your cards right and you will," she murmured.

Lily just couldn't imagine why she was so popular. "Is it my lovely hair?" she asked a friend.

"No."

"Is it my cute figure?"

"No."

"My personality?"

"No."

"Then I give up."

"That's it!"

All he had asked for was a little good-night kiss, but she haughtily rebuffed him with, "I don't do that sort of thing on my first date."

"Well," he replied with sarcasm, "how about on your last?"

The sweetest words any young man can hear from his steady girl are these: "There's really nothing to worry about—I kid you not."

The Jag zoomed along, with the native Californian sitting behind the wheel describing to his visiting chum the blind date they were on their way to meet. "She's young, she's rich and her face is a picture," said the driver.

Before the evening had grown very old, the visitor found that the young lady was indeed young, had very glowing financial prospects . . . but her looks were incredibly bad. The next morning, he challenged his friend, "I thought you said my date's face was a picture!"

His host yawned and replied, "Can I help it if you don't dig Picasso?"

The pretty young thing came slamming into her apartment after a blind date and announced to her roommate, "Boy, what a character! I had to slap his face three times this evening!"

The roommate inquired eagerly, "What did he do?!"

"Nothing," muttered the girl. "I slapped him to see if he was awake!"

"What," the girl quizzed her date, "is hot-blooded, passionate and hums?"

The young man thought a bit, then said, "I don't know."
She smiled and replied, "Hmmmmm. . . ."

"**I** nearly fainted when the fellow I was out with last night asked me to pet," exclaimed the sweet young thing to her date.

"Really?" said the date. "Then you're gonna die when you hear what *I* have in mind."

The pretty young thing was a trifle taken aback at her first visit to the Cheetah in New York City. After watching the wildly gyrating couples doing the latest in *discothèque* steps, she declined her escort's invitation to join them on the dance floor.

"Come on, pussycat," implored the young man. "You can do it."

"I know I can," the girl replied, "but not standing up."

One of the most expensive things in the world can be a gal who is free for the evening.

The disgruntled miss was complaining bitterly to her roommate about last night's blind date.

"Not only did the nogoodnik lie to me about the size of his yacht," she said, "but he made me do the rowing."

As the young couple parked in a crowded lovers' lane, she sighed romantically: "It's lovely out here tonight—just listen to the crickets."
"Those aren't crickets," her date replied. "They're zippers."

"Not that I believe in reincarnation," said the young man to his hyperprudish date, "but what were you before you died?"

As their car stopped on the shoulder of a secluded road, the young man asked his date: "If I try to make love to you, will you yell for help?"
Cooed his date: "Only if you really need it."

The lad was parked in a secluded lovers' lane with the sexy high school cheerleader. "Wow!" he exclaimed. "It's so dark I can't see my hand in front of my face."
"I happen to know," the girl sighed, "that neither of your hands is in front of your face."

"How about making the evening a Dutch treat?" cooed the delectable blonde to her handsome escort. "You pay for dinner and drinks—and the rest of the evening will be on me."

During a conversation with a kindly old minister, the young man asked, "Is it really such a sin to sleep with a girl?"
"Oh, no," answered the minister, "but you young boys—you don't sleep."

Last summer a friend of ours vacationed at a popular resort where he met a young and charming girl. She prided herself on being a good sport and demonstrated this by enjoying just about everything with our friend—dining, dancing, swimming, tennis, horseback riding, motoring—just about everything, in short, except that special enjoyment he was really interested in.
"Oh, come on," he entreated, "you're always saying what a good sport you are. Why draw the line at this?" Appealing to her sense of good sportsmanship finally turned the trick, and the last evening of their vacation was the most enjoyable of all.
Back on the job, our friend had almost forgotten the incident when, just a week ago, the phone rang.
"Do you know who this is?" a sweet, feminine voice asked.
He didn't, of course.

"The girl from the lake this summer," she said. "The good sport."

She said she had something important to tell him and wanted to meet him for a drink after work. Remembering the pleasant interlude at the end of their vacation, he made a date for that very evening.

Over Manhattans, the girl confided that she was in a family way and asked him what he was going to do about it.

Our friend was understandably unnerved.

"I—I don't know what I *can* do," he said, gulping down his drink. "This summer was just for laughs. I'm engaged to be married to another girl. The question is, what are *you* going to do about it?"

"Well," she said, almost in tears, "I suppose I could kill myself!"

"Gee!" He breathed a sigh of relief. "You *are* a good sport!"

The couple was afloat in a canoe when a sudden thunder squall flashed across the lake. "Oh Lord," the young man prayed, "save us and I'll give up smoking and drinking . . . I'll give up betting on the ponies . . . I'll give up—"

Above the noise of the thunder came the girl's earnest plea: "Don't promise to give up *everything*, George! Paddle!"

He drank with curvy Mabel,
The pace was fast and furious.
He slid beneath the table—
Not drunk, but merely curious.

Martinis, my girl, are deceiving:
Take two at the very most.
Take three and you're under the table.
Take four and you're under the host.

She was a gorgeous girl.
And he was a loving male.
He praised her shape in English,
French, Italian and Braille.

Latest comment from the pundits regarding the population explosion: If the birth rate keeps increasing, there will soon be standing room only on the earth, at which time the birth rate should stop increasing pretty quickly.

Having repaired to what they thought was an isolated spot in the cemetery, the couple was proceeding to make love when a cop surprised them. "Didn't you see the sign at the entrance?" he railed. "NO ADMITTANCE AFTER DARK. "

"No," explained the young man, "we came in the other way, past the one that reads GET LOTS WHILE YOU'RE YOUNG."

A medical journal reports that the most foolproof birth-control pill developed to date is an aspirin tablet—held firmly between the knees.

One of the members of the smart cabana club asked the lifeguard how he might teach a young lady of his acquaintance to swim.

"It takes considerable time and technique," the lifeguard said. "First you must take her into the water. Then place one arm about her waist, hold her tightly, then take her right arm and raise it slowly . . ."

"This certainly will be helpful," said the member, "and I know my sister will appreciate it."

"Your sister?" said the lifeguard. "In that case, just push her off the end of the pier."

The sweet young thing was telling her mother about the great time she had at the mountain resort: "I met a man in the recreation hall and we played Ping-Pong all afternoon. What fun, Mother!"

"Why, dear," remarked the mother, "I never knew you enjoyed Ping-Pong."

"I do now," the daughter said. "I'd hit the ball the wrong way and we'd both go after it under the table. Then he'd hit the ball the wrong way and we'd both go after it under the table. We played all afternoon. It was wonderful."

"But I don't understand," said the mother. "Where does the fun come in?"

"Under the table, silly."

"I went golfing with Scott yesterday," the attractive student told her sorority sister.

"Does he use the woods well?" asked her friend.

"I really don't know," sighed the first girl. "He insisted on playing golf all day."

The young man relaxed on the bed, enjoying a cigarette; his girl friend lay beside him, lost in thought.

"Darling," she said unexpectedly, as girls are wont to do, "let's get married."

The young man took a long drag on his cigarette and without turning said, "Dearest, who would have us?"

"I'm going to have a little one,"
Said the girl, so gay and frisky.
And the boyfriend up and fainted
(Then she told him she meant whiskey).

"My, what an attractive baby," said the handsome astrologer to the sweet young thing pushing the perambulator. "Do you happen to know what sign he was conceived under?"

"Yes," blushed the young mother. "It was KEEP OFF THE GRASS."

A twist on a well-known safety poster goes like this: IF YOU DRINK —DON'T PARK. ACCIDENTS CAUSE PEOPLE.

The Southern boy was trying to make time up North. "Honey chile," he purred to a luscious Yankee, "would it be all right if Ah kissed yo' all?"

Snapped she: "Aren't my lips enough?"

An old-fashioned gentleman took a modern miss for a ride in his car and after finding a suitable spot to park, kissed her several times lightly on the cheek and then announced, "This is called *spooning.*"

"Okay," she said, "but I think I'd rather *shovel.*"

"The trouble with Harold," commented the svelte model to her roommate, "is that once he starts kissing you, he never knows where to stop."

"That's funny," countered her friend. "The last time I went out with him, he found a great place."

A songwriter friend of ours, the same nifty word-merchant who comes up with all those jukebox hits, has turned out another catchy one: *I Used to Kiss Her on the Lips, But It's All Over Now.*

A girl's kisses usually leave something to be desired: the rest of her.

The well-stacked redhead stormed into police headquarters and shouted at the desk sergeant that a man had grabbed and kissed her while she was walking through the park.

"What did he look like?" the desk sergeant asked.

"I really don't know," the girl replied.

"Lady, it's the middle of the afternoon on a clear, sunny day," the sergeant said in an exasperated voice. "How could a man grab and kiss you without you seeing what he looked like?"

"Well," the redhead answered, "for one thing, I always close my eyes when I'm being kissed!"

"Did you follow my advice kissing your girl when she least expects it?" asked the sophisticated college senior of his younger fraternity brother.

"Oh, hell," said the fellow with the swollen eye, "I thought you said *where*."

It's no fun to kiss a girl over the phone unless you happen to be in the same booth with her.

The beautiful Belinda knew that Mervin had relatively little experience as a lover and she was surprised when he parked the car in a dark and romantic spot, then swept her into a passionate embrace. After several minutes filled with kisses, he drew back rather proudly, straightened his tie, and asked, "How was *that?*"

"You know, Mervin," she confided, "you're the first man I've met whose kisses make me sit up and open my eyes."

"Really?" he said, quite obviously pleased.

"Yes," she admitted. "Usually they have the opposite effect."

Some girls think it's fun to fight against being kissed, while others prefer to just take it lying down.

The party was a smoothly swinging scene, with all the lights turned low, and Clark espied a female form alone in a corner. He crept up behind her, and before she became aware of his presence, he'd clasped her in a passionate embrace and kissed her soundly.

"How dare you!" she shrieked indignantly, pulling away.

"Pardon me," Clark bluffed smoothly, "I thought you were my sister."

"You chowderhead," she responded tartly, "I *am* your sister."

"Give me a kiss," the fellow ordered his lovely date.

"You'll have to make me," she teased.

"Not so fast," he protested. "All I want now is a kiss."

"Before we get married," said the young man to his fiancée, "I want to confess some affairs I've had in the past."

"But you told me all about those a couple of weeks ago," replied the girl.

"Yes, darling," he explained, "but that was a couple of weeks ago."

"**G**ee," mused the pretty young high school girl as she stared longingly at her older sister's new engagement ring. "It must be wonderful when you're married."

"As far as I'm concerned," her sister replied, "it's wonderful whether you're married or not."

The loving young couple wanted to marry immediately—but the girl's strong-willed and domineering mother adamantly opposed the union.

"I can't help it," said the distraught girl to her boyfriend. "Mother thinks you're effeminate."

Reflecting for a moment, he replied: "You know, compared with her, maybe I am."

Then there was the chap who was engaged to a beautiful contortionist—until she broke it off.

With their wedding date finally set, the bride-to-be snuggled up to her fiancé and said, "Darling, I want to make love *before* we get married."

"But it won't be long until July, dear," he replied.

"Oh," she exclaimed enthusiastically. "And how long will it be then?"

While attending an engagement party given by his friends, the young fellow boasted of his past sexual exploits. "You know," he declared, looking over the assembled guests, "I've slept with every girl here, with the exception of my sister and my fiancée."

"That's interesting," his friend responded dryly. "Between the two of us, we've had them all."

The young man had invited his fiancée to meet his parents over cocktails at the Plaza. After his family had departed, the girl wanted to know whether she had made the proper impression on them.

"I'm sorry to have to tell you this, dearest," the fellow said, "but while you were in the ladies' room, my mother told me that she considered you rather uncouth."

"Did you tell them that I attended Bennington *and* Mt. Holyoke?" she asked in surprise.

"Yes, dearest."

"Did you remind them that my family enjoys a particularly high standing in Bar Harbor?"

"Yes, I did."

"And I hope you told them of my considerable interest in the arts."

"Of course," said the young man.

"Then what's this 'uncouth' crap all about?" she asked.

Friends were surprised, indeed, when Frank and Jennifer broke their engagement, but Frank had a ready explanation:

"Would you marry someone who was habitually unfaithful, who lied at every turn, who was selfish and lazy and sarcastic?"

"Of course not," said a sympathetic friend.

"Well," retorted Frank, "neither would Jennifer."

Aware of his prospective father-in-law's flair for sarcasm, the young groom-to-be was nervous over the prospect of asking for his daughter's hand. Summoning the necessary courage, he approached the girl's father and, with the utmost politeness, asked, "May I have your daughter for my wife?"

"I don't know," came the reply. "Bring your wife around and I'll let you know."

The young man addressed his prospective father-in-law: "Sir, I would like to marry your daughter."

"I'm afraid, son," the older man replied, "that you couldn't support her in the manner to which she is accustomed."

"Your daughter and I have talked it over, and she has consented to live on what I earn."

"That's fine. But remember that after a while a little one may come along, and that will mean added expense."

"Well, that's true, sir," the youth agreed, "but we've been lucky so far."

3
MARRIAGE

The sweet young thing was shopping for her wedding gown.
"Have you been married before?" asked the salesgirl.
"Why, no—why do you ask?"
"Well, when a girl has been previously married, it's customary to wear lavender rather than white."
"Oh. Well let's see what you have in white with lavender trim."

Nobody gave the bride away, but several young men at the wedding could have.

The reason no one ever gives the groom a shower is that everyone figures him to be all washed up anyway.

To the astonishment of his friends, Martin, as gay a blade as ever cut a swath through a gaggle of girls, announced his intentions to marry. Speculation ran high as to what his conduct would be after the nuptials, but Martin put an end to all doubt when he toasted the bridesmaids at the reception.
"Girls," he said warmly, his eyes flitting lightly over their charms, "I want to wish you all the best of luck, and to extend the hope that each of you will, in the near future, take the place of the bride."

It was a beautiful reception, but the mother of the bride was worried that the newlyweds wouldn't have time to change and pack their clothes in time to catch their honeymoon flight to Rio. Seeing that the party was nowhere near breaking up, she finally approached the groom and whispered: "Don't you children think it's time to go upstairs and get your things together?"

A young couple had been married in a large, expensive church ceremony, and they had finally reached the resort hotel where they were going to spend their honeymoon. The bride was extremely tired and nervous after the tension of the day, and she launched into an impromptu criticism of large weddings, emphasizing both the bother and the expense of such affairs. "It's ridiculous," she said finally. "Why, this wedding set my family back over five thousand dollars."

"Honey," interrupted the groom, "if you'll just shut up and come to bed, I'll try to give you your money's worth!"

We've heard about a preacher who officiated at so many shotgun weddings that he decided to rename his church Winchester Cathedral.

We recently attended a wedding where the bride was six months pregnant—the guests all threw puffed rice.

'Twas the night before the nuptials and the bride-to-be's father was unmercifully teasing his future son-in-law. "Are you going to be a man and do it tonight, or are you going to be a mouse and wait until tomorrow night?" he smirked.

Before he could stop himself, the nervous young man blurted out, "I guess I'm a rat, sir—I did it *last* night!"

The Olympic swimming champ got married to a beautiful girl and, on their honeymoon, treated her to an exhibition of his swimming prowess. He leaped into the hotel pool, cleaved the water with expert strokes and came up on the opposite side in a matter of seconds. His proud smile faded slightly when his lovely wife dived in and repeated his feat in half the time.

But, masking his bruised ego, he took her in his arms and exclaimed, "Darling, you're wonderful! Why didn't you tell me you were a swimming champion too?"

"I'm not," she replied. "I was a street-walker in Venice."

It was her wedding night and the sweet young thing was in a romantic haze. "Oh, darling," she sighed, "we're married at last. It's all like a wonderful dream!" Her husband didn't answer.

A few moments passed, she sighed again, and said: "I'm afraid I'll awaken in a moment and find it isn't true." Still no response from her spouse.

Another pause and another sensuous sigh, then, softly: "I just can't believe that I'm really your wife."

"Damn it," growled her mate, "as soon as I get this shoelace untied you will!"

Adjusting to marriage sometimes poses problems. We met a good friend of ours recently, the morning after his wedding, brooding over a drink in a local bar.

"What's the trouble?" we asked. "I should think you'd be the happiest man in the world today."

He shook his head sadly.

"What creatures of habit we are," he said. "This morning when I rose, half asleep, without thinking, I pulled a five dollar bill from my wallet and left it on the pillow."

We tried to console him—told him his wife wouldn't think anything of it.

"You don't understand," he said. "Half asleep, without thinking, she gave me three dollars change."

The young bride's mother had some old-fashioned ideas of marriage and passed them on to her daughter. "Never let your husband see you in the nude," she advised. "You should always wear something."

"Yes, Mother," replied the obedient girl.

Two weeks after the wedding, the girl and her brand-new husband were preparing to retire when the fellow asked, "Dear, has there ever been any insanity in your family?"

"Not that I know of," she answered. "Why?"

"Well," said her husband, "we've been married two weeks now and every night you've worn that silly hat to bed."

News item: Arthur Proctor, of this city, was today accused of signing a false name when applying for a marriage license. The new Mrs. Proctor came to his defense, saying, "Arthur didn't mean to do that —it's just that he's become so accustomed to hotel registers."

"Darling, I have a confession to make," said the shy young bride at their first breakfast together. "It isn't a big thing, but I feel I should have told you before. I suffer from asthma."

"Thank heavens," said the groom, smiling. "Last night I thought you were hissing me."

A young bride's mother was helping unpack after the honeymoon and was shocked to find her daughter's trousseau badly torn.

"Darling," she gasped, "didn't your husband like your trousseau?"

"Oh, yes," the blushing bride replied, "he liked my trousseau, mother. It's just that he liked my torso more than my trousseau—that's why my trousseau is tore so."

One of the executive secretaries had just returned from her honeymoon and was discussing it with the girls at the office.

"How did your husband register at the hotel?" one little co-worker wanted to know.

"Fine," the secretary said, beaming. "Just fine!"

The newlyweds entered the elevator of their Miami Beach hotel. The operator, a magnificent blonde, looked at them in surprise and said, "Why, *hello*, Teddy, how are you?"

A frosty silence prevailed until the couple reached their room, when the piqued bride demanded: "*Who* was that *woman?!*"

"Take it easy, honey," said the groom, "I'm going to have trouble enough explaining you to *her*."

Proud and pleased as she could be, the petite young bride, Mrs. Stanford Summers, strode briskly up to the teller's cage at the bank to cash her husband's pay check for the first time. When the teller told her the check would have to be endorsed, the bride grabbed the pen and unhesitatingly wrote on the back, "I heartily recommend my husband, Mr. Stanford Summers."

The newlyweds were obviously suffering from exhaustion and after a routine examination, their doctor advised, "It's not unusual for a young couple to overdo things during the first weeks of marriage. What you both need is more rest. For the next month I want you to limit your sexual activity to those days of the week with an 'r' in them. That is, Thursday, Friday and Saturday."

Since the end of the week was approaching, the newlyweds had no immediate difficulty following the doctor's orders. But on the first evening of scheduled rest the young bride found herself unusually passionate. Hubby fell asleep quickly, but she tossed and turned interminably and finally nudged her spouse into partial wakefulness.

Expecting daylight and confused because it was still dark, he asked, "What day is it?"

"Mondray," said his bride, cuddling against him.

After the lavish wedding reception, the newlyweds retired to their honeymoon suite. The groom turned down the lights and found something suitably romantic on the radio. Then he excused himself and returned in pajamas and robe. He opened a bottle of champagne and poured them each a drink, then he took his bride by the hand and tenderly led her toward the bedroom.

"Damn," she muttered, "every time I go out with a guy it ends up the same way."

The young bride was having her new house decorated and, while changing into something suitable for her afternoon bridge club, she noticed what appeared to be her husband's handprint on the wall in the bedroom that had been freshly painted the day before. She slipped into a filmy but adequate covering and, going to the head of the stairs, called down to the painter who was now working in the living room.

"Pardon me, but would you like to come up here and see where my husband put his hand last night?" she said.

"I'd love to, lady," replied the painter, "but I've got to get done with this painting first."

Mary and Bob were in their upper berth on the train to Niagara Falls, and she was so wonderstruck that she kept repeating over and over again: "Bobby, I just can't believe that we're really married."

Finally, a sleepy voice bellowed out from below: "For chrissake, Bobby, convince her—we wanna get to sleep!"

Never try to keep up with the Joneses; they might be newlyweds.

Sam and Arthur, expectant fathers both, nervously paced the floor in the waiting room of a maternity hospital.

"What tough luck," grumbled Sam. "This had to happen during my vacation."

"You think you've got troubles?" said Arthur. "I'm on my honeymoon."

Margie was an enthusiastic newlywed and, after discussing the family budget with her husband, she decided she should get a temporary job. Bouncing into the public library, she approached the attentive old maid sitting at the reference desk.

"Could you please give me the name of a good book on positions?" she inquired.

"What kind of positions did you have in mind?" asked the old librarian with a starched smile.

"Oh, you know—" explained the bright-eyed young girl, "—the different kinds of positions a bride might take."

Carter had been back from his honeymoon only a week when a friend asked him how he enjoyed married life.

"Why, it's wonderful!" was his enthusiastic reply. "It's almost like being in love."

After an engagement of several years, George and Gloria were finally married. When they returned from their honeymoon, a bright-eyed friend asked Gloria how she enjoyed married life. Absent-mindedly, the bride replied: "To tell the truth, I can't see a bit of difference."

The TV quiz show m.c. was interviewing a pair of newlyweds, and his usual forced smile had grown so wide that the lower part of head seemed completely surrounded by teeth.

"So you've only been married six days?" he cried.

"That's right," the pretty bride replied hastily, "but it seems like six months!"

"How is that?" the m.c. boomed jovially.

"Well," the girl answered thoughtfully, "I guess it's because we've done so much in such a short time."

Sheila and George were spending the first night of their honeymoon in a quaint medieval town in France. To add piquancy to the evening, Sheila suggested coyly that they make love every time the old night watchman rang his hourly bell. George smiled in delight at this prospect, but four rings later he pretended that he had to go out to get some cigarettes and staggered off to the watchman's tower.

"Listen, old man," he wheezed to that worthy, "do me a favor, will you? For the rest of the night, ring that bell of yours at two-hour intervals instead of hourly!"

"Ah," replied the ancient watchman, fingering his mustache, "I would be happy to oblige, *monsieur*, but I cannot do this."

"Why not?" George demanded. "I'll give you money, if that's what's troubling you!"

"Not at all," the old man responded. "You see, a beautiful young lady has already bribed me to ring the bell every half hour."

Hoping to avoid the embarrassing attentions that most hotels bestow on newlyweds, the honeymooners carefully removed the rice from their hair, took the JUST MARRIED sign off their car and even scuffed their luggage to give it that traveled look. Then, without betraying a trace of their eagerness, they ambled casually into Miami Beach's Fontainebleau Hotel and up to the front desk, where the groom said in a loud, booming voice, "We'd like a double bed with a room."

The king had arranged a regal marriage for his daughter—a bond that would unite two great nations. Yet, because the young couple seemed so terribly formal to each other, the old monarch was worried that the union would not be a success. Posting a spy outside the royal bridal chamber, he demanded a full acount of the wedding night's progress.

"It is hard to tell," said the king's spy the next morning. "When the prince entered the chamber, I heard the princess say, quite formally, 'I offer you my honor.' Then the prince said, with equal courtliness, 'Madame, I honor your offer.' And that is the way it went all night long —honor, offer, honor, offer."

On the first night of their honeymoon the bride slipped into a flimsy bit of silk and crawled into bed, only to find that her husband had settled down on the couch. When she asked why he was apparently not going to make love to her, he replied, "Because it's Lent."

"Why, that's the most ridiculous thing I've ever heard," she exclaimed, almost in tears. "To whom, and for how long?"

"I must insist on knowing one thing," said the groom as he lay beside his bride in the darkness of their honeymoon suite. "Am I the first man to sleep with you?"

"You will be, darling," said his bride, "if you doze off."

Have you heard about the newlywed who was so lazy that he took his wife to the bridal suite of a San Francisco hotel and waited for an earthquake?

The shy young man, wed three months, met his doctor on the street and very unhappily reported that—due to similar shyness on his bride's part—theirs was still a marriage in name only. "Your mistake," the doctor advised after hearing the gloomy details of repeated ineptitudes, "is in waiting until bedtime to make advances. The thought of the approaching moment creates tensions and impairs any chance of success. What you must do is take advantage of the very next time you both are in the mood." The young man thanked the doctor and hurried home to tell his bride of the heartening advice he'd received.

A week later, the doctor happened to meet the man again, and noticed that he was now smilingly self-possessed. "My advice worked, I take it?" he inquired.

The young man grinned. "Perfectly. The other night, we were having supper, and as I reached for the salt—so did she! Our hands touched. . . . It was as if an electric current ran through us. I leaped to my feet, swept the dishes from the table, threw her down upon it and there and then consummated our marriage!"

"That's wonderful. I'm pleased to hear things worked out so well," said the doctor, about to go on his way. The young man laid a hand upon his arm.

"There's just one hitch, though, doctor," he said, uncomfortably.

"What's that?" asked the medical man, puzzled by the other's sudden uneasiness.

"Well—" said the young man, "we can never go back to The Four Seasons again. . . ."

When one of the two first-grade teachers at the posh suburb's new school left on her two-week honeymoon, the other volunteered to teach both classes in her absence. A few weeks later, at a housewarming party given by the newlyweds, the guests were somewhat taken aback as the groom introduced them to his wife's teaching colleague:

"And this, ladies and gentlemen," announced the grateful husband, "is the lovely lady who substituted for my wife during our honeymoon."

After spending his wedding night in a motel, the young man approached the desk clerk and asked for his bill.

"Our charge for a double room is seven dollars apiece," advised the clerk. The newlywed grumbled something about the price being a bit steep, then dug out his wallet and handed the clerk forty-two dollars.

Before leaving on her honeymoon ocean voyage, the lovely bride made a last-minute stop at a nearby drugstore to purchase some necessary pharmaceutical provisions. Rushing up to the man behind the prescription counter, the blushing newlywed exclaimed, "I've got to have a hundred seasick pills and a three-month supply of birth-control pills right away."

The druggist smiled knowingly, then with a note of genuine concern in his voice asked, "I know it's none of my business, young lady. But if it makes you sick, why do it?"

The honeymoon is over when a quickie before dinner refers to a short drink.

After a Sunday-morning wedding, the newlyweds boarded a plane for Bermuda and several hours later arrived in the bridal suite of a magnificent hotel. Overwhelmed with the sheer splendor of the resort, the bride nervously remarked, "I'm sorry to bother you, honey, but I don't have any idea of what to wear tonight."

"Darling," said her smiling mate, "you're putting me on."

"We're newlyweds and we'd like a suite," said the groom to the hotel clerk.

"Bridal?" inquired the clerk.

"Oh, no!" blurted out the bride. "I'll just hang onto his ears until I get used to it."

Then there was the sleepy bride who couldn't stay awake for a second.

The groom awoke the morning after his wedding to find his bride in tears. "Why are you crying?" he asked.

"Look," she sobbed, pointing to him. "We almost used it all up the first night!"

While inspecting their honeymoon motel room, the bride discovered a little box attached to the bed. "What's this for?" she asked her husband.

"If you put a quarter in," he answered, reaching into his pocket, "the bed starts vibrating."

"Save your money," she cooed. "A quarter in and I start vibrating, too."

Before retiring on his wedding night, the young minister turned to his bride and murmured, "Pardon me, darling, I'm going to pray for guidance."

"Sweetheart," his wife answered, "I'll take care of the guidance. You pray for endurance."

The reception had ended and the newlyweds had just sneaked off to the honeymoon resort. After supper and champagne, the groom retired to the bedroom, but the bride pulled a chair up to the window and sat gazing out at the stars.

"Aren't you coming to bed?" called her impatient husband.

"No," she announced. "My mother told me this would be the most beautiful night of my life—and I don't want to miss a minute of it."

We know an octogenarian who married a woman in her late seventies—they spent their honeymoon trying to get out of the car.

The recently married gentleman came home after a day at the office to find his young wife stretched languorously on the sofa, dressed in a revealing negligee. "Guess what I've got planned for dinner?" she cooed seductively. "And don't tell me you had it for lunch!"

On their wedding night, the honeymoon couple checked into an expensive Miami Beach hotel. Next morning, the groom telephoned room service and ordered a breakfast of bacon and eggs for himself and a plate of lettuce for his bride. "Would the lady care for anything else?" the puzzled clerk asked.

"Not right now," replied the chap. "I just want to see if she eats like a rabbit, too."

On their wedding night, the rather pious young man entered the bedroom and found his bride lying languorously on top of the covers. "I expected to find you on your knees by the side of the bed," he said with a frown.

"Well, I will if you insist," she answered, "but it gives me the hiccups."

As the young newlywed was telling a girlfriend how she had successfully taught her husband some badly needed manners, he suddenly dashed into the living room and said breathlessly, "Come on, honey, let's fuck."

The friend sat stunned as the husband scooped his bride into his arms and carried her into the bedroom. Some time later, the girl returned, smiling and adjusting her clothing. "See what I mean?" she beamed. "A week ago, he wouldn't have asked!"

Sounds drifting from the honeymoon suite kept the bellboy glued to the door. Between gasps, a male voice was saying, "Now will you let me?"

Throughout the night, the same exchange held the bellboy with his ear at the keyhole. As he was about to give up, he heard the man, in a plaintive voice, say, "Honey, it's almost dawn. *Now* will you let me?"

"Oh, all right," sighed a sweet voice. "Go ahead and take it out."

We overheard a couple of modern young ladies chatting at cocktails the other afternoon. "Did you hear about Joanne getting married again?" asked the first.

"No!" exclaimed the other in surprise. "I didn't even know she was pregnant."

One day, after a phone call from his wife, the braggart office manager strutted into the steno pool, chest puffed out with self-satisfaction, and proclaimed loudly, "Well, girls, my wife is pregnant!"

After a moment's silence, a small voice in the back of the room replied, "Whom do you suspect?"

"It all happened so fast," sighed the sweet young thing trying on a bridal gown. "First he said 'I do' and then I said 'I do'—and now we have to get married.

Our Research Department informs us that today's most common form of marriage proposal is: "You're *what!?*"

The beautiful eighteen-year-old girl, sobbing quietly at the funeral service for her seventy-five-year-old husband, was overheard confiding to a solicitous neighbor: "We had such a happy marriage for the six months it lasted. Every Sunday morning he would make love to me, and he'd keep time with the church bells that summoned you all to services." She sobbed a little, then said with rising animation, "And he'd still be alive today if it weren't for that damned fire engine that went clanging by!"

Eighty-five-year-old Will Jones hobbled down to the local bar to have a cold one and shoot the breeze with his friends. Mr. Jones was the talk of the town, as he had recently married a beautiful nineteen-year-old girl. Several of the boys bought the old man a drink in an effort to get him to tell of his wedding night, and sure enough, the old rascal fell right into the swing of it. "My youngest son carried me upstairs and lifted me onto the bed with my young bride," the octogenarian re-called. "We spent the night together and the next morning my three other sons carried me off the bed." The small circle of men scratched their heads and asked the old boy why it took three of his sons to carry him off the matrimonial mattress when it took only his youngest boy to put him on. Proudly, he replied, "I fought them!"

About to marry a girl in her early twenties, the spry octogenarian went to a marriage counselor and asked how he might keep his prospective bride happy. Shaking his head, the counselor could only say: "I think you should take in a youthful boarder."

Several months later, the old gent returned to the counselor and reported that his new wife was pregnant. "I see you took my advice about the boarder," said the counselor, chuckling.

"Yep," said the octogenarian, "and she's pregnant, too."

The two old maids lived their lonely lives together until, rather unexpectedly, a stranger arrived on the scene and whisked one of them away in matrimony. After the honeymoon, the new bride visited her unmarried friend and painted an ecstatic picture of married life.

"Our honeymoon," she said, "was like a cruise down the Mediter-ranean, a sail into a glorious sunset. It was *wonderful!*"

The second old maid was very much impressed and determined to get a man for herself. She showed her bankbook around town and eventually nailed a local gigolo. They were married at once and began their honeymoon.

They climbed into their wedding bed and in a short time the husband was flushed with excitement. The bride, however, was cool as a cucumber and decidedly unaffected by the proceedings.

"I simply don't understand it," she said rather indignantly. "My friend told me that marriage was like a cruise down the Mediterranean —like a sail into a glorious sunset."

"Oh, she did, eh?" said the guy, now trembling with uncontrollable excitement. "Well, bon voyage, baby—I'm sailing without you!"

An optimist is a man who looks forward to marriage. A pessimist is a married optimist.

It was the first day for Joyce, the newly hired salesgirl in the maternity shop, and a hectic day it had been. The store had been crowded from the moment its doors opened, and the girl had sped from one customer to another without stopping. Now, just as she concluded a large sale and anticipated a breathing spell, the doors opened and a fresh flood of obviously expectant ladies poured in.

"Ye gods!" the exhausted salesgirl cried in anguish. "Doesn't *any- one* do it for fun any more?"

The understanding employer was only too glad to give his clerk the rest of the day off, after the young man explained that his wife was going to have a baby. When the clerk came to work the following morning, the boss called him into his office to offer his congratulations and inquired, "Was it a boy or a girl?"

"Oh, it's much too soon to tell," the clerk replied. "We have to wait nine months to find that out."

The unusually high birthrate in a suburb near our city was recently explained to us. Every morning at 6:15 the Express comes roaring through town blowing its whistle.

It's too early to get out of bed, and too late to go back to sleep.

The rural lady had been coming into the city hospital regularly to give birth to her annual child. When she was packing up to go home after her tenth trip, the nurse said, "Well, Mrs. Slocum, I suppose we'll be seeing you again next year, as usual?"

"No, ma'm," drawled Mrs. Slocum. "My husband and I jest found out what's been causin' it."

Our Research Department informs us that the bathroom is no longer the room where the most household accidents occur. It's the bedroom.

A priest engaged in social work attempted to explain the Church's views on birth control to a tough but friendly gang of teen-agers that had gathered around him on the sidewalk in front of a favorite juke joint.

"When you're married, you have two choices," he said, "periodic abstinence and complete continence."

The teen-agers thought about that for several moments, then a cool cat standing on the curb announced, "I get it, man—rhythm and blues!"

Our Research Department reports that these miraculous new hearing aids may be instrumental in lowering the birth rate. They bolster this fantastic assumption by the following case history:

John and Susan X had produced a bouncing baby every single year of their married life until quite recently when Susan, who is hard of hearing, acquired the aforementioned apparatus. As Susan explains it: "Every night when we retire, John always turns to me and asks, 'Well, shall we go to sleep or what?' And before I got my hearing aid, I always answered, 'What?' "

"Darling," she whispered, "will you still love me after we are married?"

He considered this for a moment and then replied, "I think so. I've always been especially fond of married women."

If you must get married, it is always advisable to marry a ravishing beauty. Otherwise, you'll never find anybody to take her off your hands.

A none-too-likable, middle-aged office gal of our acquaintance has announced that she much prefers the business world to marriage. "In my younger days," she boasts, "I could have married any man I pleased."

"Obviously," observes a waggish friend of ours, "she never pleased anyone."

Interviewing the sixty-five-year-old rodeo champion in Amarillo, Texas, the New York newspaperman remarked, "You're really an extraordinary man, to be a rodeo champion at your age."

"Heck," said the cowboy, "I'm not nearly the man my Pa is. He was just signed to play guard for a pro football team, and he's eighty-eight."

"Amazing!" gasped the journalist. "I'd like to meet your father."

"Can't right now. He's in Fort Worth standing up for Grandpa. Grandpa is getting married tomorrow. He's a hundred and fourteen."

"Your family is simply unbelievable," said the newspaperman. "Here you are, a rodeo champion at sixty-five. Your father's a football player at eighty-eight. And now your grandfather wants to get married at a hundred and fourteen."

"Hell, mister, you got that wrong," said the Texan. "Grandpa doesn't *want* to get married. He *has* to."

Getting married is a good deal like going into a restaurant with friends. You order what you want, then when you see what the other fellow has, you wish you had taken that.

We know a man who thinks marriage is a fifty-fifty proposition, which convinces us that he either doesn't understand women or percentages.

It was while they were crushed together in passionate embrace that Harry decided the psychological moment was at hand to tell Marge.

"Honey," he whispered. "I want you to know that I think you're a wonderful person and that I certainly appreciate your—uh—company, but as far as I'm concerned, wedlock is nowhere."

In reply, Marge uttered only a small sigh of pleasure.

"I mean," Harry went on doggedly, "you're more like a sister to me."

At that, Marge's lovely eyes opened, and her lips parted in surprise. "My God," she murmured, "what a home life you must have!"

Sunday was to be the day of Joe's wedding, and he and his father were enjoying a nightcap together before they retired to gather strength for the next day's event.

Lifting his glass in a toast to his father, Joe asked: "Any advice before I take the big step, Dad?"

"Yes," the father said. "Two things. First: Insist on having one night out a week with the boys."

"Makes sense. And second?"

"Second: Don't waste it on the boys."

The gods gave man fire, and he invented fire engines. They gave him love, and he invented marriage.

George knew just what he wanted in a woman. "The girl I marry," he used to tell us," will be an economist in the kitchen, an aristocrat in the living room and a harlot in bed."

Now he's married and his wife has all the required traits—but not in the same order. She's an aristocrat in the kitchen, a harlot in the living room and an economist in bed.

We've come across a refreshingly unique proposal of marriage: "Honey, how would you like to do this *every* night?"

Returning from his vacation, Roger asked for two weeks more in which to get married.

"But you just had two weeks off," protested his boss. "Why didn't you get married then?"

"What," exclaimed Roger, "and ruin my vacation?"

Marriage is like a long banquet with the dessert served first.

In her own eyes, Peggy was the most popular girl in the world. "You know," she said, with characteristic modesty, "a lot of men are going to be miserable when I marry."

"Really?" said her date, stifling a yawn. "How many are you going to marry?"

"I'll never marry a man who snores," said the pretty young thing.

"All right," replied her mother, "but be careful how you find out."

Marriage starts with billing and cooing but only the billing lasts.

The young man stood in the doorway unnoticed for several minutes before he had the courage to speak. Then, clearing his throat, he said, "Excuse me for interrupting you, sir, but I've come to ask for your daughter's hand in marriage."

"I see," replied the father, giving the youth a swift appraisal. "And tell me, young man, do you think you can make my little girl happy?"

"Oh, I can do that all right, sir," the boy exclaimed, obviously pleased to have been asked something to which he could respond with such a strong affirmative. "You should have seen her when I had her up in my room earlier this evening . . . !"

We've heard of a persistent suitor who spent so much money on a girl over a two-year period that he finally married her for *his* money.

We know a fun-loving young lady who insists she won't even consider marriage until she's gotten some experience under her belt.

The middle-aged suburban father was reading his newspaper when his daughter's boyfriend came to the house and asked to speak to him. "I realize this is only a formality," the young man declared, "but I want to ask for your daughter's hand."

"And where did you get the idea that this was just a formality?"

"From her obstetrician," replied the boy.

Census takers have found that one tenth of all married couples aren't.

Sleeping the sleep of the just in his upper berth, the gentleman was awakened by a persistent tapping from below.

"Oh, Mr. Forsythe, are you awake?" asked the middle-aged lady in the berth below.

"I am now," he said groggily.

"It's frightfully cold down here, Mr. Forsythe. I wonder if you would mind getting me a blanket."

"I've a better idea, lady," he said. "Let's pretend we're married."

He could hear her giggling softly below him. "That sounds like a lovely idea," she said.

"Good," said he, rolling over. "Now go get your *own* damn blanket."

Florence and Emily, two pretty young housewives, had arranged to have cocktails and lunch together, but as soon as they met, Emily could see that something serious was bothering her friend.

"Out with it, Florence," she commanded. "What's depressing you so?"

"I'm ashamed to admit it," Florence wailed, "but I caught my husband making love."

"Why let that bother you?" laughed Emily. "I got mine the same way."

The boss had listened in sympathetic silence as Sylvester went through the reasons why he needed, and felt he deserved, a raise. Then, with a benevolent smile, he patted the younger man on the shoulder.

"Yes, Sylvester," he said kindly, "I know you can't get married on the salary I'm paying you—and someday you'll thank me for it."

Mrs. Farnsworthy felt bereaved but sympathetic when she got the news that Juliette, her jewel of a French maid, was leaving to get married.

"Ah, well," she said, seeing the glow of happiness on the girl's beautiful young face, "I am overjoyed for you, Juliette. You will have it much easier now that you're getting married."

"Yes, Madam," said the girl, with a tingle of anticipation that made her trim figure tremble, "and more frequently as well."

A man is incomplete until he's married—then he's really finished.

4
HUSBAND
& WIFE

One guy we know is so suspicious that when his wife gave birth to twins, he flew into a rage because only one of them looked like him.

The fellows were kidding the one married man among them. "You've been married five years now, George," one of them said. "How come you have no children? Is your wife—" (and here he tried a very bad pun)"—*unbearable?*"

"Or," interjected another, "is she inconceivable?"

"Maybe she's, uh, impregnable," joked a third.

The married man shook his head. "No, boys, you're all wrong. She's insurmountable and inscrutable."

"That wife of mine is a liar," said the angry husband to a sympathetic pal seated next to him in the bar.

"How do you know?" the friend asked.

"She didn't come home last night and when I asked her where she'd been, she said she had spent the night with her sister, Shirley."

"So?"

"She's a liar. *I* spent the night with her sister, Shirley."

The husband was disturbed by his wife's indifferent attitude towards him and the marriage counselor suggested he try being more aggressive in his lovemaking.

"Act more like a romantic lover and less like a bored spouse," he was advised. "When you go home, make love to her as soon as you meet —even if it is right inside the front door."

At the next consultation, the adviser was pleased to hear that the husband had followed instructions. "And how did she react this time?" the consultant asked.

"Well, to tell the truth," the husband replied, "she was still sort of indifferent. But one thing I've got to admit: Her bridge club went absolutely wild!"

The husband came strolling in the front door to discover his wife in the passionate embrace of his best friend.

"I love him, John," she said to her surprised spouse.

"See here," said the friend, "we're all too sophisticated to let a situation like this get out of hand. Tell you what let's do—we're both sportsmen—I'll play you a game of gin rummy for her."

The husband thought about that for a moment.

"All right," he said, "but let's play for a penny-a-point on the side, just to keep it interesting."

The ship's captain returned from a two-year voyage to find his wife nursing a month-old baby. "Who did this?" he demanded. "Was it my friend Mike Fitzpatrick?"

"No," his wife said softly.

"Well then, was it my friend Bob Bigelow?"

His wife shook her head.

"Bill Connery," he demanded, "could it have been my friend Bill Connery?"

"*Your* friends, *your* friends," his wife said impatiently, "all the time, *your* friends. Don't you think I have any friends of my own?"

"A man is responsible for the good name of his family," said the lecturer grandly. "Is there a man among us who would let his wife be slandered and not rise to her defense?"

One meek little fellow in the back of the room stood up.

"What's this?" exclaimed the speaker. "You, sir—would you permit your wife to be slandered and not protest?!"

"Oh," apologized the little fellow, resuming his seat, "I thought you said 'slaughtered.'"

"You want to know why I've come home half loaded?" said the soused spouse. "Because I ran out of money, that's why."

Demonstrating once again the importance of the lowly comma, this telegram was sent from a wife to her husband: "NOT GETTING ANY, BETTER COME HOME AT ONCE."

"You used to be the life of the party in the old days," reminisced one buddy to the other. "Does your wife still find you entertaining after six years of marriage?"

"No," answered the live one, "she usually doesn't catch me."

We know an honest, if henpecked, husband who tells us that he really doesn't mind being in the doghouse as long as he can get his tail outside.

"For twenty long and wonderful years," mused the gentleman at the bar, "my wife and I were deliriously happy."

"Then what happened?" asked the bartender.

"We met."

She knew that these were to be her last few hours on this earth, so she called her husband to her side and in a halting voice told him her last request.

"I know," she said, "that you and Mother have never gotten along. But would you, as a special favor to me, ride to the cemetery in the same car with her?"

"All right," replied the unhappy husband, "but it will spoil my whole day."

Over Gibsons, two animated gentlemen were having a rousing battle about the charms of Kim Novak.

"I say she's overrated," said one. "Take away her eyes, her hair, her lips and her figure and what have you got?"

"My wife," said the other with a heavy sigh.

Walter arrived at his office late one morning and was greeted with giggles from the pretty receptionist.

"What are you laughing at?" asked Walter.

"There's a big black smudge on your face," said the girl.

"Oh, that!" said Walter. "That's easy to explain. I saw my wife off on a month's vacation this morning; I took her to the station and kissed her good-bye."

"But what about the smudge?"

"As soon as she got on board, I ran up and kissed the engine."

Arthur sat brooding at his favorite bar. "Charley," he said to the bartender, "I'm a rat. I've a lovely wife at home and instead of appreciating her, I've been out getting into trouble with another woman.

But a guy can reform. I'm going home right now, Charley, and I'm going to tell her everything, beg her to forgive me and start anew as a model husband."

Thereupon, Arthur paid his tab, went home, told his wife everything and begged her to forgive him so he could start anew as a model husband.

"I'll forgive you on one condition, Arthur," his wife said. "I want to know the name of the woman." But Arthur was too gallant to tell.

"Was it Susan Adams?" she asked.

"I can't tell you, dear," he said.

"I'll bet it was Mrs. Simpson," the wife declared.

"My lips are sealed," said hubby.

"I know," exclaimed the wife, "it's that hussy Mrs. Higgins."

The next day Arthur was seated again at his favorite bar and as he sipped on a vodka Martini, the bartender asked how he'd made out with his good resolution of the night before.

"Not bad," said Arthur. "My wife didn't forgive me, but she gave me three pretty good new leads."

"What are you nagging me about?" complained the husband. "I was in last night by a quarter of twelve."

"You were not, you liar!" cried the irate wife. "I heard you come in and the clock was striking three."

"Well, stupid," said hubby, "isn't three a quarter of twelve?"

Henry was helping his son fly a kite in the back yard, but was having trouble getting it to stay up. His wife stood watching them from the porch. Henry had just run the entire length of the yard, trying to pull the kite into the air, only to have it thrash about uncertainly and plummet to the ground.

"Henry," said the wife, "you need more tail."

"I wish you'd make up your mind," said Henry, panting heavily. "Last night you told me to go fly a kite!"

Sam, the private eye, was giving his curvesome client a report.

"I trailed your husband into four bars and a bachelor's apartment," he said.

"Aha!" exclaimed the wife. "Go on, go on! What was he doing there?"

"Well, lady," Sam responded in an embarrassed tone, "near as I could make out, he was trailing *you*."

The suburban couple, middle-aged and married for very nearly twenty-two years, were out for the Saturday-afternoon ritual with the grass, the bushes and flowers. He was putting Vigoro on the crab grass and she was pruning the rose bushes, but somehow their minds didn't seem to be on their work. The wife seemed especially discontent and was mumbling under her breath about something; then, quite unexpectedly, she stalked over to where the husband was standing, examining at close range a tree fungus on his favorite elm, and gave him a short kick to the ankle.

"Ow-ouch!" exclaimed the husband, seizing the bruised appendage. "What the hell did you do that for?!"

"That," she said, stalking back to her rose bushes, "is for being such a lousy lover!"

The husband thought about this unexpected attack for a minute or two, then he turned and—just as resolutely as she had a few moments before—stalked over and gave his wife a swift and well-placed foot to the behind as she bent over, about to pluck an American Beauty.

"OW!" she wailed. "You brute—why did you do *that?*"

"THAT," said he, returning to his elm, "is for knowing the difference!"

The two Madison Avenue types met on the suburban train platform.

"Hi, Charley," greeted the one, "how's your wife?"

"Compared to what?" responded the other dryly.

A young politician, eager to gather votes, accepted the invitation of a local woman's club to speak on the subject of sex. However, fearing that his wife wouldn't understand, he told her that he planned to lecture on sailing.

A week after the speech, his wife ran into one of the ladies of the club who mentioned how entertaining his talk had been.

"I just can't understand it," said the wife, "he knows so little about it."

"Come on, darling, don't be coy. His talk showed intimate acquaintance with the subject," said the matron.

"But he's only tried it twice," protested the wife. "The first time he lost his hat and the second he became seasick."

Although he kept bachelor's hours, Harry quite piously demanded absolute fidelity from his wife. Almost every night he would leave her at home with the children, bidding her farewell with a cheery, "Good-night, mother of three."

Then one night she called back just as cheerfully, "Good-night, father of one."

Now Harry stays home.

Some men are so interested in their wives' continued happiness that they hire detectives to find out the reason for it.

Two men met at a cocktail party, and as they stood talking, one glanced across the room and remarked, "Get a load of that ugly woman over there, with a nose like a pomegranate and what looks to be a fifty-five-inch waistline!"

"That's my wife," said the other man.

"Oh, I'm sorry," said the first man.

"*You're* sorry?!!"

Some wives claim that if you give a man enough rope, he'll claim he's tied up at the office.

Then there was the man who wanted to get something for his wife, but no one would start the bidding.

A henpecked husband was heard to remark after his third Martini, "Give my wife an inch and she thinks she's a ruler!"

At a suburban dinner party, a curvaceous blonde was the center of attraction. She stood in the middle of the room surrounded by almost every male in the place. Finally, one woman turned to her husband and meowed, "I don't see what they see in her."

"I don't either," replied her husband as he started across the room. "I think I'll take a closer look."

A not-so-young housewife was bragging to her husband about her slim figure. "I can still get into the same skirts that I had before we were married," she said.

Without glancing up from his newspaper, her spouse replied, "I wish the hell *I* could."

"And my husband is very absent-minded," wailed the embarrassed bride to the marriage counselor. "Last night, while we were making love, the doorbell rang; and without saying a word, he jumped up and answered it."

"You mean he just got up and left you lying there?" the incredulous counselor asked.

"No, sir," she sobbed, "he took me with him!"

A young wife whose husband had grown neglectful decided that the best way to arouse his dormant interest would be to shock him into jealousy.

"Darling," she purred one night, "the doctor I visited today said I had the most flawless face, full, well-rounded breasts and the loveliest legs he'd ever seen."

"And did he say anything about your fat ass?" her husband asked her.

"Oh no, dear," she said calmly, "your name wasn't mentioned once during our talk."

A beautiful but obviously overwrought young woman tearfully admitted to her doctor that after almost a year of marriage, her husband had not yet made love to her.

"No wonder you're nervous and upset," said the astonished physician. "Bring your husband to my office tomorrow afternoon and I'll have a talk with him."

The following day, she returned with her husband.

"I dislike prying into your personal life, my good man," the doctor said, "But you're not fulfilling your marital obligations."

"What do you mean, doctor?" the naïve husband replied. "I'm considerate, gentle, devoted and a good provider."

"But what about your *sexual* obligations?" the doctor demanded.

"I don't understand," the husband replied.

The doctor tried to explain, but the husband was too stupid to comprehend.

"All right," said the doctor at last, in exasperation, "then I'll *show* you."

He then asked the pretty wife to disrobe. After she had wriggled out of her clothes, the good medic proceeded to make passionate love to her. When he was finished, the doctor said "And *that's* what every married woman needs at least twice a week."

Seeing the happy glow on his wife's face, the husband could only agree. "Very well, doctor," he said, "we'll be back on Friday for another treatment."

Worried about their lackluster sex life, the young wife finally persuaded her husband to undergo hypnotic treatment. After a few sessions, his sexual interest waxed anew; but during their lovemaking, he would occasionally dash out of the bedroom.

Overcome by curiosity, she followed him to the bathroom. Tiptoeing to the doorway, she saw him standing before the mirror, staring fixedly at himself and muttering, "She's not my wife . . . she's not my wife. . . ."

"My sex life has improved immeasurably since my wife and I got twin beds," the business executive confided to an associate.

"How can that be?" the associate asked.

"Well," replied the exec, "hers is in Connecticut and mine's in Manhattan."

"I've got an idea," said the attractive wife to her husband. "Let's go out tonight and have some real fun."

"Suits me," he answered. "If you get home first, leave the light on in the hallway."

At her wit's end, the young wife finally took pen in hand and wrote to a lovelorn columnist:

"I'm afraid I married a sex maniac. My husband never leaves me alone—he makes love to me all night long, while I'm in the shower, while I'm cooking breakfast, while I'm making the beds and even while I'm trying to clean the house. Can you tell me what to do?

Sign me,
Worn-out

P.S. Please excuse the jerky handwriting."

Wishing to surprise her husband with a new wig she had just bought, the wife put it on and strolled unannounced into his office. "Do you think you could find a place in your life for a woman like me?" she asked sexily.

"Not a chance," he replied. "You remind me too much of my wife."

During a session with a marriage counselor, the wife snapped at her husband: "That's not true—I *do* enjoy sex!" Then, turning to the counselor, she added: "But this fiend expects it three or four times a year!"

"Your Honor," said the distraught woman, pointing to her husband, "he won't give me enough money to feed and clothe our four children."

"Young lady," the judge announced, "I'm going to see to it that you get at least a hundred dollars a week."

At this, the husband jumped up and exclaimed: "That's mighty kind of you, your Honor. And I'll try to give her a couple of bucks myself."

"I think I've finally cured my husband of coming home in the wee hours of the morning," the wife proudly announced on New Year's Day. "Last night, when I heard him fumbling downstairs, I yelled: 'Is that you, Harold?' "

"How has that cured him?" questioned her friend.

"His name is Charles."

"I always worry when you leave on a business trip," sobbed the salesman's lovely young wife.

"Don't worry about me, honey," he answered soothingly. "I'll be back before you know it."

"I know," she said. "That's what worries me."

Sitting in the doctor's office, the frustrated fellow unburdened himself of a tale of woe. His beautiful young wife, who had been delightfully passionate before they were married, had now lost all interest in sex.

"Try giving her these," said the doctor, handing him a bottle of pills. "One each evening with dinner."

The man complied, but the first night brought no reaction. On the second evening, he gave his wife two pills, but still no reaction. On the third night, he gave her half the bottle and, in disgust, swallowed the rest himself. Soon, his wife stretched out languorously on the couch. "Oh, darling," she said, "I want a man."

"That's funny," said her husband. "So do I."

"My wife is the most suspicious woman in the world," complained the harried husband to a sympathetic friend. "If I come home early, she thinks I'm after something. And if I come home late, she thinks I've already had it."

The young, attractive housewife was a bit surprised when her husband's best friend dropped by one afternoon and offered five hundred dollars to make love to her. Thinking that the extra money would come in handy, she led him into the bedroom and fulfilled her part of the bargain. Later that afternoon, her husband returned from work. "Did David stop by today?" he asked casually.

"Yes, he did," she stammered. "Why do you ask?"

"Well," her spouse replied, "he was supposed to return the five hundred dollars I lent him last week."

We know a fellow who, upon being told by his shrewish wife that she would dance on his grave, promptly provided for a burial at sea.

When the shrew learned her husband had taken a mistress, she demanded, "Does this mean that you've had enough of me?"

"No, my dear," he coolly replied. "It means that I *haven't* had enough of you."

The nonchurchgoer's wife persuaded him to attend a service on a hot summer Sunday. He was ignorant of the various rituals involved and his spouse seemed to constantly be whispering, "Stand up," "Sit down," "Kneel," "Stand up," "Sit."

Perspiring from all the activity, he took out a handkerchief to mop his brow and then laid it on his lap to dry. Seeing this, his wife leaned over and whispered, "Is your fly open?"

"No," he replied testily. "Should it be?"

We know a happily married philanderer who justifies his amours with the comment, "My wife doesn't care where I get my appetite, as long as I eat at home."

"I've just invented a cotton gin," Eli Whitney declared proudly as he emerged from his workshop.

"Big deal," his wife grumbled. "Who needs a fluffy Martini?"

The jaded husband called his voluptuous wife to tell her he'd discovered a *new* position for making love; his wife was excited by the prospect of something fresh in their usually uninspired intimacies—and she pressed for more information. "In this new sexual position, we'll engage in intercourse lying back to back," he said.

"Back to back?!" she said. "I don't understand how that's possible?!"

"It's quite simple," he replied. "I'm bringing home another couple."

Morning, Howard," said the commuter, getting on the train. "How's the wife?"

"Just fine, George," came the response. "How's mine?"

It was the social event of the season: the identical twin sons of a wealthy oil tycoon married the twin daughters of a millionaire textile manufacturer. Unfortunately, all four of the newlyweds got very drunk on their wedding night. Now, a year later, the newly arrived offspring are listed in *Who's Who*, but nobody is really sure who's whose.

A friend of ours sat down next to another passenger on a train recently and couldn't help overhearing his conversation out the window with a man standing on the station platform.

"Thanks for putting me up while I was here, Sam," said the passenger.

"Glad to do it," said the other man.

"Thanks for the food and the drinks—everything was wonderful."

"It was a pleasure," said the man.

"And thank your wife, Sam—she was great," said the passenger, as the train began pulling out. "I really enjoyed sleeping with her."

Our friend was rather taken aback by this exchange and he turned to his fellow passenger and said: "Pardon me sir, but I couldn't help overhearing your conversation. Did I understand you to say that you enjoyed sleeping with your friend's wife?"

"Well," said the fellow passenger, "I didn't *really* enjoy it. But Sam is a hell of a nice guy."

"Your wife will probably hit the ceiling when you get home tonight," said the bar fly to his drinking companion.

"Yeah," said the companion. "She's a lousy shot!"

The talkative lady was telling her husband about the bad manners of a recent visitor. "If that woman yawned once while I was talking," she said, "she yawned thirty times."

"Maybe she wasn't yawning, dear," said the husband, "just trying to say something."

During a chance meeting of two old friends who had not seen each other in years, one of the men inquired about the other's wife.

"Oh, but of course, you couldn't know," said the second man sadly. "Doris has gone to heaven."

"I'm sorry to hear that," said the first man, who was a bachelor. Then, realizing that this might be misunderstood, he corrected himself, saying, "I mean, I'm glad!" Then, noticing the shocked look on his friend's face, he blurted, "That is, I'm awfully surprised!"

When a funeral procession passed a golf course where four men were preparing to tee off for their regular Saturday-afternoon game, one of them turned toward the street, removed his cap and held it over his heart. "Why did you do that?" asked his partner.

"Well," replied the fellow, "I thought it was the least I could do for my wife."

An undertaker called the next of kin to confirm the funeral arrangements desired for the dear departed and, as luck would have it, the son-in-law—who was actually delighted to be rid of the old battle-ax —answered the phone.

"We're sorry to disturb you in this time of personal grief," the undertaker intoned solemnly, "but there appears to be some confusion as to whether the body of the loved one is to be buried or cremated."

"Let's not take any chances," came the prompt reply. "Do both."

We know a cynical husband who says it's better to have loved and lost than to have loved and won.

We know a young thing who had been married three times and was still a virgin: Her first husband, a psychiatrist, only talked about it; the second, a gynecologist, just looked at it; and the third was a gourmet.

While visiting the livestock exhibit at a county fair with her husband, the overbearing wife asked one of the bull breeders how many times a week his animals performed their stud function.

"Oh, about four or five times," replied the owner.

Turning to her husband with a scornful look, she said, "You see, four or five times a week is not unusual among champions."

Realizing that he had contributed to the woman's abuse of her husband, the breeder quickly added, "Of course, we never use the same cow twice."

Jealously eying her next-door neighbor's new mink stole, the young wife asked how she had been able to afford such an expensive item.

"You probably won't believe it," her neighbor replied, "but I saved up the money by charging my husband five dollars every time we made love."

That night, when her husband tried to fondle her, the young wife, determined to get a mink of her own, promptly stuck out her palm and demanded five dollars. Fumbling through his trousers, the husband complained that he had only $4.50.

"For $4.50," she rejoined stubbornly, "you can only sample my affection!"

After several minutes of extensive sampling, however, the aroused wife realized she would not be able to resist her husband's advances much longer. In a final attempt to maintain her newly acquired bargaining position, she whispered in his ear, "If it's all the same to you, dear, why don't I lend you fifty cents until tomorrow?"

Joe sat at his dying wife's bedside. Her voice was little more than a whisper.

"Joe, darling," she breathed, "I've a confession to make before I go. . . . I . . . I'm the one who took the $10,000 from your safe. . . . I spent it on a fling with your best friend, Charles. And it was I who forced your mistress to leave the city. And I am the one who reported your income-tax evasion to the government. . . ."

"That's all right, dearest, don't give it a second thought," answered Joe. "I'm the one who poisoned you."

Harry, a golf enthusiast if ever there was one, arrived home from the club to an irate, ranting wife.

"I'm leaving you, Harry," his wife announced bitterly. "You promised me faithfully that you'd be back before noon and here it is almost nine P.M. It just can't take that long to play eighteen holes of golf."

"Now, wait," said Harry. "Let me explain. I know what I promised you, but I have a very good reason for being late. I got up at the crack of dawn, as you know, and picked up Fred at six A.M. But on the way to the course we had a flat tire and when I changed it I discovered that the spare was flat, too. So I had to walk three miles to a gas station to get the tire fixed and then roll it all the way back and put it on the car.

After that, we got back into the car, drove a quarter of a mile and ran out of gas. I had to trudge all the way back to the gas station and back to the car again. Finally we got to the course and started to play. Everything was fine for the first two holes and then, on the third tee, Fred had a stroke. I ran back to the clubhouse but couldn't find a doctor. And, by the time I got back to Fred, he was dead. So, for the next sixteen holes, it was hit the ball and drag Fred, hit the ball and drag Fred. . . ."

"**I** was married twice," explained the man to a newly discovered drinking companion, "and I'll never marry again. My first wife died after eating poison mushrooms and my second died of a fractured skull."

"That's a shame," offered the friend. "How did that happen?"

"She wouldn't eat her mushrooms."

The matronly woman was alone in the house watching her favorite television program when her husband burst through the front door, stalked into the bedroom without saying a word and began packing his suitcase.

"Where are you going?" she demanded.

"I resigned from the firm today. I'm sick and tired of you and I'm going to Australia," was his reply. "I'm told that the young ladies there will gladly pay twenty dollars a night for the services of a good man and I intend to live off the earnings from my lovemaking." He then continued to pack.

Suddenly, his wife pulled her suitcase from the closet and began packing her own clothing.

"And where do you think you're going?" he demanded to know.

"To Australia," she laughed. "I want to see how you're going to live on forty dollars a month!"

News item: Mrs. Bradley Fowler was granted a divorce after she told the judge her husband had spoken to her only three times since they were married. Mrs. Fowler was awarded the custody of their three children.

The rising exec married a co-worker's ex-wife, and his spiteful predecessor persisted in reminding him that he had received second-hand merchandise. "Hey, George," quipped the first husband one day at lunch, "how do you like handling worn goods?"

"It's great," George replied, "once you get beyond the used part."

It's been said that the trouble in the Garden of Eden wasn't caused by an apple—but by a green pair.

Adam and Eve were walking in the Garden.

"Do you love me?" asked Eve.

Replied Adam, nonchalantly, "Who else?"

Returning from the funeral of his beautiful wife, the widower was disconsolate.

"I know how deeply grieved you are," his best friend said, "but you're young and in time you will forget. You'll meet someone else with whom you will share real happiness."

"I know, I know," said the husband. "but what about *tonight?*"

"I have seven children and I've just found out my husband has never really loved me," said the distraught woman to her lawyer.

"There, there, my dear," said the attorney. "Just imagine the fix you'd be in today if he *had*."

The tensions of life were threatening to get a stranglehold on Bill, and after he'd finished a good dinner it was his pleasant expectation to relax mindlessly in a soft chair next to the stereo, with a stiff drink in his hand. His wife, unfortunately, knew nothing of his nervous state, and hardly had he seated himself then she climbed onto his lap. With the thought of trying to wheedle a fur coat from him, she cuddled as close to him as she could, murmuring and fondling, until he finally exploded:

"Good heavens, Ethel, get off! I get enough of this at the office."

When Tom, the rising young insurance executive, appeared at his friend Ed's home in the early-morning hours, asking to be put up for the night, Ed was concerned by his friend's hollow-eyed appearance.

"What happened, Tom? You and your wife have a fight?"

"Yeah. When I got home tonight I was really beat, tired as hell. So when she asked me for fifty dollars for a new dress . . ."

"Yeah?"

"Well," Tom went on sheepishly, "I guess I must have been half asleep or something, because I said, 'All right, but let's finish this dictation first.' "

A pair of suburban couples who had known each other for quite some time talked it over and decided to do a little conjugal swapping. The trade was made the following evening and the newly arranged couples retired to their respective houses. After about an hour of bedroom bliss, one of the wives propped herself up on an elbow, looked at her new partner and said:

"Well, I wonder how the boys are getting along."

Martin was known among his friends for the punctuality with which he sent his wife her alimony payment each month. When asked the reason for his haste, he shivered and explained: "I'm afraid that if I ever should fall behind in my payments she might decide to repossess me."

Behind every successful man stands a surprised wife.

Many a wife thinks her husband is the world's greatest lover. But she can never manage to catch him at it.

The weeping bride poured out her heart to the eminent marriage counselor. "Isn't there some way—without turning into a nag—that I can keep my husband in line?"

The counselor scowled. "Young lady," he said, "your husband shouldn't have to wait in line!"

John Harrison was despondent. He'd been married for ten years and had nothing to show for it but twelve children; he and his wife were obviously compatible, but that was not enough. He found it impossible to get by on a single job, so he'd taken two; now the long hours were beginning to affect his health. Slowly he trudged down the basement steps.

"I can't support my family," he said to himself, though he'd said the same thing many times to his wife as well. "I'm no good to them and no good to myself." He picked up a piece of clothes line, made a noose, and placed it around his neck. "They'd be better off if I were dead," he said. He climbed up on a box, tossed the loose end of the rope over a pipe and tied it securely to the top of the washing machine. "If I were dead, they'd at least have the insurance," he said. "My sweet wife has given me everything, and I've had nothing to give her in return— nothing but twelve children to feed, and wash for, and clean up after and worry over. . . ."

He tightened the rope about his throat, shut his eyes and then his sweet wife dashed downstairs, crying out, "John! Don't do it. You're hanging an innocent man!"

During a grouse hunt in North Carolina two intrepid sportsmen were blasting away at a clump of trees near a stone wall. Suddenly a red-faced country squire popped his head over the wall and shouted, "Hey, you almost hit my wife."

"Did I?" cried the hunter, aghast. "Terribly sorry. Have a shot at mine over there."

The sexy wife of a busy husband recently won a divorce, charging her hubby with lack of attentiveness. "If anything ever happened to me," the stacked missus claimed, "my husband wouldn't even be able to identify the body."

5
SWINGING SPOUSES

"I've learned one thing about women," said the experienced one to his drinking companions. "You just can't trust a girl with brown eyes."

"It occurs to me," said one of his inebriated friends, "that I've been married nearly three years and I don't know what color eyes my wife has."

The second man finished his drink, climbed from his stool and hurried home to investigate this disturbing possibility. His wife was in bed asleep. He crept up to her and carefully lifted an eyelid.

"By God! *Brown!*" he exclaimed.

"How the hell did you know I was here?" said Brown, crawling out from under the bed.

Pete was the playboy of the office. He kept the typewriter set bug-eyed with juicy tales of his conquests. One afternoon a bachelor in the office cornered him and asked, "Pete, how the hell do you do it? You're a married man, but you make Casanova look like a two-bit amateur. Come on, buddy, what's your secret?"

Pete was in a conversational mood. "I wouldn't do this for everybody, Eddie," he said, "but you're a friend, so I'll tell you my secret. Like all great plans, it's really very simple. It's all in the *approach!*

"Tonight, take the 5:21 out of Penn Station and get off at Great Neck. You'll find dozens of dolls there waiting for their husbands. Now there are always *some* husbands who have to work late. So all you have to do is be charming and let nature take its course."

The system was indeed simple, but it also seemed foolproof. Eddie boarded the 5:21 that night with Pete's instructions fixed firmly in his mind. But he dozed en route and didn't waken till two stops after Great Neck. He got off the train in a hurry and was about to catch a cab back to his destination when he noticed an unescorted female standing on the platform looking very, very available.

He sauntered over casually, lit her cigarette, and asked whether she'd like to have a nice quiet drink with him.

"I'd love to," she said, "but let's go to my place. It's near here and it's very, very quiet."

Everything went as planned. They had a small dinner at her place, some drinks, then they retired to the pleasures of the bedroom. They'd been enjoying themselves only a few minutes, however, when the door swung open and the lady's husband entered.

"Goddammit, Betty," he cried, "what the hell goes on here? So this is what you do when my back is turned! And as for you, you muttonhead —I thought I told you to get off at Great Neck!!"

Two Englishmen struck up a conversation with an American in the club car of a train headed east out of Chicago.

"I say," queried the younger Englishman, "have you ever been to London?"

The American laughed. "It was my home for two years during the war," he said. "Had some of the wildest times of my life in that old town."

The older Englishman, a little hard of hearing, asked, "What did he say, Reggie?"

"He said he's been to London, father," the younger Englishman replied.

After a little lull in the conversation, the young man asked, "You didn't, by any chance, meet a Hazel Wimbleton in London, did you?"

The American almost fell off his chair. "Hot-Pants Hazel?!" he exclaimed. "My God, I shacked up with that broad for three months just before I came back to the States."

"What did he say, Reggie?" the older Englishman wanted to know.

"He says he knows mother," the younger Englishman responded.

Paul Revere's horse galloped down the country road. The life of the colonies depended on his warning the people that the British were coming. He approached a farmhouse.

"Is your husband at home?" he called to the woman feeding chickens in the yard.

"He's back in the barn, Paul," she answered.

"Tell him to get his musket and go to the village square. The Redcoats are coming!"

The exchange of words had taken but an instant; Revere's horse had not broken its stride. The famous patriot thundered off towards the next farm.

"Is your husband at home?" Revere called to the woman in the doorway of the next farmhouse he approached.

"He's asleep in his room, Paul," she said.

"Tell him to get on his clothes," Revere cried. "The Minute Men are meeting at the village square. The British are coming!"

Horse and rider galloped on to still another home.

"Is your husband at home?" he called to the handsome woman who leaned out the window.

"He's gone to New Amsterdam and won't be back till Sunday," she said.

"Whoa-a-a!"

The husband finally wised up to the fact that his wife was something less than faithful. He put a private investigator on her tail, and within a week had the name and address of the "other man."

"No sonofabitch is going to break up my home," the husband snarled indignantly to himself. "My loving wife would be true to me today if this sneaky guy hadn't come on the scene!"

Still, the husband prided himself on his sophistication, and determined to handle the situation in a businesslike way. He called in his secretary and dictated this letter:

"Sir: It has been called to my attention that for some time now you have been carrying on an affair with my wife. So that we can settle this matter intelligently, please see me in my office at three P.M. sharp on Friday."

The "other man," amused by the husband's formal manner, called in his own secretary and dictated this reply:

"Dear Sir: Received your circular letter this morning. You are advised that I will attend the scheduled conference on time."

Before he went off to the wars, King Arthur locked his lovely wife, Guinevere, into her chastity belt. Then he summoned his loyal friend and subject, Sir Lancelot.

"Lancelot, noble knight," said Arthur, "within this sturdy belt is imprisoned the virtue of my wife. The key to this chaste treasure I will entrust to only one man in the world. To you."

Humbled before this great honor, Lancelot knelt, received his king's blessing and took charge of the key. Arthur mounted his steed and rode off. Not half a mile from his castle, he heard hoofbeats behind him and turned to see Sir Lancelot riding hard to catch up with him. "What is amiss, my friend?" asked the king.

"My lord," gasped Lancelot, "you have given me the wrong key!"

His Lordship awoke with an all too infrequent feeling of virility and joyfully announced his condition to his valet. Impressed, the servant asked, "Shall I notify M'lady?"

"No, just hand me my baggy tweeds," replied his Lordship. "I shall smuggle this one into town."

A married man we know quite well relaxed on a recent business trip by enjoying a lively weekend with a lively blonde. Not long after returning to the home office, however, a rather shifty individual paid him a visit and said, with the nasty innuendo of a professional blackmailer, "Remember that trip you took? Remember that blonde?" The answer to both questions was "Yes."

"Well, mister," said the unsavory one, "it just so happens that I have photographs of everything that you and her did."

"Everything?" gulped our friend.

"Everything! See?" He spread a half-dozen highly detailed snapshots on the desk and after giving them a chance to make the proper impression, asked, "What are you gonna do about it, mister?"

"Well," drawled our friend coolly, "I'll take one of these, two of those, and five of this one over here. Can I have them tinted?"

A sharp rap on the door startled the two lovers.

"Quick, it's my husband," exclaimed the frightened woman. "Jump out the window!"

"But we're on the thirteenth floor," the Casanova gasped.

"Jump," cried the woman. "This is no time to be superstitious."

Mrs. Culpepper was almost in tears. "Oh, Marie," she said to her maid, "I believe my husband is having an affair with his secretary."

"I don't believe it," snapped Marie. "You're just saying that to make me jealous."

"Doctor," said the man on the phone, "my son has scarlet fever."

"Yes, I know," replied the doctor. "I came by your house and treated him yesterday. Just keep him away from the others in the house and. . . ."

"But you don't understand," said the distraught parent. "He's kissed the maid!"

"Well, that's unfortunate. Now we'll probably have to quarantine her. . . ."

"And, doctor, I'm afraid I've kissed the girl myself."

"This is getting complicated. That means you may have contracted the disease."

"Yes, and I've kissed my wife since then."

"Damn it," exclaimed the doctor, "now I'll catch it too!"

Mrs. Applebottom grew angry with the French maid and after a series of stinging remarks regarding the young girl's abilities as a cook and housekeeper, she dismissed her. But the girl's Gallic ancestry wouldn't allow such abuse to go unanswered: "Your husband considers me a better cook and housekeeper than you, Madame. He has told me so himself."

Mrs. Applebottom looked at the girl scornfully and made no comment.

"And furthermore," said the angry girl, "I am better than you in the bed!"

"And I suppose my husband told you that, too," snapped Mrs. Applebottom.

"No, Madame," said the maid, "the chauffeur told me *that!*"

Two longtime friends sipped Scotch in a local bar and talked about their troubles.

"And on top of everything else," said the first, "my wife has cut me down to just once a week."

"That's too bad," agreed his friend, "but it could be worse. I know two guys she's cut off altogether."

"Get this," the husband chuckled. "That ridiculous janitor of ours claims he's made love to every woman in the building except one."

"Hmmmm," said his wife, assuming a thoughtful, faraway expression, "must be that stuck-up Mrs. Frobisher on the fourth floor."

Jim Morgan had just returned from a month-long trip to New York and he met a good friend just outside his office.

"Jim," said the friend, "what's wrong? Your eyes are so red and bloodshot!"

"It happened on the trip," said Jim. "My very first evening in New York, I met this very attractive young woman in a cocktail lounge. We had a few drinks, then dinner and a show. One thing led to another and she spent the night with me at my hotel.

"When I woke the next morning, she was sitting on the edge of the bed crying. I asked her what was troubling her and she told me she was married and that she was very ashamed of herself.

"Well, that got me to thinking about my wife and kids back here, so we both sat there on the edge of the bed and cried for about a half hour."

"But, Jim," said the puzzled friend, "that was almost four weeks ago. What does that have to do with your eyes being bloodshot today?"

"Well, look," Jim exclaimed, "you can't sit and cry your eyes out every morning for four weeks without making them a little red!"

One of our friends has a real problem. He received a note through the mail advising him, "If you don't stop making love to my wife, I'll kill you." The trouble is, the note wasn't signed.

Lord Duffingham returned from his grouse shooting somewhat earlier than usual and found Lady Duffingham in a rather compromising situation with his best friend, Sir Archibald Carpley. Lord Duffingham stood stiffly in the bedroom doorway and loudly berated his wife for her infidelity. With thunder in his voice, he reminded her that he had taken her from a miserable existence in the London slums, given her a fine home, provided her with servants, expensive clothes and jewels.

As Lady Duffingham was by this time crying inconsolably, his Lordship turned his wrath on his supposed friend: "And as for you, Carpley —you might at least stop while I'm talking!"

The king was waving to his loyal subjects from the steps of the palace when he spotted a beggar in the crowd who looked, beneath the dirt and rags, amazingly like his royal self. He had a guard bring the beggar to him and the crowd was likewise struck by the remarkable resemblance. The king was amused, for he knew that the king before him had a well-deserved reputation as a ladies' man, as did he himself.

"Tell me, my good fellow," said the king, smiling, "was your mother perhaps a servant in the royal palace?"

"No, Your Highness," said the beggar, "but my father was."

The outraged husband discovered his wife in bed with another man.

"What is the meaning of this?" he demanded. "Who is this fellow?"

"That seems like a fair question," said the wife, rolling over. "What *is* your name?"

The jealous husband returned home from a business trip a day early and, discovering a strange coat in the front closet, stormed into the living room with the accusation that there was another man in the apartment.

"Where is he?" the husband demanded, as he stalked from room to room, searching.

"You're mistaken, dear," the wife insisted. "That coat must have been left by one of your friends the last time you threw a poker party. Since you've been gone, I haven't even *looked* at another man."

The husband searched through the entire apartment and, finding no one, decided his wife must be telling the truth. Apologizing for his unwarranted display of temper, he then went to the bathroom to wash up. He was running water in the basin when he noticed that the shower curtain was pulled closed. Rather peculiar, he thought. He ripped the curtain open and—sure enough—there was a strange man. But before the astounded husband could utter a word, the man jerked the curtain closed again, saying, "Please! I haven't finished voting yet."

The very swank men's club had for years forbidden the presence of women in any of its stately rooms. One night a dignified member walked in and was shocked to discover a covey of chirruping ladies gathered in the very center of the study.

"What is the meaning of this?" he demanded of the club manager.

"We've decided to let members bring their wives in for dinner one evening a month," was the reply.

"But that's unfair," complained the disgruntled fellow. "I'm not married. Could I bring my girlfriend?"

The manager thought for a moment, and then replied slowly, "I think it might be all right . . . provided she's the wife of a member."

"Anything else, sir?" asked the attentive bellhop, trying his best to make the lady and gentleman comfortable in their penthouse suite in the posh hotel.

"No. No, thank you," replied the gentleman.

"Anything for your wife, sir?" the bellhop asked.

"Why, yes, young man," said the gentleman. "Would you bring me a post card?"

The hungover couple dawdled over a mid-afternoon breakfast, after a particularly wild all-night party held in their fashionable apartment.

"Dearest, this is rather embarrassing," said the husband, "but was it you I made love to in the library last night?"

His wife looked at him reflectively, and then asked, "About what time?"

"Do you cheat on your wife?" asked the psychiatrist.

"Who else?" answered the patient.

"You beast. You animal," cried the young thing. "I'm going back to Mother."

"Never mind," said the guy. "I'll go back to my wife."

"Your continual unfaithfulness proves you are an absolute rotter," stormed the outraged wife, who had just caught her husband for the seventh time in a sportive romp with another woman.

"Quite the contrary," came the cool reply. "It merely proves that I'm too good to be true."

The young married couple had moved into an apartment next to a sexy fashion model, and whenever the husband went over to borrow something it usually took him much longer than his wife thought it should. On one especially extended trip, his wife lost all patience and pounded several times on the wall between the two apartments. Receiving no answer, she called the model on the phone.

"I would like to know," the wife said huffily, "why it takes my husband so long to get something over there!"

"Well," replied the model coolly, "these interruptions certainly aren't helping any."

"**Y**es, you heard correctly," said Phillip rather pensively to the cute cigarette girl. "My wife has run off with my very best friend."

"Oh, I'm terribly sorry, sir," said she. "I suppose he was a handsome scoundrel."

"I don't really know," said Phillip, brightly. "I've never met the chap."

The meek little bank clerk had his suspicions. One day he left work early and, sure enough, at home he found a strange hat and umbrella in the hallway and his wife was on the couch in the living room in the arms of another man. Wild for revenge, the husband picked up the man's umbrella and snapped it in two across his knee. ·

"*There!*" he exclaimed. "Now I hope it rains!"

Arriving home unexpectedly from a business trip, the husband found his wife in bed with his best friend, in what may be delicately described as a compromising position.

"See here," exclaimed the husband, "just what do you two think you're doing?"

"See!" said the wife to the man beside her. "Didn't I tell you he was stupid?"

Joe had been out on the town with a dazzling blonde, and as he returned home the rosy tints of dawn began to color the skies. Marshaling his inner resources, he managed an air of quiet sobriety before the suspicious eye and clapping tongue of his wife.

Suddenly, as he was undressing, she punctuated her harangue with a sharp, gasping intake of air.

"Joe," she asked through clenched teeth,. "Where's your underwear?"

Blearily, Joe perceived that his boxer shorts were, indeed, missing. Then inspiration struck.

"My God!" he cried, with aggrieved dignity, "I've been robbed!"

With deep concern, if not alarm, Dick noted that his friend Conrad was drunker than he'd ever seen him before.

"What's the trouble, buddy?" he asked, sliding onto the stool next to his friend.

"It's a woman, Dick," Conrad replied.

"I guessed that much. Tell me about it."

"I can't," Conrad said. But after a few more drinks his tongue and resolution both seemed to weaken and, turning to his buddy, he said, "OK. It's your wife."

"My wife!"

"Yeah."

"What about her?"

Conrad pondered the question heavily, and draped his arm around his pal. "Well, buddy-boy," he said, "I'm afraid she's cheating on us."

As they ran for their respective trains, Ralph called to his fellow-commuter Paul:

"How about a game of golf tomorrow?"

"Sorry," Paul called back, "but it's the kids' day off, and I've got to take care of the maid."

Carol was furious when she came home unexpectedly and caught her Harry in bed with a lady midget.

"You promised me two weeks ago that you would never cheat on me again," she stormed.

Harry shrugged his shoulders and murmured airily, "Well, as you can see, I'm tapering off."

Homer and his pretty wife were about to check out of the hotel, when Homer expostulated over the amount of the bill.

"But that, sir," explained the hotel manager, "is our normal rate for a double room with bath and TV."

"Yeah? Well, as it happens, we didn't use the TV."

"I'm sorry, sir," the manager replied firmly. "It was there for you to use if you'd wanted it."

"OK," Homer said, "but in that case, I'm going to charge you for making love to my beautiful wife."

"But, sir," spluttered the manager, "I did no such thing!"

"That's OK," Homer said, "she was there for you to use if you'd wanted her."

At this reply, the manager became so flustered that he actually reduced Homer's bill. Homer was exultant at his *coup*, and for months afterward he told and retold the story at parties with great relish, while his wife rolled her lovely eyes heavenward to indicate her opinion of his boorishness. Finally, they took another trip. Homer was determined to pull the same stunt and, up to a point, he achieved the same success:

"Sir, that's our normal rate," said the young clerk.

"Very well, but we didn't use the TV."

"But, sir, it was there for you to use if you'd cared to."

Homer's eyes brightened in anticipation. "Well, in that case," he said, "I'll have to charge you for making love to my beautiful wife."

To Homer's chagrin, the clerk became very red in the face and began to stammer. Then he said, "OK, OK, I'll pay you. But keep your voice down, will you? I'm new at this hotel and you're apt to get me fired."

Beauregard discovered his wife in the arms of her lover and, mad with rage, killed her with his .38 revolver. A jury of his Southern peers had brought in a verdict of justifiable homicide, and he was about to leave the courtroom a free man, when the judge stopped him.

"Just a point of personal curiosity, suh, if you're willing to clear it up?"

In reply, Beauregard bowed.

"Why did you shoot your wife, instead of her lover?"

Beauregard ran his finger lightly over his mustache.

"Suh," he replied, "I decided it was better to shoot a woman once than a different man each week."

"Say," said the operator in his usual confidential tone, "there's a lot of good stuff at this party. If I find a chick who's ready, would you mind if I used your extra bedroom for a quick tryst?"

"Not at all," replied the gracious host, "but what about your wife?"

"Nothing to worry about," said the operator. "I'll only be gone a few minutes and she'll never miss me."

"No, I'm sure she won't miss you," agreed the host, "but fifteen minutes ago *she* borrowed the extra bedroom."

Noah Webster's wife, returning from a long trip, discovered the lexicographer *flagrante delicto* with a pretty chambermaid.

"Mr. Webster!" she gasped, "I am surprised!"

"No, my dear," said Webster with a reproving smile. "You are shocked; *I* am surprised."

After two years in Korea, a Marine was shipped back to the States. Naturally, after a tearful shipside reunion, he and his beautiful wife went immediately to a hotel. Much later that night, a drunk, wandering through the hall, banged on their door, shouting, "Let me in!"

"Good Lord," said the Marine, leaping from the bed only half awake, "I'll bet that's your husband!"

"Don't be silly," his wife sleepily reassured him, "he's in Korea."

Then there was the band leader who spent all week working on a new arrangement and then discovered that his wife wasn't going out of town after all.

"I had everything a man could want," moaned a sad-eyed friend of ours. "Money, a handsome home, the love of a beautiful and wealthy woman. Then, bang, one morning my wife walked in!"

"I think you've made a mistake in my bill," said the patron, after three excellent highballs in a swank New York bar. "You've only charged me fifteen cents."

"No mistake, replied the bartender. "I only charge a nickel a drink."

"Fantastic," said the delighted patron. "But how, at a nickel a drink, can you afford to operate such a plush bar? Are you the owner?"

"No," confided the bartender. "The owner's upstairs with my wife. And what he's doing to her up there I'm doing to him down here!"

The defense attorney was bearing down hard: "You say," he sneered, "that my client came at you with a broken bottle in his hand. But didn't *you* have something in *your* hands?"

"Yes," said the battered plaintiff, "His wife. Charming, of course, but not much good in a fight."

Harry constantly irritated his friends with his eternal optimism. No matter how bad the situation, he would always say, "It could have been worse."

To cure him of this annoying habit, his friends decided to invent a situation so completely black, so dreadful, that even Harry could find no hope in it. Approaching him at the club bar one day, one of them said, "Harry! Did you hear what happened to George? He came home last night, found his wife in bed with another man, shot them both, then turned the gun on himself!"

"Terrible," said Harry. "But it could have been worse."

"How in hell," asked his dumfounded friend, "could it *possibly* have been worse?"

"Well," said Harry, "if it had happened the night before, I'd be dead now."

In former times, people who committed adultery were stoned; today, it's often the other way around.

It had promised to be a sensational divorce case, with the wife accused of incredible escapades, but thus far it had all proved rather disappointing, with nothing more than a few insinuations and vague generalities tossed back and forth. But this was the day when the wife was to take the witness stand for the first time, and the courtroom was filled to capacity. Testifying before her own lawyer, she projected an image of sweet innocence, as she told a tale of wifely fidelity and sacrifice. At long last the wife's direct testimony came to an end, and the husband's attorney was given the opportunity to cross-examine.

He first re-established her name, relationship to the plaintiff and other details of identification. Then he picked up a paper from the table, studied it a moment, turned to her and asked, "Is it not true, Madam, that on the night of June twelfth, in a driving rainstorm, you had sexual intercourse with a certain circus midget on the handle bars of a careening motorcycle that passed through the center of Libertyville at speeds in excess of sixty miles per hour?"

The wife turned pale, but retained her remarkable self-control, and her voice was almost serene in its innocence as she asked, "What was that date again?"

Originally scheduled for all-night duty at the station, Patrolman Michael Fenwick was relieved early, and thus arrived home four hours ahead of schedule. It was nearly two A.M., and hoping to get into bed without waking his wife, he decided to undress in the dark. But as he crossed the room to climb into bed, his wife sat up and sleepily asked, "Mike, dearest, would you go down to the all-night drugstore in the next block and get me a box of aspirin? My head is splitting."

"Certainly, sweetheart," he said, and feeling his way across the room, he crawled back into his clothes and stumbled out of the house and down the street to the drugstore. As he arrived, the pharmacist looked up in surprise.

"Say," said the druggist, after taking Fenwick's order, "aren't you Officer Fenwick of the Ninth Precinct?"

"Yes, I am," said Fenwick.

"Well, then, what in the world are you doing in the fire chief's uniform?"

Having just returned from an extended business trip, the executive lay asleep beside his wife, who was dreaming she was in her lover's arms. Suddenly, in her dream, she imagined she heard a familiar step outside the bedroom door.

"Heavens!" she cried aloud in her sleep. "Get out, my husband's coming!" With that, her spouse leaped out of bed and bounded into the closet.

A wild-eyed young man rushed into Tony's crowded one-man barbershop at nine o'clock one morning and asked: "How many ahead of me?" "Three" came the answer, and he ran out the door. At shortly after twelve he returned, asked the same question, the barber replied "Four" and again the young man sped off.

At three P.M. and five P.M. the previous scenes repeated themselves, but with only one difference: There was a noticeable decline in the young man's vigor as the day proceeded, and some of the spring had gone out of his step. The barber, concerned about a good and regular customer, instructed his bootblack to follow the lad and report back on what he was doing that was tiring him so.

Minutes later the bootblack returned and announced: "Better call your home right away, Tony, and tell your wife you're ready for that young man right now!"

A young zoologist entered a cocktail lounge and ordered a triple Martini, explaining to the bartender that he was celebrating his first major achievement in the field of genetics. The shapely miss at the other end of the bar asked if she might join him, since she was also there to commemorate an outstanding personal accomplishment.

"What a coincidence," said the zoologist. "I've just succeeded in breeding a very rare blue-eyed female pheasant for the first time in captivity. What did you do?"

"Nothing quite so significant," replied the girl. "It's just that, after ten long years of marriage, my doctor tells me I am finally pregnant. But how did you ever manage to breed your blue-eyed pheasant?"

"It was simple," he explained. "All I did was keep changing mates until I found the right biological combination."

"Really," said the girl, with a knowing smile. "What a coincidence!"

Two successful restaurateurs were discussing business when one suddenly dropped his head and solemnly announced, "Did you know that my married daughter is having an affair?"

"Is that so," said the other. "Who's catering it?"

Have you heard about the man who never worried about his marriage, until he moved from New York to California and discovered that he still had the same milkman?

The husband had arrived home unexpectedly, and now he stared suspiciously at a cigar smoldering in an ashtray. "Where did that cigar come from?" he thundered, as his wife cowered in their bed.

There was a pregnant pause, then from the closet a shaky masculine voice answered, "Cuba!"

A pediatrician we know informs us that infants don't have nearly as much fun in infancy as adults have in adultery.

While riding home from work one evening, three commuters became friendly in the club car and after the third round, they began to brag about the relative merits of their respective marital relationships. The first proudly proclaimed, "My wife meets my train *every* evening, and we've been married for ten years."

"That's nothing," scoffed the second, "my wife meets me every evening, too, and we've been married *seventeen* years!"

"Well, I've got you both beat, fellows," said the third commuter, who was obviously the youngest in the group.

"How do you figure that?!" the first fellow wanted to know.

"I suppose you've got a wife who meets you every evening, too!" sneered the second.

"That's right," said the third commuter, "and I'm not even married!"

It was late afternoon in a small Nevada town and Joe, the owner of the local beer parlor, was lazily polishing glassware when his friend Mike, obviously agitated, came running in.

"Joe, baby," he shouted, "get over to your house quick. I just stopped off to see if you were home and I heard a stranger's voice in your bedroom. So I looked in the window and there—well, I hate to tell you, but your wife is in bed with another man."

"Is that so?" Joe replied calmly. "What does this guy look like?"

"Oh, I don't know—he's tall and completely bald."

"And did he have a thick red mustache?" asked Joe.

"Right, right!" Mike yelled.

"And did you notice if he had a gold front tooth?"

"Dammit, man, you're right!"

Pouring his friend a beer, Joe remarked philosophically, "Must be that jackass Cal Thompson—he'll make love to *anything!*"

The young wife was in the bedroom toweling off from her morning shower when she heard the back door slam. Thinking it was her husband, she called out, "I'm in here, darling. I've been waiting for you."

To which a deep voice answered, "I think you ought to know, madam, that I'm not your regular milkman!"

King Arthur, going on a two-year dragon-hunting expedition, ordered Merlin the Wise to make a chastity belt for Guinevere to wear while he was away. Merlin came up with a very unorthodox design— one that had a large gaping aperture in the area that would normally be most strongly fortified.

"That's absurd," said Arthur. "It's not functional."

"Yes it is," said Merlin. Picking up a spare magic wand, he passed it through the opening. Instantly, a guillotine-like blade came down and chopped the wand in two.

"Ingenious!" cried Arthur. After outfitting Guinevere with the belt, he rode off to slay dragons, his mind at peace.

Two years later, when Arthur came back, his first official act was to assemble all the Knights of the Round Table and send them to the court physician for a special "inspection." His frown grew severe as he learned that every member of the Round Table was nicked, cut or scratched. All but one. Sir Lancelot was impeccable. Arthur called for him immediately and smiled at his best knight.

"Sir Lancelot," he declared, "you are the only one of my knights who did not assail the chastity of my lady Guinevere while I was off slaying yon dragons. You have upheld the honor of the Round Table, and I am proud of you. You shall be rewarded. You may have anything in the kingdom you desire. You have but to name it. State your wish, Sir Lancelot!"

But Sir Lancelot was speechless.

After a round of golf, two men were changing their clothes in the country-club locker room. One of the men started putting on a girdle and the other, quite astonished, said, "Since when did you start wearing that thing?"

Shaking his head resignedly, the first man replied, "Ever since my wife found it in the glove compartment of our car."

After twenty years of marriage, a couple decided upon an amicable divorce. To celebrate the granting of the decree, they dined out together. After the third glass of champagne, the husband confessed: "There's one thing I've always wanted to ask you, but I never had the nerve. Now that we're splitting up, your answer can't possibly hurt me, so please be honest. Why is it that five of our six children have black hair, but little Tommy is a blond? Whose child is Tommy, anyway?"

"I can't tell you," said the wife after a long pause. "It would hurt you too much."

"Oh, don't be ridiculous," the husband insisted. "I don't care who the father is. I'm just curious."

Finally, the wife acquiesced: "Well, if you really want to know, Tommy is *your* child."

Returning home for a forgotten briefcase, the husband found his pretty wife standing naked on the bathroom scales. Not bothering to enter the room, he reached in, patted her on the bottom and asked: "How much today, baby?"

"The same as always," she answered. "Two quarts of milk and a pound of butter."

"His family wasn't too pleased about our engagement," sighed the party girl to her roommate. "In fact, his wife was furious."

"Darling," cooed the wife sweetly over morning coffee, "do you remember those trout you spent two weeks fishing for back in April?"

"Sure," mumbled her husband through his newspaper.

"Well," she continued, "one of them called last night to say you're going to be a father."

"I don't really mind him being unfaithful," sighed the wife to the marriage counselor, "but I just *can't* sleep three in a bed."

After several years of marriage, the youthful stockbroker still couldn't keep away from other women; but he was fast running out of excuses to satisfy his jealous wife. One afternoon, he accompanied his good-looking secretary to her apartment—and made love to her far into the night.

"My God!" he exclaimed, grabbing his watch from the nightstand. "It's three o'clock in the morning." Then, inspired, he dialed his wife. When she answered the phone, he declared: "Don't pay the ransom, dear. I've just escaped."

Creeping around to the bedroom window, the private detectives saw their client's wife in bed with another man.

"Just as I suspected," said the first. "Let's go in after him."

"Great idea," the other replied. "How soon do you think he'll be finished?"

A middle-aged husband went to a doctor and explained that his wife was constantly nagging him about his vanishing potency. After giving him a bottle of pills, the doctor assured him that they would work wonders. A month later, the man returned, obviously satisfied with the results.

"The pills are terrific," he said. "I've been doing it three times a night."

"Wonderful," the doctor replied. "What does your wife say about your lovemaking now?"

"How should I know?" the fellow shrugged. "I haven't been home yet."

Suspecting her husband of infidelity, the woman attempted to put an end to it by arousing his jealousy. "What would you say if I told you that I've been sleeping with your best friend?" she asked provocatively.

"Well," he mused, "I'd say that you're a Lesbian."

Noticing that her husband's relationship with the alluring miss across the street was becoming more intimate, the suspicious wife awoke one morning to find herself alone in bed. Angered, she dialed her attractive neighbor and bellowed into the phone, "Tell my husband to get his ass across the street."

"Ma'am," a soft, sexy voice replied, "that's where he's been getting it for some time now."

Early one evening, the shrewish wife of a stock-market analyst returned home unexpectedly from a bridge game and discovered her husband in bed with a shapely blonde. "Harry, what the hell are you doing?" she bellowed.

"Don't you know?" the quick-thinking chap replied. "I've gone public."

We know a swinging suburban housewife who says there's as much difference between husbands and lovers as night and day.

While passionately making love, the couple was interrupted by the phone ringing. The girl answered it, returning to bed a few seconds later. "Who was that?" her companion questioned.

"My husband," the curvaceous young thing sighed, snuggling up against her bed partner. "He wanted to tell me he'll be out late because he's playing poker with you and some of the other fellows."

As the time drew near, the patient asked her obstetrician, "Will my husband be permitted to stay with me during the delivery?"

"Oh, yes," answered the physician. "I feel that the father of the child should also be present at its birth."

"I don't think that would be a very good idea," the woman said. "He and my husband don't get along too well together."

Fred and Elaine had been married for ten years when one evening at dinner Fred announced his intention of taking a mistress. His wife was shocked, but Fred pointed out that his two partners, Jim and Bob, both had mistresses and their wives had adjusted to the situation very nicely.

"All three girls dance in the chorus of the same night club," Fred explained, "and tomorrow night, I'm going to take you there to see them."

The next evening, Fred and Elaine went to the night club, and when the showgirls began their opening number, Fred said, "The blonde on the left is Jim's. The redhead next to her is Bob's. And the pretty brunette on the end is mine."

Elaine stared at the girls long and hard before answering: "You know something, darling? Of the three, I like ours best."

Have you heard about the husband who took a mistress just to break the monogamy?

A retired four-star general ran into his former orderly, also retired, in a Manhattan bar and spent the rest of the evening persuading him to come to work for him as his valet.

"Your duties will be exactly the same as they were in the army," the general said. "Nothing to it—you'll catch on again fast."

Next morning promptly at eight o'clock, the ex-orderly entered the ex-general's bedroom, pulled open the drapes, gave the general a gentle shake, strode around to the other side of the bed, spanked his employer's wife on her bottom and said, "OK, sweetheart, it's back to the village for you."

The Madison Avenue exec was dallying with both his secretary and the French maid, and on this particular evening he called home to make his excuses for a night out with the secretary. Babette, the French maid, answered the phone and the executive said in a very business-like manner, "Tell Madam she'd better go to bed and I'll be along as soon as I can."

"*Oui, monsieur,*" purred Babette, "and who shall I say is calling?"

A wife made to order can't compare with a ready maid.

The preacher's sermon was on the Ten Commandments. When he reached "Thou Shalt Not Steal," he noticed one of his parishioners, a little man sitting in the front row, became very agitated. When the preacher reached "Thou Shalt Not Commit Adultery," the man suddenly smiled and relaxed.

After the service, the preacher approached the man and asked him the reason for his peculiar behavior.

The man replied with an embarrassed smile, "When you talked about the Commandment, 'Thou Shalt Not Steal,' I suddenly discovered my umbrella was missing. But when you said 'Thou Shalt Not Commit Adultery,' I remembered where I'd left it."

In quest of his first mistress, the eager executive was plying a sweet young thing with food and drink. "I've rented a town house for you," he said, "and you shall have your own bank account and credit at all the best *couturiers.* I'll visit you a couple of nights during the week and we'll spend all our weekends together. And if we find we've made a mistake, why, we can always separate."

After toying with the idea for a moment, the girl smiled and replied, "Sounds fine; but what'll we do with the mistake?"

A sure sign that social barriers no longer exist, observed a society matron of our acquaintance, is the number of cute French maids who enter a home by the servants' entrance and leave in a family way.

Within a year after marrying one of a set of gorgeous identical twins, the exec found himself in court, asking for a divorce. When the judge demanded his reasons, the exec replied, "It's this way. My wife's sister visits us a lot and I sometimes come home and make love to her by mistake."

"But surely there's some difference between the two women," the judge said.

"You bet there is," responded the exec. "That's why I want a divorce."

Waxing eloquent on the sins of the flesh, the dynamic young preacher raised himself to full height, leaned over the pulpit and boomed, "Brothers and sisters, if there are any among you who have committed adultery, may your tongue cleave to the woof of your mowf."

The surest sign that a man is in love is when he divorces his wife.

After the professional golfer made a five-footer on the practice green, his wife sued for divorce.

We know a religious fellow who loves his neighbor—but can't stand her husband.

6
DOCTORS, LAWYERS, INDIAN CHIEFS

A few friends had gathered in Bob's basement rec room for an evening of drinks and dancing. With the party in full swing, one of the girls excused herself to go the the john. This room, it seems, had been newly painted in a charming pastel blue; it was supposed to be a fast-drying enamel, but it hadn't dried fast enough, and the young lady found herself stuck. Her shrieks brought Joe's girlfriend, who, unable to do anything about the situation herself, summoned Joe. After several minutes of uncontrolled laughter, Joe managed to produce a screwdriver and detach the thing, permitting the girl to stand up. But they still couldn't get it off, so they called a doctor.

"Did you ever see anything like this before, doctor?" the girl asked in embarrassment when the M.D. arrived.

"Well, yes," the doctor replied truthfully, "but I believe this is the first time I've ever seen one framed."

The young Georgia miss came to the hospital for a checkup.
"Have you been X-rayed?" asked the doctor.
"Nope," she said, "but ah've been ultra-violated."

The attractive young lady was worried about her sailor boyfriend, away at sea, and complained to her doctor that she couldn't sleep at night. She requested some sleeping tablets, but the doctor suggested she try a psychological technique before resorting to drugs. "Since counting sheep and the other more usual methods have failed," he said, "try repeating this little ritual each night when you retire: 'Toes go to sleep, feet go to sleep, ankles go to sleep, legs go to sleep, thighs go to sleep' and so on, all the way to the top of your head. Concentrate on each separate part of your body as you direct it to sleep, and before you know it, you'll be in dreamland."

The young lady was dubious, but that very night, after turning out the light and getting into bed, she tried the doctor's suggestion.

"Toes go to sleep," she began. "Feet go to sleep, ankles go to sleep, legs go to sleep, thighs go to sleep. . . ."

Suddenly the door to her apartment burst open and in walked her sailor boyfriend.

"Everybody up," she exclaimed, *"Everybody up!"*

The doctor had just finished giving the young man a thorough physical examination.

"The best thing for you to do," the M.D. said, "is give up drinking and smoking, get to bed early and stay away from women."

"Doc, I don't deserve the best," said the patient. "What's next best?"

The new patient was airing his woes to an understanding doctor: "After the first, I'm tired, Doc. After the second, my chest aches and I start getting pains in my legs. After the third, I feel like fainting and it takes half-an-hour for my heart and respiration to return to normal."

"Why don't you quit after the first?" inquired the doctor.

"How can I do that, Doc?" the patient asked. "I live on the third."

"Dear Dad," read the young soldier's first letter home. "I cannot tell you where I am, but yesterday I shot a polar bear. . . ."

Several months later came another letter: "Dear Dad, I still cannot tell you where I am, but yesterday I danced with a hula girl. . . ."

Two weeks later came yet another note: "Dear Dad, I still cannot tell you where I am, but yesterday the doctor told me I should have danced with the polar bear and shot the hula girl. . . ."

"I just examined Sophia Loren," said the bug-eyed doctor at the Hollywood film studio.

"And how is she?" his fellow physician wanted to know.

"My only wish is that the whole world should be in such good shape."

"I don't know what's wrong with me, doctor," said the curvy call girl. "I feel tired, dragged out. Pooped. No pep. No get up and go. Is it vitamin deficiency, low blood count or what?"

The medico gave her a top-to-toe examination and then his verdict: "Young lady, there's really nothing wrong with you. You're run-down, that's all. You've been working too hard. I suggest you try staying out of bed for a few days."

The good doctor had been an inspiration to the jungle natives. He had cured their sick and taught them the religious and moral values of his own England. He was loved and respected by every native in the village, but on this particular afternoon the chief was obviously troubled as he entered the doctor's hut.

"You live among my people long time now," said the chief. "You tell us not right for man and girl to be close together before marriage and we believe what you say. This morning white child born to woman in village. You only white man in jungle. What I tell my people?"

The doctor smiled and led the chief to a window. "My son," he said, "I won't attempt to give you a full scientific explanation for the phenomenon known as an albino. But look at the flock of sheep upon that hill. Every one is snow white except one. The white baby born to the woman in your village means nothing more or less than that one black sheep in the white flock. It is simply one of nature's mysterious accidents."

The black chief became embarrassed and looked at his feet. "OK, doc," he said. "You no tell—I no tell."

"Have you ever performed one of these delicate brain operations before?" asked the patient, as a nurse prepared to put him under an anesthetic.

"Oh, yeah," said the man in white standing over him, "nothing to it."

"It's funny," said the patient, "but you look exactly like a bartender who works in a bowling alley where I bowl every Thursday night."

"I am," said the fellow with a smile, "but I'm also a man who thinks for himself."

A rather naïve young man named Lester had recently reached manhood and had no idea why he was continuously nervous and tense. He went to see his doctor. The M.D. was not in, but his nurse was, a red-headed vixen who wore her uniform so tight that Lester's jitters noticeably increased. She asked him what was wrong and he told her. She eyed him appraisingly.

"That's easy to fix," she said. "Come with me." She led Lester into a small examination room, and there relieved his tensions.

As he was preparing to leave, she said, "That will be twenty dollars." And quite satisfied, Lester was pleased to pay.

Several weeks went by, and Lester found the same unrest growing in him again. He returned to the doctor's office and this time the doctor was in. He listened to Lester's symptoms, then wrote out a prescription on a piece of paper and handed it to him.

"This is for tranquilizers," the doctor said. "You can have it filled downstairs. That will be five dollars, please."

Lester looked at the small piece of paper for a few moments, then looked up at the doctor and said, "If it's all the same to you, doc, I'd just as soon have the twenty-dollar treatment."

The voluptuous blonde entered the dentist's office in an obvious state of agitation. She sat down in the chair and fidgeted nervously as the dentist prepared his utensils.

"Oh, doctor," she exclaimed, as he prepared to look into her mouth, "I'm so afraid of dentists. Why, I think I'd rather have a baby than have a tooth drilled."

"Well, miss," said the dentist impatiently, "better make up your mind before I adjust the chair."

With a bushel of apples, you can have a hell of a time with the doctor's wife.

The head doctor at the hospital was making his rounds and he paused before a group of newborn babies.

"What's the matter with this little fellow," he asked. "He seems awfully puny and underweight."

"He's one of those artificial insemination babies," said the sweet young nurse, "and he's been coming along rather slowly, I'm afraid."

"Confirms a pet theory of mine," said the doctor, with a twinkle in his eye. "Spare the rod and spoil the child."

An exceedingly well-formed young nurse walked calmly along the hospital corridor with a portion of her bosom exposed. A staff doctor, passing by, noticed the delightful exposure and scolded her for this improper show of her charms. Blushing, the nurse murmured, "I'm sorry, sir, but it's these darn interns—they never put anything back when they're through with it."

A new shop opened in the heart of the little town, with no sign of any sort on its awning, door or window, the nearest thing to identification being the large clock in the window. A gentleman whose watch had stopped happened to be passing by, and he went inside and asked if they would repair it.

"I'm sorry," said the clerk, "but this is not a watch-repair shop. This is a branch of the hospital in the next block. All we do here is perform hemorrhoid operations."

The man begged the clerk's pardon and started to leave, then turned with a puzzled frown. "Then what's the significance of the clock in the window?" he asked.

"Well," said the clerk, "what else *could* we put in the window?!"

Completing his examination of the uncommonly well-built, beautiful blonde, the doctor said solemnly, "You are a very sick young lady. I don't want you returning to work this afternoon. Go home, get undressed and get into bed. Drink about a third of this bottle of medicine I'm preparing for you . . . it will make you drowsy. I don't want you to answer your phone or let anybody into your apartment until you hear three short knocks. . . ."

A lovely young thing entered a doctor's office on her lunch hour and addressed a handsome young man in a white coat. "I've had a pain in my shoulder for a week. Can you help me?"

"Lie down on this table," he said, "and I'll massage it for you." After a few minutes, the beauteous patient exclaimed, "Doctor, that isn't my shoulder!"

The young man smiled and replied: "No, and I'm not a doctor, either."

One cold winter's day a lady midget hobbled into a doctor's office. After waiting her turn for an hour, she finally got in to see the doctor and reported that she was suffering from a severe irritation between the legs.

"Is the pain a constant one?" he asked.

"No," she said. "I notice it mostly when I go out on cold, snowy days."

"Well, sit up on this table and let's examine you," said the doctor. He instructed her to lift her skirt, studied the situation, then produced a pair of medical shears from among his instruments. While she waited fearfully, he began snipping.

"Aren't you going to use an anesthetic?" she asked.

"That won't be necessary," he reassured her. "All right," he said at last. "Get down from the table and try walking now."

She did so, and reported, amazed, "Why, I feel wonderful! What did you do?"

"It was simple," said the doctor, "I just cut two inches off the tops of your galoshes."

A recent survey showed that the nine out of ten doctors who preferred Camels have switched back to women.

A young man approached his family physician and said, "Doc, I'm afraid you'll have to remove my wife's tonsils one of these days."

"My good man," replied the doctor, "I removed them six years ago. Did you ever hear of a woman having two sets of tonsils?"

"No," the husband retorted, "but you've heard of a man having two wives, haven't you?"

"Doctor," said the voluptuous young girl, "I'd prefer being vaccinated where it won't show."

"All right," replied the physician, "but that will cost you ten dollars in advance."

"Why do I have to pay in advance?" the girl protested.

"Because the last time a patient as pretty as you made that request," he explained, "I got so wrapped up in what I was doing I forgot to charge her."

Every newspaper in New York sent a reporter and a staff photographer to the office of a local ophthalmologist when it was learned that he had recently performed a successful sight-saving operation on the wife of the country's most celebrated pop artist, who, in addition to paying the doctor's usual fee, had gratefully insisted on painting one of his contemporary masterpieces across an entire wall of the doctor's waiting room. The mural turned out be an immense multicolored picture of a human eye, in the center of which stood a perfect miniature likeness of the good doctor himself. While cameras clicked and most of the newsmen crowded around the famous artist for his comments, one cub reporter drew the eye specialist aside and asked: "Tell me, if you can, Doctor—what was your first reaction on seeing this fantastic artistic achievement covering an entire wall of your office?"

"To tell the truth," replied the physician, "my first thought was, thank goodness I'm not a gynecologist!"

The doctor had just completed his examination of the teen-age girl:

"Madam," he said to her mother, "I'm afraid your daughter has syphilis."

"Oh, dear," exclaimed the embarrassed mother. "Tell me, Doctor, could she have possibly caught it in a public lavatory?"

"It's possible," replied the physician after a moment's reflection, "but it would certainly be uncomfortable."

The intern on duty at the hospital emergency room received a phone call late one night from a distressed mother who exclaimed, "Doctor, what shall I do—my husband just discovered that our two year old has eaten a whole tube of contraceptive jelly."

"Well," the intern drawled, "if it's really an emergency, why don't you have one of those all-night drugstores deliver?"

A lovely young thing decided to confide in her roommate. "The strangest thing has been happening to me," she said. "Every time I sneeze, I'm overtaken by an unbelievable sensation of wild passion."

"I've never heard of such a strange illness," her friend answered. "What do you take for it?"

Came the smiling reply: "Black pepper!"

The harried stockbroker was suffering from insomnia, never got to sleep before dawn, then slept right through the alarm and so never made it to the office on time. Upon being reprimanded by his boss, he decided to consult a doctor. The doctor gave him some sleeping pills, and that night he fell asleep immediately and experienced a pleasant rest. In the morning, he awoke before the alarm rang, jumped out of bed with new verve and vigor. When he arrived at his office promptly, he told his boss: "Those pills I got from my doctor really work. I had no trouble at all waking up this morning."

"That's nice," the boss replied. "But where were you yester-day?"

A young man sat next to a beautiful blonde in a bar and offered to buy her a drink. After some casual conversation, he asked her if she would care to go to his apartment for a nightcap and she agreed. Up in his apartment, she resisted his advances for over an hour until, in desperation, he exclaimed, "If you don't want to have sex with me, why did you agree to come with me in the first place?"

"I don't enjoy sex in the usual way," she explained. "But I'll let you make love to me if you promise to do it *my* way."

He was too aroused to argue.

"Then remove your shoe and stocking," she said passionately, "and take me with your big toe."

A few days later, his toe began to throb and he decided to have it examined by a doctor. The doctor looked at the toe and shook his head.

"I'm sorry to have to tell you this," the doctor said, "but you have gonorrhea of the big toe."

"I've never heard of such a thing," the young man said.

"It's a medical rarity," the doctor agreed, "but no rarer than the case I had this morning."

"Oh," said his patient, "what was that?"

"I treated a young woman with a case of athlete's vagina."

"No need for me to come out to the house," the doctor told the worried caller. "I've checked my files and your uncle isn't really ill at all—he just thinks he's sick."

A week later, the doctor telephoned to make sure his diagnosis had been correct. "How's your uncle today?" he asked.

"Worse," came the reply. "Now he thinks he's dead."

Then there was the Eskimo who rubbed noses so indiscrimi-nately that he contracted snyphilis.

After a heart-transplant operation, the patient was receiving instructions from his doctor. He was placed on a strict diet, denied tobacco and advised to get at least eight hours' sleep a night. Finally, the patient asked: "What about my sex life, Doc? Will it be all right for me to have intercourse?"

"Just with your wife," responded the doctor. "We don't want you to get too excited."

The voluptuous miss was perched on the examination table when the doctor placed his hand on her bare breast. "You know what I'm doing, of course," he said, reassuringly.

"Yes," the patient murmured. "You're checking for breast cancer."

Encouraged, the doctor proceeded to caress her stomach. "Of course," he continued, "you know what I'm doing."

"Yes," she smiled. "You're checking my appendix."

At this point, the doctor could no longer control himself. He stripped off his clothes and began to make passionate love to her. "You know what I'm doing, don't you?" he gasped.

"Yes," his patient answered. "You're checking for V.D.—and that's what I came here for."

"I just can't find a cause for your illness," the internist said. "Frankly, I think it's due to drinking."

"In that case," replied his attractive patient, "I'll come back when you're sober."

During her annual checkup, the well-constructed miss was asked to disrobe and climb onto the examining table.

"Doctor," she replied shyly, "I just can't undress in front of you."

"All right," said the physician, "I'll flick off the lights. You undress and tell me when you're through."

In a few moments, her voice rang out in the darkness: "Doctor, I've undressed. What should I do with my clothes?"

"Your clothes?" answered the doctor. "Put them over here, on top of mine."

We know an ingenious doctor who prescribed sex for insomnia. His patients didn't get any more sleep, but they had more fun staying awake.

When the handsome gynecologist asked his new patient to disrobe, the pretty young thing started to blush. "Haven't you ever been examined before?" he questioned.

"Oh, yes," she whispered, "but never by a *doctor.*"

The tired doctor was awakened by a phone call in the middle of the night. "Please, you have to come right over," pleaded the panic-stricken mother. "My child has swallowed a contraceptive."

The physician dressed quickly; but before he could get out the door, the phone rang again.

"You don't have to come over, after all," the woman bubbled. "My husband just found another one."

Upon finishing examining his cute new patient quite thoroughly, the obstetrician smiled and said, "I've got good news for you, Mrs. Smith—"

"Pardon me," interrupted the young lady, "but it's *Miss* Smith."

"Oh, I see," gulped the physician. "Well, Miss Smith, I've got bad news for you. . . ."

The sixty-year-old patient explained his predicament to the doctor. He had recently married a gorgeous girl in her twenties, but unfortunately, every night at bed time, when he and the lovely bride were ready and willing, he would fall asleep.

The doctor scribbled out a prescription and handed it to the patient. The old man's face lit up as he said, "You mean that now I'll be able to—"

"No," the doctor interrupted, "I'm afraid I can't do anything about *that.* But now at least she'll fall asleep, too."

Doctor Jones was called to examine his friend Frank, who at sixty-four had married a woman less than half his age. The doctor noticed that she was an extremely attractive and voluptuously proportioned girl. After a thorough examination, he knew that the cause of his friend's illness was exhaustion. He wrote a prescription and was preparing to leave when the patient asked:

"Well, Doc, what's wrong with me? Am I overweight?"

"No, Frank," answered the doctor with a sidelong glance at the buxom young bride, "overmatched."

"You're in remarkable shape for a man your age," said the doctor to the ninety-year-old man after the examination.

"I know it," said the old gentleman. "I've really got only one complaint—my sex drive is too high. Got anything you can do for that, Doc?"

The doctor's mouth dropped open. "Your *what?!*" he gasped.

"My sex drive," said the old man. "It's too high, and I'd like to have you lower it if you can."

"*Lower* it?!" exclaimed the doctor, still unable to believe what the ninety-year-old gentleman was saying. "Just what do you consider 'high'?"

"These days it seems like it's all in my head, Doc," said the old man, "and I'd like to have you lower it if you can."

A scientific friend informs us that celibacy isn't an inherited trait.

After an examination, the curvaceous blonde phoned her gynecologist and asked, "Doctor, would you see if by chance I left my panties in your office?"

He looked in the examining room, returned to the phone and told her, "I'm afraid they're not here."

"Sorry to trouble you, doctor," she replied. "I'll try the dentist."

Which reminds us of the dental joke about the Texas oilman who went in to see his dentist and, when asked which tooth was bothering him, replied, "Oh, just drill anywhere, doc. I feel lucky today!"

A man was complaining to a friend about an uncle who was staying with him: "I didn't mind when he wore my suits, I didn't object when he smoked my best cigars, drank my bourbon and borrowed my car every night. But when he sat down at the dinner table and laughed at me with my own teeth—that was too much!"

Science is making so many strides ahead, almost daily, that it gets increasingly difficult for the layman to keep up. Latest invention we've heard about is a toothpaste with built-in food particles, for people who can't eat between every brushing.

An inmate at the insane asylum was being examined for possible release. The first question the examining doctor asked was: "What are you going to do when you leave this institution?"

"I'm gonna get me a sling shot," said the patient, "and I'm gonna come back here and break every goddam window in the place!"

After six more months of treatment, the patient was again brought before the examining doctor for possible dismissal, and the same question was put to him.

"Well, I'm going to get a job," the patient replied.

"Fine," said the doctor. "Then what?"

"I'm going to rent an apartment."

"Very good."

"Then I'm going to meet a beautiful girl."

"Excellent."

"I'm going to take the beautiful girl up to my apartment and I'm going to pull up her skirt."

"Normal, perfectly normal."

"Then I'm gonna steal her garter, make a sling shot out've it and come back here and break every goddam window in the place!"

After the attractive blonde had seated herself, the young psychiatrist asked, "What seems to be the trouble?"

"Well," the shapely thing answered, blushing, "I think I may be a nymphomaniac."

"I can probably help you," said the doctor, "but I must tell you that my fee is fifty dollars an hour."

"That's not bad," the girl quickly replied. "How much for all night?"

A young virgin, suffering from acute nervousness due to repressed desires, paid a visit to a highly recommended psychiatrist. The doctor took one look at the voluptuous maiden and lost all his professional objectivity. "Take off your clothes," he ordered, scarcely able to disguise the lust in his voice. "Now lie down on this couch. Now close your eyes and, very slowly, spell the word, 'bedroom.'"

She began: "B . . . E . . . D . . . R . . . *Oh! . . . Ohhhhhhhhhh . . . Mmmmmmmmmmmm.*"

She was cured.

"I've good news for you," said the psychiatrist. "You're a well man. It won't be necessary for you to continue the analysis any longer."

"How wonderful, doctor," said the patient. "I'm so very pleased, I wish there were something special I could do for you in return."

"Oh, that's not necessary. You've paid your bill and that's all that's expected."

"But really, doctor, I'm so elated I could kiss you!"

"No, don't do that. Actually, we shouldn't even be lying here on the couch together."

The new inmate at the mental hospital announced in a loud voice that he was the famous British naval hero, Lord Nelson. This was particularly interesting, because the institution already had a "Lord Nelson." The head psychiatrist, after due consideration, decided to put the two men in the same room, feeling that the similarity of their delusions might prompt an adjustment in each that would help in curing them. It was a calculated risk, of course, for the men might react violently to one another, but they were introduced and then left alone and no disturbance was heard from the room that night.

The next morning, the doctor had a talk with his new patient and was more than pleasantly surprised when he was told: "Doctor, I've been suffering from a delusion. I know now that I am *not* Lord Nelson."

"That's wonderful," said the doctor.

"Yes," said the patient, smiling demurely, "I'm Lady Nelson."

Have you heard about the psychiatrist who gave his son a set of mental blocks for Christmas?

During the last day of a psychiatrists' convention, one of the doctors present at the closing lecture noticed an attractive female Ph.D. being pawed by the man seated next to her.

"Is he bothering you?" the gallant observer asked the woman.

"Why should I be bothered?" she replied. "It's *his* problem."

"Doctor," said the obviously disturbed young man to his psychiatrist, "my biggest problem is that I always dream about baseball. Nothing but baseball."

"Don't you ever dream about girls?" asked the headshrinker.

"I don't dare," said the young man. "I'm afraid I'll lose my turn at bat."

The mother took her young daughter to a psychiatrist and explained to the headshrinker that the girl thought she was a chicken. The doctor soothed her, observing that an overactive imagination is not uncommon in children, and asking how long the girl had suffered from the delusion.

"Almost two years," said the mother.

"Your daughter has imagined she is a chicken for nearly two years?!" the psychiatrist exclaimed. "Why have you waited so long before bringing her in?"

The woman looked embarrassed, then confessed: "We needed the eggs, doctor."

"**P**sychoanalysis is a lot of bunk," one imbiber said to his bar companion.

"Why do you say that?"

"I've been undergoing analysis for six months and today my analyst tells me I'm in love with my umbrella! Have you ever heard anything so ridiculous?"

"That's pretty crazy," agreed the friend.

"I would say that we certainly hold a sincere affection for each other. But *love?* Ridiculous!"

"**O**h, Doctor, you mean I'm finally cured?" the woman sighed happily.

"Yes Miss Willoughby," said the psychoanalyst, "I believe we now have your kleptomania firmly under control and you can go out in the workaday world just like anybody else."

"Oh, Doctor, I'm so grateful," said the woman. "I don't know how I'll ever repay you for your help."

"My fee is all the payment I expect," said the kindly analyst. "However, if you should happen to have a relapse, you might pick up a small transistor radio for me."

Beverly stretched out on the psychiatrist's couch, looking forlorn but comely. With genuine emotion she cried, "I just can't help myself, doctor. No matter how hard I try to resist, I bring five or six men with me into my bedroom every night. Last night there were ten. I just feel so miserable, I don't know what to do."

In understanding tones, the doctor rumbled, "Yes, I know, I know, my dear."

"Oh!" the surprised girl exclaimed. "Were you there last night too?"

The analyst was concerned about the results of a Rorschach Test he had just given, for the patient associated every ink blot with some kind of sexual activity.

"I want to study the results of your test over the weekend," he said, "then I'd like to see you again on Monday morning."

"OK, Doc," the man agreed, and then as he was slipping on his coat, he said, "I'm going to a stag party tomorrow night. Any chance I might be able to borrow those dirty pictures of yours?"

Natalie, a pretty but distraught model, took her troubles to a psychiatrist.

"Doctor, you must help me," she pleaded. "It's gotten so that every time a man takes me out, I wind up in bed with him. And then afterwards I feel guilty and depressed all day long."

"I see," nodded the psychiatrist. "And you want me to strengthen your will power."

"Heavens, no!" exclaimed the model. "I want you to fix it so I won't feel guilty and depressed afterward."

An ingenious psychiatrist we know claims there are millions to be made on his invention—a double couch.

A cute young thing was consulting a psychiatrist. Among other questions, the doctor asked, "Are you troubled at all by indecent thoughts?"

"Why, no," she replied, with just the hint of a twinkle in her eye. "To tell you the truth, doctor, I rather enjoy them."

With apologies to the noble science of psychiatry and the hope that the good doctors have not lost the ability to laugh at themselves, another analyst was listening to a voluptuous beauty with a problem of her own. "It's liquor, doctor," she sobbed. "I'm really a very nice girl, but just as soon as I've had a drink or two, I become uncontrollably passionate and I want to make love to whomever I happen to be with."

"I see," the analyst said thoughtfully. "Well, suppose I just mix us up a couple of cocktails here and then you and I can sit down, nice and relaxed, and discuss this compulsive neurosis of yours."

The psychiatrist leaned back and placed the tips of his fingers together while he soothed the deeply troubled man who stood before him.

"Calm yourself, my good fellow," he gently urged. "I have helped a great many others with fixations far more serious than yours. Now let me see if I understand the problem correctly. You indicate that in moments of great emotional stress, you believe that you are a dog. A fox terrier, is that not so?"

"Yes, sir," mumbled the patient. "A small fox terrier with black and brown spots. Oh, please tell me you can help me, doctor. If this keeps up much longer, I don't know what I'll do. . . ."

The doctor gestured toward his couch. "Now, now," he soothed, "the first thing to do is lie down here and we'll see if we can't get to the root of your delusion."

"Oh, I couldn't do that, doctor," said the patient. "I'm not allowed up on the furniture."

The psychiatrist was not expecting the distraught stranger who staggered into his office and slumped into a chair. "You've got to help me. I'm losing my memory, Doctor," he sobbed. "I once had a success-ful business, a wife, home and family; I was a respected member of the community. But all that's gone now. Since my memory began failing, I've lost the business—I couldn't remember my clients' names. My wife and children have left me, too; and why shouldn't they—some nights I wouldn't get home until four or five in the morning. I'd forget where I lived. . . . And it's getting worse. Doctor—it's getting *worse!*"

"This is not an unusual form of neurosis," the psychiatrist said soothingly. "Now tell me, just how long ago did you first become aware of this condition?"

"Condition?" The man sat up in his chair. "What condition?"

A wild-eyed man dressed in a Napoleonic costume and hiding his right hand inside his coat entered the psychiatrist's office and nervously exclaimed, "Doctor, I need your help right away."

"I can see that," retorted the doctor. "Lie down on that couch and tell me your problem."

"I don't have any problem," the man snapped. "In fact, as Emperor of France I have everything I could possibly want: money, women, power—everything! But I'm afraid my wife, Josephine, is in deep men-tal trouble."

"I see, said the psychiatrist, humoring his distraught patient. "And what seems to be *her* main problem?"

"For some strange reason," answered the unhappy man, "she thinks she's Mrs. Schwartz."

Obviously on the verge of hysteria, the distraught woman en-tered the psychiatrist's office and, between sobs, managed to explain that her husband was suffering under the delusion that he was a refrig-erator. "You can see what this is doing to me," the poor woman cried. "It's been weeks since I had a good night's sleep."

"I understand, my dear," the doctor reassured her. "But if you don't stop staying awake nights worrying about your husband's condi-tion, you'll make yourself sick as well."

"It's not his condition that keeps me up," she wailed. "It's that damn little light that goes on every time he sleeps with his mouth open!"

Sinking uneasily into the depths of the psychiatrist's couch, the patient sighed, "Doctor, I have a problem." He loosened his collar and continued, "I've got one son in Harvard and another at Yale. I've just gifted them with twin Ferraris. I have a town house on upper Fifth Avenue and a summer home at Easthampton and a sprawling ranch in Venezuela."

"Well!" smiled the psychiatrist, obviously impressed. "Either I missed something or you really don't have a problem."

"Doc," the harried chap croaked, "I only make seventy-five dollars a week."

The woman was enthusiastic about psychoanalysis and confided to a friend that she had undergone therapy. "You never knew this," she said, "but for years I was under the delusion that I was a fox terrier."

"And now you're completely cured?" asked the friend.

"That's right," said the woman proudly. "Just feel my nose."

"Doctor," explained the frustrated junior exec, "every night I have the same strange dream. Beautiful girls sneak into my apartment and try to seduce me."

"Well, what do you do?" asked the doctor.

"Nothing. I keep pushing them away."

"And what do you want me to do?"

"Please, doc," pleaded the man, "break my arms."

"Doctor," the worried exec told the psychiatrist, "I'm afraid I'm schizophrenic."

"Well," replied the doctor, "that makes four of us."

When the gorgeous young girl walked into the psychiatrist's office, she was immediately led to his couch. Without saying a word, he undressed her and made love to her. Finally he stood up, adjusted his tie and said, "Well, that takes care of *my* problem—now what's yours?"

"I'm in love with my horse," the nervous young man told his psychiatrist.

"Nothing to worry about," the psychiatrist consoled. "Many people are fond of animals. As a matter of fact, my wife and I have a dog we're very attached to."

"But, doctor," continued the troubled patient, "I feel *physically* attracted to my horse."

"Hmmm," observed the doctor. "Is it male or female?"

"Female, of course!" the man replied curtly. "What do you think I am, queer?"

"I'm always forgetting things," the distraught man grumbled to the psychiatrist. "What should I do?"

"The first thing to do," the doctor prescribed, "is pay me in advance."

On his first visit to the psychiatrist, the nervous young man explained that his family made him seek help because he preferred cotton socks to woolen ones. "That's no reason for you to see me," retorted the physician. "In fact, I myself prefer cotton socks."

"Really?" the happy patient exclaimed. "Do you like yours with oil and vinegar or just a squeeze of lemon?"

"I'm perpetually exhausted," Joe told the psychiatrist. "Every night, I dream I'm driving a truck from Galveston to Chicago and in the morning, I wake up dead tired."

"Beginning tonight," advised the analyst, "you stop at Tulsa and I'll take it on to Chicago."

Later, at a bar, the relieved patient listened to a friend's problem. "Each night," related his buddy, "I dream that I'm being forced to satisfy four beautiful women. It's killing me."

Joe recommended his psychiatrist; but the next time the acquaintance came around, he was in worse shape than ever.

"What happened?" Joe asked him. "Didn't my shrink do anything about your problem?"

"Oh, he took away the chicks, all right," moaned the guy, "but now every night I dream I've picked up a damn truck in Tulsa and I have to drive it all the way to Chicago."

The worried bachelor consulted a psychiatrist about his nymphomaniac girlfriend. "Doctor," he exclaimed in a shaky voice, "she'll stop at nothing to satisfy her bizarre sexual desires and unholy cravings—"

"I've heard enough, interrupted the psychiatrist. "Does she have a friend?"

"Have faith and ye shall be healed!" intoned the evangelist at the revival meeting. A woman on crutches and a man came forward. The evangelist asked, "What is your name, my good woman?"

"I'm Mrs. Smith," she answered, "and I haven't been able to walk without crutches for twenty years."

"Well, Mrs. Smith," he said, "go behind that screen and pray."

Turning to the man, he asked, "Now, sir, what is your name?"

"My name ith Thamualth," he answered, "and I have alwayth thpoken with a lithp."

"All right, Mr. Samuals," the evangelist said, "go behind that screen with Mrs. Smith and pray." After several minutes had passed, the revivalist announced: "I think the time has come. Witness these miracles. Mrs. Smith, throw your left crutch over the screen." The audience gasped as it sailed over. "Mrs. Smith, throw your right crutch over the screen." The crowd cheered as the second crutch appeared.

Encouraged, the evangelist commanded: "Mr. Samuals, say something in a loud, clear voice, so we can all hear you."

Samuals answered: "Mithuth Thmith jutht fell on her ath!"

We overheard two young ladies discussing their marriage plans on a northbound subway last week. "I understand your boy friend graduates from law school this June. I suppose you'll be getting married then."

"Oh, no, not right away," replied the other. "I want him to practice for at least a year first."

Concluding his final lecture before the holidays, the professor of criminal law observed, "Remember, gentlemen, if you have an affair with a girl under age, with or without her consent, it's rape; if you have an affair with a girl *of* age, without her consent, that's rape; but if you have an affair with a girl of age, *with* her consent, Merry Christmas!"

We just got the word about the legal secretary who told her amorous boyfriend, "Stop and/or I'll slap your face."

A lawyer friend tells us that you can't take it with you—especially when crossing a state line.

The editor of a small weekly newspaper, in a rage over several government bills that had recently been passed, ran a scathing editorial under the headline: "HALF OF OUR LEGISLATORS ARE CROOKS." Many prominent local politicians were outraged, and tremendous pressure was exerted on him to retract the statement. He finally succumbed to the pressure and ran an apology with the headline: "HALF OF OUR LEGISLATORS ARE NOT CROOKS."

A well-known lawyer friend of ours informs us that the difference between making love to a girl and making love to a woman can be as much as twenty years in some states.

When a utility company started moving its heavy equipment into the quiet suburban neighborhood, the local residents formed a protest committee and invited the offending firm's attorney to attend the committee's first meeting. Before the meeting could be called to order, however, the attorney decided to take the initiative and question each homeowner separately. Turning to a pretty widow on the committee, the lawyer said: "Now, as I understand it, the utility company is running its equipment around the clock, and the noise is disturbing your rest."

"What rest?" she interrupted. "*You* try spending a night in my bedroom. I promise you won't get a wink of sleep."

"Really, madam!" exclaimed another homeowner reproachfully. "If you're going to make offers like that, you might at least give the fellows from your own neighborhood first chance."

A sexy female attorney we know consistently breaks speed limits but never gets a ticket. Every time a policeman stops her, she simply lays down the law.

Then there was the lady barrister in London who dropped her briefs and became a solicitor.

A young major was apprehended, completely nude, while chasing a woman through the lobby of a large hotel. However, his lawyer soon had him freed on a technicality. The Army manual specifically states that an officer need not be in uniform, provided he is properly attired for the sport in which he is engaged.

And, of course, you've heard about the lady lawyer who moonlighted as a call girl. She was a prostituting attorney.

Then there was the Indian chief who installed electric lights in the tribal latrine, thus becoming the first Indian ever to wire a head for a reservation.

We overheard an Indian matron explaining the facts of life to her daughter. She pointed out: "Stork not bring papoose, it come by beau and error."

Two Indian scouts watched silently from their place of concealment behind some shrubbery as the first white settlers set foot on the North American continent. After solemnly surveying the scene for several minutes, the one Indian turned to the other and said, "Well, there goes the neighborhood."

In a little New Mexico town, a pretty young tourist watched with considerable interest as an Indian said "Chance" to every passing female. Finally, when curiosity got the best of her, she walked up to him and said "Hello"—to which he answered, "Chance."
Instead of strolling on, she turned to him and said, "I thought all Indians said 'How.'"
Replied the Indian: "I *know* how—just want *chance.*"

One late fall day, the Indian chief called together his tribe and announced that he had news to give them—some good and some bad. He went on to say he would give them the bad news first, and stated that due to their own improvidence, they would have nothing to eat during the winter months except buffalo dung. He then said, "Now for the good news—we have an ample supply of buffalo dung."

While driving through an Indian reservation, the salesman was approached by a very lovely Algonquin maid, who offered herself to him for fifty dollars. "That's a lot of money," he said. "Manhattan Island cost only twenty-four."
"True," she agreed, "but Manhattan Island just lies there."

The Indian agent on a South Dakota reservation tells us that the Sioux squaws have been practicing a variation on suburban wife-swapping. They call it passing the buck.

7
MISS-
DEMEANOR

The judge looked down at the sweet young thing. "You claim that the defendant stole your money from your stocking?" he asked.

"That's right, Your Honor," she answered.

"Well, why didn't you resist?" the judge asked.

The girl blushed and lowered her eyes. "I didn't know he was after my money, Your Honor," she said.

A husband returning from a trip was informed by his wife that a burglar had entered their apartment while he was gone.

"Did he get anything?" the husband anxiously inquired.

"I'll say he did," replied the wife. "In the dark, I thought he was you."

An attractive young thing met her maiden aunt downtown for lunch one afternoon and during the meal, the older woman asked her niece to deposit a paycheck for her at the bank where the girl worked. On her way back from lunch, the girl was accosted by a purse snatcher.

"Help, help," she screamed at a passing cop. "That man has taken my aunt's pay—he's taken my aunt's pay!"

"OK, lady," said the cop. "Cut out the pig latin and tell me exactly what happened."

The voluptuous redhead was walking down a dimly lit street when a man jumped out of the bushes.

"Give me your money," he demanded.

"I d-don't have any," she managed to reply.

"Give me your money or I'll search you!" he threatened.

She repeated that she didn't have any, then gasped as he made a tentative search.

"You'd better give me your money now," he said menacingly, "or I'm going to *really* search you!"

"But I don't have any!" she protested, almost in tears.

So he *really* searched her.

"I guess you were on the level," he finally muttered angrily, "you don't have any money on you."

"For heaven's sake," she wailed, "don't stop now. I'll write you a check."

A friend of ours reports that he was innocently walking down the street the other day, when he was accosted by a fellow flashy in features and dress—the very model of a con man.

"Hey, buddy," the con man said confidentially, "you wanna buy a hot?"

"A hot what?" our friend asked.

"You name it," said the flashy one with a smile. "I'm having a very good season."

The bank robbers arrived just before closing and promptly ordered the few remaining depositors, the tellers, clerks and guards to disrobe and lie, face down, behind the counter. One nervous blonde pulled off her clothes and lay down on the floor facing upwards. "Turn over, Maybelle," whispered the girl lying beside her, "this is a stick-up, not an office party."

Moving along a dimly lighted street, a friend of ours was suddenly approached by a stranger who had slipped from the shadows nearby.

"Please, sir," asked the stranger, "would you be so kind as to help a poor unfortunate fellow who is hungry and out of work? All I have in the world is this gun."

"Police?" came the voice on the phone. "I want to report a burglar trapped in an old maid's bedroom!" After ascertaining the address, the police sergeant asked who was calling. "This," cried the frantic voice, "is the burglar!"

A psychiatrist we know says that one good thing about being a kleptomaniac is that you can always take something for it.

On a road ten miles from Palermo, an American motorist was stopped by a masked desperado who, brandishing a revolver, demanded in a thick Sicilian accent that he get out of the car.

The motorist obeyed, pleading, "Take my money, my car, but don't kill me!"

"I no kill-a you," replied the brigand, "if you do what I say." Whereupon, he told the motorist to unzip and masturbate then and there. Though shocked, the motorist did what he was told.

"Good," said the masked stranger. "Now-a do it again." The motorist protested, but the gun was menacingly waved, so, with extreme difficulty, he repeated the act.

"Again," commanded the desperado, "or I kill-a you!" Summoning superhuman resources, the exhausted motorist Portnoyed himself yet a third time.

The bandit gave an order and a beautiful young girl stepped from behind the rocks. *"Now,"* said the highwayman, "you can give-a my sister a ride to town!"

Before his daring escape from prison, an infamous criminal had been photographed from four different angles. The FBI sent copies of the pictures to police chiefs all across the land, with orders to notify Washington the moment an arrest was made.

The next day, the Bureau received a teletyped reply from the ambitious sheriff of a small Southern town: "PICTURES RECEIVED. ALL FOUR SHOT DEAD WHILE RESISTING ARREST."

It was tea-time in the pad, and the air hung heavy in thick blue folds as the beat bunch and their tourist friends lit up. Suddenly, a loud voice in the hall demanded that they open the door in the name of legality. The smokers frantically gathered their still-smoking weeds and stuffed them in the cuckoo clock. The police entered, searched diligently, found nothing and left. The bunch breathed a sigh of relief and made for the cuckoo clock just as the clock's hands announced three A.M. The little door popped open, the bird poked his head out and said, "Hey mannn, what time is it?"

The advance proofs of a cookbook for hipsters recently came our way. Wildest recipe is for a salad: You cut up lettuce, tomatoes, cucumbers and green peppers. Then you add a dash of marijuana, and the salad tosses itself.

We know a cool chick who thinks a potholder is a cigarette case.

Well launched on an LSD trip, the two acidheads were happily relating the details of their hallucinations to each other. Said the first, "Right now, I've a mind to buy all the jewels in the world. In fact, I'm going to buy up all the world's gold, its oil, its yachts and, yes, all those lovely naked women who are now dancing in front of me."
Raising an eyebrow querulously, his friend replied, "And where, may I ask, did you get the idea that I'd be willing to sell?"

The doting father came home one night and was shocked to find his daughter and her friends smoking marijuana. Pulling the stick of pot out of the girl's mouth, he exclaimed, "What's a joint like this doing in a nice girl like you?"

A hip chick we know gets her kicks by taking LSD with her birth-control pills. She wants to take a trip—but not to Dr. Spock.

An underground newspaper suggested recently that the marijuana question could easily be settled by a joint session of Congress.

Have you heard about the hippie group in San Francisco that is trying to force a plebiscite on the legalization of marijuana? They're calling it a reeferendum.

The two stoned hippies were staggering along a railroad track when one tiredly complained to the other, "I sure wish we'd get to the bottom of this flight of stairs."

"The stairs aren't the worst of it," grumbled the second. "It's the low handrail that bugs me."

We hear there's a new type of tranquilizer that doesn't relax you —just makes you dig being tense.

And, of course, you've also heard about the ingenious chemist who invented an aphrodisiac insecticide. It didn't kill any bugs, but you could always swat two at a time.

We also know a hip couple who mixed LSD with an aphrodisiac and spent the night making love on the ceiling.

And, of course, you've heard about the nymphomaniac who got stoned on pot one night and found herself in a strange apartment—her own.

The rape of the Sabine women by the Romans is a famous historical incident, but our research department has uncovered a hitherto unrevealed story.

It seems that Trebonius, the tallest, strongest, handsomest soldier in the Roman legions broke into a house where he found two luscious, sloe-eyed sisters and their elderly nurse. Chuckling with glee, he roared, "Prepare thyselves for conquest, my pretties!"

The lovely girls fell to their knees and pleaded with him. "Ravish us if thou wilt, O Roman, but spare our faithful old nurse."

"Shut thy mouth," snapped the nurse. "War is war!"

The man standing at the bar (in court, unfortunately) was well-dressed, alert and obviously intelligent. The judge asked him how he pleaded to the charge of rape and, much to the magistrate's surprise, he replied, "Not guilty by reason of insanity, Your Honor."

"Insanity?" exclaimed the judge.

"Yes, sir," said the defendant. "I'm crazy about it."

Then there was the girl who didn't know she'd been raped until the check bounced.

Sauntering across the hot desert, the grimy cowpoke encountered an attractive young woman, completely naked, tied to the ground by four stakes. Leaning forward in his saddle, he inquired, "What's going on here, ma'am?"

"Oh, thank heavens you've come," she gasped. "A terrible thing has happened! Six Indians intercepted our wagon, killed my husband, tied me up like this and raped me, and then rode off with our children, leaving me here to die."

Slowly dismounting and unbuckling his gun belt, the cowboy said, "Well, ma'am, it looks like today just ain't gonna be your day."

"It wouldn't have been so bad if he'd just done it once," explained the sweet young thing to the judge. "But every time we went out, it was rape, rape, rape."

"Please help me," panted the shapely career girl, running into the police station. "I've just been raped by an imbecile."

"How do you know he was an imbecile?" asked the desk sergeant.

"He must have been," she replied. "I had to show him what to do."

The sweet young thing and her handsome escort for the evening became embroiled in a heated discussion on the subject of rape. The young man contended that any normal male could win a girl's favors by assault, whether she was willing or not. The young lady was equally certain that no woman could be won without her consent.

To settle the argument, they decided to conduct an experiment. They began to wrestle and, though the girl fought valiantly for her cause, the young man eventually proved his point.

Although conquered, the girl was undaunted. "You didn't win fairly," she exclaimed. "I lost my footing on the carpet. Let's try again."

The confident defense attorney approached the witness stand. "My client is only five feet tall and you are five feet, eleven—and yet you claim that he raped you, standing up," rasped the lawyer. "Could you explain to the court how this was possible?"

Squirming in her chair, the blushing victim admitted: "I guess I might have stooped a little."

The headmistress of a girls' boarding school was abruptly awakened one night by one of her students, a rather mature-looking sixteen year old.

"Miss Forbes, Miss Forbes," she cried, "I've just been raped!"

"Now, be calm, Melissa," the headmistress told her firmly. "The first thing you must do is go to the refrigerator and eat half a lemon."

"Half a lemon?" asked the surprised student. "Will that keep me from getting pregnant?"

"No," admitted the headmistress, "but it *will* get rid of that silly grin."

A college sophomore at a staid Eastern girls' school entered the office of the dean of women and began to weep bitterly. "A strange man jumped me, knocked me out and violated me while I was unconscious," she sobbed. "It was terrible!"

"That *is* terrible," the dean declared. "You missed the best part."

Two young girls were returning home from church one night when they were accosted by a pair of hoodlums in a dimly lit alley. "Dear Lord," prayed one girl, "forgive them, for they know not what they do."

"Sh," whispered the older. "This one does."

Then there was the ninety-year-old man who tried to seduce a fifteen-year-old girl and was charged with assault with a dead weapon.

A seventy-year-old man met a fellow geriatric on the street one day and asked him what he'd been doing lately. The friend said he'd just spent six months in jail, after being convicted of rape. "Rape!" shouted the first man. "At your age? That's the most ridiculous thing I ever heard of."

"I know," replied the other, "but I was so flattered, I pleaded guilty."

A stranger in town found his way to the most luxurious bordello. He entered, selected a gorgeous redhead and was escorted to a resplendent bed chamber of Hollywood proportions. Half an hour later, a satisfied smile on his face, he sought out the madam and took his wallet from his pocket. But the madam would not accept payment. She opened the drawer of a solid-gold cash register, counted out a hundred dollars and handed the money to him. Stunned and speechless, he staggered out.

A week later, he returned, chose a succulent blonde and was presented with *two* hundred dollars by the madam. Still puzzled, he took the money and left, feeling himself a very lucky fellow indeed.

The next night, he decided to pay another visit. After enjoying the services of a beautiful brunette, he walked up to the madam, held out his hand and waited for the money. He was unpleasantly surprised when she said, "Twenty-five dollars, please."

"Now, look here," he rejoined. "The first time I came in here, *you* gave *me* a hundred dollars. The second time, you gave me two hundred. How come I don't get paid tonight?"

"Tonight," replied the madam, "you were *not* on television!"

Back in the good old days, a traveler stopped at the mining town's best sporting house for a few hours of pleasure. As he cuddled up with a sweet blonde, he noticed some men across the street digging around the foundation of a church. "What's going on?" he asked.

"Oh, that," she replied. "Last week, the town council passed a law that no bawdyhouse could be located within three hundred feet of a place of worship. So they've got till the end of the month to move that church."

I met a woman who was willin'—
Now I'm usin' penicillin.

The lanky Texas ranch hand was still a virgin at twenty-one, so, on his first trip to the big city, he decided to visit a brothel and find out what he'd been missing. Upon securing the address of a rather exclusive establishment, he soon found himself lying in bed with an attractive partner. Sensing the lad was somewhat inexperienced, the professional gently took his hand and placed it on the source of her income. "Is this what you're looking for?" she whispered seductively.

"Well, I don't rightly know, ma'am," the cowboy shyly murmured. "I'm a stranger to these parts."

It was the young Englishman's first visit to the States and, in his innocence, he sought lodging in the city's red-light district. His money, however, was as green as his outlook, and the madam gladly offered him a room for the night. When a friend questioned him about his accommodations over lunch the following day, the young Briton replied:

"Well, the room was very pretentious, you know, but *gad,* what maid service!"

Obsessed with the idea of pleasing all manner of customers with girls of the very highest order, an enterprising madam set up a three-story house of sport. She had ex-secretaries, selected for their efficiency, on the first floor; ex-models, selected for their beauty, on the second; and ex-schoolteachers, selected for their intelligence, on the third. As time went on, the madam noticed that almost all the play went to floor number three. She asked why, and the answer to the puzzle finally came from one of the steady customers:

"Well," said the sporting gentleman, "you know how those school-teachers are—they make you do it over and over, until you get it right."

Then there was the young man who saved for years to buy his mother a house, only to find that the police department wouldn't let her run it.

"Though there are two dozen houses of ill fame in our town," said the candidate for mayor to his attentive audience at the political rally, "I have never gone to one of them!"

From the back of the crowd a heckler called out, "Which one?"

Upon entering the taxi and noticing the driver was a woman, the young man decided to have a little fun: "Take me to the cheapest brothel in town," he said.

"Mister," the female cabbie replied, "you're in it!"

"Signore," the Italian guide announced to his American client, "we are now passing the most fabulous brothel in all of Rome."

"Why?" asked the tourist.

Having put in over three hundred miles behind the wheel during the first day of a cross-country business trip, the weary salesman was prepared to stop at the first motel along the road when he spotted a sign advertising: GRANDMA'S WHOREHOUSE 30 MILES AHEAD. His spirits understandably cheered, the salesman drove on to Grandma's place, where he was greeted by a sweet old lady who silently led him to a plushly decorated waiting room and motioned for him to sit down. Without uttering a single word, she then left the room and returned momentarily with a picture of a beautiful young girl and a note stating that if he liked what he saw in the photo, the salesman should pay her fifty dollars and use the door at the far end of the room. The excited traveler quickly handed her the prescribed amount and rushed through the designated doorway, only to find himself standing back outside in the cold night air. Turning abruptly, he discovered a message painted across the door which read: CONGRATULATIONS! YOU HAVE JUST BEEN SCREWED BY GRANDMA.

Shortly after a new police commissioner took office, the local house of pleasure was raided and the girls were lined up outside for questioning by the fuzz. A little old lady chanced to walk by and, noticing the commotion, asked what was happening. As a joke, one of the chicks told her they were standing in line for free lollipops. A few minutes later, a constable approached the elderly woman and asked, "Aren't you a bit old for this?"

"Officer," she cackled, "as long as they keep making them, I'll keep sucking them."

Here are a couple of salesman jokes worth a retelling:

A big store buyer had been on the road for nearly two months. Each week he would send his wife a telegram saying: "CAN'T COME HOME YET. STILL BUYING."

His wife knew that these buying trips usually involved more than business. She tolerated this particular jaunt for a while, but when the third month rolled by and she'd still seen nothing of her husband but the weekly telegrams, she wired him: "BETTER COME HOME. I'M SELLING WHAT YOU'RE BUYING."

A salesman friend of ours spent a couple of days in Miami last fall. His first night there, a good-looking blonde approached him in a bar and said, "I'm selling—you buying?"

Our friend bought and thought no more about it till, a week later, he discovered he had a "case."

He visited a doctor and had it taken care of, and two months later business again took him to Miami and again he visited the same bar. Sure enough, the same blonde was there, and once again she approached him with, "I'm selling—you buying?"

"Well, that depends," said our friend, sipping his drink thoughtfully. "What are you selling tonight—cancer?"

Then there was the professional lady who bought a bicycle and peddled it all over town.

A street-walking acquaintance of ours has a new slogan that's certain to revolutionize her trade: "It's a business to do pleasure with you."

A doctor and his wife were out walking when a buxom blonde in tight-fitting sweater and skirt nodded hello from a nearby doorway.

"And who was that?" questioned the wife.

"Oh, just a young woman I know professionally," said the doctor, reddening visibly.

"I'm sure of that," said the wife, "but your profession or hers?"

Then there was the middle-aged businessman who took his spouse to Paris. After traipsing with her from one *maison de la couture* to another, he begged for a day off to rest and got it. With the wife gone shopping again, he went to the Ritz Bar and picked up a luscious Parisienne. They got on well until the question of money came up. She wanted fifty American dollars; he offered ten. They couldn't get together on the price, so they didn't get together. That evening he escorted his wife to one of the nicer restaurants on the Rue de Rivoli and there he spotted his gorgeous babe of the afternoon seated at a table near the door.

"See, *monsieur?*" she said, as they passed her. "Look what you got for your lousy ten bucks."

Bill's sister was one of the most popular girls in Manhattan. She had more boyfriends than she knew what to do with and she never wanted for a thing. Bill was an impecunious musician, always in debt and constantly asking his sister for spending money.

"I don't understand you, Bill," she said in obvious annoyance one afternoon when he had tried to put the bite on her for a ten spot. "I don't have any trouble saving money, so why should you?"

"Sure, sure," he said, "but you've got money coming in all the time from the very thing that's keeping me broke."

A curvilinear young secretary, just returned from a magnificent vacation in a South American republic, walked into the foreign-exchange section of her New York bank and dropped a wad of foreign currency on the counter. The teller counted it carefully and gave her fifty-three cents in exchange.

"Do you mean to tell me that's all I get?" gasped the lovely thing.

"I'm afraid so, miss," said the teller. "That's the legal exchange rate."

"Damn," the girl hissed. "And like a fool I gave him breakfast too."

Business was brisk for the pretty little call girl at the bar, with a number of would-be customers gathered about her. "Bill," she said, "you can come over about seven-ish, and you, George, around eight-ish. Frank, I'll have time for you around nine-thirty-ish."

Then, obviously pleased with the prospects of a busy, busy evening, she spun around on her bar stool, surveyed the crowded club and caroled, "Ten-ish, anyone?"

"I'm through going to psychiatrists," asserted the call girl. "I just can't get used to a guy who tells me to lie down on a couch and then sends me the bill."

One of the recent cases investigated by the Director of Internal Revenue was that of a young girl who listed her apartment rent as "expenses incurred while entertaining clients."

Charlie was taking his out-of-town pal, George, for a stroll through the city. They were admiring the scenery, when George observed:

"Say, will you look at that good-looking girl over there. She's smiling at us. Do you know her?"

"Oh, yes: Betty—twenty dollars."

"And who's that brunette with her? Man, she's really stacked!"

"Yep: Dolores—forty dollars."

"Ah, but look what's coming. That's what I call really first class!"

"That's Gloria—eighty dollars."

"My God," cried George, "aren't there any nice, respectable girls in this town?"

"Of course," Charlie answered. "But you couldn't afford their rates!"

In Rio on a business trip, Al found himself hampered, after working hours, by the fact that he didn't know the language. He was at once delighted and dismayed, therefore, when a plunging neckline surrounded by femininity of surpassing comeliness sat down at his restaurant table.

"Can you speak English?" he ventured hopefully.

"*Si,*" she said with a bright white smile, "bot jus' a leetle beet."

"Just a little bit, eh?" Al repeated joshingly. "How much?"

"Twenty-five dollars," was the prompt reply.

Roger, the handsome real-estate agent, couldn't remember when he'd rented an apartment to a more desirable tenant. As she bent over his desk to sign the lease, he became aware that his pulse was beating in his ears with the sound of bongo drums.

"Well," he said, "that's that. I wish you much happiness in your new apartment, and here are the two keys that come with it."

She straightened up, accepted the keys and favored him with a dazzling smile.

"And here is a month's rent in advance, honey," she replied. And she handed him back one of the keys.

Said Flo, a lady of the evening, to Dolores (another pro): "Would you please lend me ten dollars until I get back on my back?"

Though Wilbur Simpson appeared to be in good health for a man in his middle forties, his doctor informed him that his blood pressure was disturbingly high and, unless he quit his job at once and took a complete rest for at least a year, he should not expect to be around to enjoy his middle fifties. Like many a man before him, Wilbur had been so busy keeping up with the Joneses, he'd neglected to put anything away for an emergency, but his loving wife, Mildred, expressed a real willingness to go to work and support them both till he was back on his feet. Unfortunately, Wilbur had not married his sweet wife for her brains, and there were very few jobs about for even as attractive a middle-aged woman as she that would produce anything close to the kind of income they had been used to living on. So, with understandable reservations, but recognizing it was truly a matter of life or death, they decided that the only profession for which the unskilled Mildred could hope to qualify, and earn any real money, was the world's oldest.

Wilbur choked back his misgivings as he watched his wife depart on the first day's adventure, but he credited himself with being a sophisticated and worldly man, and he had to admit that this was the one profession for which Mildred was well suited. She was still a well-proportioned and attractive woman, and, if she could just remember to keep track of her earnings, she might do very well, indeed. But at the end of the first day, Mildred arrived home a sorry sight, her clothes dirty and disarranged, in a state of near exhaustion.

"It certainly looks as though you've been a busy girl on your first day," said Wilbur sympathetically. "How much did you earn, dear?"

"Thirty-six dollars and a quarter," moaned Mildred.

"That isn't very much money for twelve hours," said Wilbur. "Who gave you the quarter?"

Mildred collapsed on the sofa and smiled weakly. "Why, silly," she said, *"all* of them, of course!"

Rustic Ron stared at the bellhop in disbelief. "Twenty-five dollars for a girl? That's ridiculous! Why, in Tennessee I can get a girl to clean my house, wash my clothes, cook my meals and sleep with me all night for four pork chops a day."

"Then what," said the bellhop, "are you doing in Chicago?"

"Buying pork chops."

George, after tying on a whopper the night before, woke up in the morning to find a pathetically unattractive woman sleeping blissfully beside him. He leaped out of bed, dressed quickly, and furtively placed a twenty dollar bill on top of the bureau. He then proceeded to tiptoe out of the room. But as he passed the foot of the bed, he felt a tug at his trouser cuff. Glancing down, he saw another female almost as homely as the one he'd left in bed. She gazed up at him soulfully and asked, "Nothing for the bridesmaid?"

Then there was the Japanese call girl who went broke because no one had a yen for her.

Seeing an attractive girl sitting alone in the cocktail lounge, the young man approached her politely and offered to buy her a drink.

"A motel!" she shrieked.

"No, no," he said, embarrassed, "I said a drink. . . ."

"You expect me to go to a motel with you!" she shrieked even louder.

Definitely daunted, the young man fled to a dim rear booth of the lounge, to avoid the stares of the other patrons. A few minutes later, the girl came back to where he was seated and said softly, "I'd like to apologize for making you so uncomfortable at the bar. You see, I'm studying psychology at the university, and I wanted a chance to study the reactions of the people here."

To which the young man replied, in a resounding roar, "Seventy-five dollars!"

A business executive on an out-of-town sales trip was about to check in at a hotel when he noticed a lusciously proportioned young woman smiling at him provocatively. Very casually he walked over to her and spoke a few inaudible words. He returned to the desk with her clinging to his arm and they registered as man and wife. After a two-day stay, he checked out and was handed a bill for seven hundred and fifty dollars. "There's some mistake here," he protested. "I've only been here two days."

"Yes," the clerk explained, "but your wife has been here for two months."

After an evening at the theater and several nightcaps at an intimate little bistro, the young man whispered to his date, "How do you feel about making love to men?"

"That's *my* business," she snapped.

"Ah," he said. "A professional!"

A French actress, returning from a visit to the United States, brought back a superb mink coat.

"How beautiful," remarked an envious script girl at the studio. "Where did *mademoiselle* get that?"

"I met a gentleman," said the haughty actress disdainfully, "who had five thousand dollars . . . *et voilà!*"

That summer the script girl took her vacation in the U.S. On her return, she sported a mink coat equally as beautiful as the actress'.

"*Sacré bleu!*" exclaimed the astonished actress, "how did you get that?"

"The same way as *mademoiselle,*" replied the script girl icily. "Only in my case, I met a hundred gentlemen, and each had fifty dollars."

The American diplomatic courier had just arrived in the tiny Latin American capital and as he strode briskly out of the airport terminal, he was obviously charged with the sense of his own self-importance —snapping instructions at the porters carrying his luggage and looking about impatiently for the car that was supposed to be there to meet him. He certainly had no time for the dirty little street urchins who trailed after him trying to sell everything from a shoeshine to their sisters.

"Hey, American," called out one lad especially worldly-wise for his years. "I get what you like, if you pay—feelthy pictures, marijuana, girls . . . boys . . . ?"

"I can't be bothered with this vermin," the undiplomatic messenger disdainfully proclaimed, brushing his ragged pursuers aside. "My business here is with the American ambassador!"

"Can do, *señor,*" responded the boy. "But for an ambassador, you weel have to pay extra."

During an out-of-town business trip, the young executive picked up a lovely creature in the hotel bar and took her up to his room for a nightcap. After a few drinks, the girl sat on his lap and cooed, "Would you like to hug me?"

"Sure," said the businessman, pressing her close to him.

"And would you like to kiss me?" the girl whispered passionately.

"Of course," he replied, planting a big buss on her inviting lips.

"OK, honey," she continued, "Brace yourself—because here comes the fifty dollar question."

The wages of sin are high unless you know someone who'll do it for nothing.

One evening, after conducting a real old-fashioned revival meeting, the visiting evangelist decided to take a walk, and happened to wander into a nearby red-light district. On a corner, he saw a streetwalker leaning against a lamppost. The evangelist stopped and, in a powerful voice, he intoned, "Woman, I prayed for you last night."

"Well, you could've had me if you'd come around," she purred. "I was standing right here all night long."

A ravishing professional girl of our acquaintance gets a grand and glorious feeling whenever a man makes love to her—but the grand always comes first.

Have you heard about the ingenious call girl who found a better-paying position?

The cooperative Chicago call girl coupled with the charming gent and when they were done, he handed her two hundred dollars. The girl was flabbergasted, for she'd never before been given more than twenty dollars for her favors.

"Think nothing of it," said the man. "You come back here tomorrow night at the same time and there'll be another two hundred dollars for you where that came from."

The following evening she returned, and when they were finished making love, true to his word, the fellow handed her another two hundred. Again she thanked him profusely, and again he replied, "Think nothing of it. Come back here tomorrow night and there'll be another two hundred dollars for you where that came from."

She returned the third night, and after she had satisfied him once again, he gave her another two hundred dollars.

"You're the most generous man I've ever met," she said. "Tell me, where are you from?"

"Atlanta."

"Atlanta!" she exclaimed. "Isn't that a coincidence. My mother lives in Atlanta."

"I know," said the man. "When she learned I was coming to Chicago, she gave me six hundred dollars to give to you."

Then there was the prostitute who was so dumb she wound up working in a warehouse.

The impecunious young couple finally hit on a way to save money. Each time they made love, the husband would deposit all his change in a huge porcelain piggy bank in their bedroom.

After about a year of this, they decided to break open the bank and spend the money. Counting up all the proceeds, the husband remarked: "This is really strange—there's all this currency here. Fives, tens, even some twenties. I don't remember putting in any bills."

"No," responded his wife, "but not everyone is as cheap as you are."

When one of the prostitutes passed away, the girls moped disconsolately around the house. "Good old Gloria," lamented one. "She could handle twenty men a night, drink a fifth of whiskey and still have the strength to roll five drunks."

Hearing this, one of the others burst into tears. "Why is it," she sobbed, "that a girl has to die before anyone says anything nice about her?"

The dazzling blonde met a well-attired gentleman at a plush cocktail lounge and they soon struck up an amiable conversation about human nature. "Would you sleep with a complete stranger for a million dollars?" the gentleman hypothesized.

"Yes, I think I would," the girl declared.

"Would you sleep with me for twenty-five dollars?" he asked.

"What do you think I am?" she retorted indignantly.

"We've already established that," he responded. "Now we're just haggling over the price."

The bartender presented the conventioneer with the bill, and the customer was outraged. "New York is the most expensive place in the world," he complained. "Why, back in Sioux City, you can drink as much as you want without paying, sleep in a fancy hotel for free and wake up and find fifty dollars on your pillow."

"Come on, now," questioned the bartender. "Has that ever happened to you?"

"No," the man admitted. "But it happens to my wife all the time."

Then there was the Old Testament prostitute who was arrested for trying to make a prophet.

The luxurious Las Vegas hotel was engulfed in flames as the firemen battled the blaze and attempted to rescue the trapped guests. Just then, a man clad only in a towel came running from the hotel. "Have you seen a blonde girl running around naked?" he asked breathlessly.

"No, I haven't," a fireman replied.

"Well, if you do, you can have her," the man said. "She's already paid for."

Having leased an apartment to an attractive receptionist, the landlord appeared promptly on the first of the month and rapped sharply on the door. "Who is it?" a feminine voice called out.

"It's the landlord," he shouted. "I've come to collect the rent."

"Could you come back in an hour?" she asked. "I'm still paying my grocery bill."

Then there was the airline stewardess who turned to prostitution but couldn't break the habit of greeting her customers with "Welcome aboard."

On a southbound train a few months after the Civil War, a young belle suddenly moved from her seat next to a businessman and sat beside a Confederate veteran who was on his way home from the battle lines. "That carpetbagger offered me ten dollars to spend the night with him," the offended girl indignantly told the soldier.

The Southerner immediately drew his gun and shot the man. "Let that be a lesson to any other damn Yankees," he proclaimed in a loud voice. "Don't come down here and try to double the price of everything."

We know a swinging call girl who's a pleasure to be with—but she doesn't come cheap.

"I was in a phone booth talking to my girl, Your Honor," said the defendant, "and this cop came up, opened the door, grabbed me by the coat and dragged me out."

"What did you do?" the judge asked.

"I didn't do anything, not until he grabbed my girl and dragged her out, too."

In olden days, man's greatest fear was that a woman would take it to heart; today, his greatest fear is that a woman will take it to court.

She was standing before the judge, crying out her story: "Your Honor, he gets up every morning and starts knocking me around the bedroom. He hits me in the head with his fist, and sometimes he uses a shoe. If I don't fix his meals just the way he likes them, he conks me with the pots and pans. If I dare to talk back to him or say anything he doesn't care for, he belts me on the skull with a beer bottle. Your Honor, that man ought to be in jail."

Turning to the defendant, the judge asked, "What have you to say for yourself?"

"You can't believe a word that woman says, Your Honor," said the man. "She's obviously punch-drunk."

Perjury charges were recently filed against a jury of six men and six women who, after being locked up together for twelve hours, came out saying, "Not guilty."

There was a generous area of disagreement between the sexy young widow and a bachelor friend she said had sired the latest addition to her brood. So they took their problem to court.

"Did you sleep with this woman?" asked the judge.

To which our hero replied, sincerely, "Not a wink, Your Honor. Not a wink."

The courtroom was pregnant with anxious silence as the judge solemnly considered his verdict in the paternity suit before him. Suddenly, he reached into the folds of his robes, drew out a cigar and ceremoniously handed it to the defendant.

"Congratulations!" said the jurist. "You have just become a father!"

"You are charged," said the judge, "with the serious offense of assault and battery upon your husband. How do you plead?"

"Innocent," said the shapely defendant. "I hit him because he called me a vile name."

"And just what did he call you?" asked the jurist.

"It's really too terrible to repeat—he . . . he called me a 'two-bit whore'!"

"That *is* bad," said the judge. "What did you hit him with?"

"A bag of quarters, Your Honor."

Then there was the freaky WAC who was court-martialed for contributing to the delinquency of a major.

Have you heard about the bed-wetting racist who went to Klan meetings in a rubber sheet?

A weekend golfer, having four-putted the last hole, threw his clubs into the golf cart and drove toward the clubhouse. Arriving there, he saw a squad car parked by the entrance. As he walked toward the locker room, a policeman stopped him. "Did you drive from the fifteenth tee about half an hour ago?" the officer asked.

"Yes."

"Did you hook your ball over those trees and off the course?"

"Yes, as a matter of fact, I did," replied the puzzled golfer.

With anger in his voice, the policeman continued, "Your ball sailed out on the highway, cracked the windshield of a woman's car; she couldn't see where she was going and ran into a fire truck; the fire truck couldn't get to the fire and a house burned down! What are you going to do about it?"

The golfer pondered a moment, picked up his driver, and said: "Well, I think I'm going to open my stance a little and move my left thumb around farther toward my right side."

"Gentlemen of the jury," said the defense attorney, now beginning to warm to his summation, "the real question here before you is, shall this beautiful young woman be forced to languish away her loveliest years in a dark prison cell? Or shall she be set free to return to her cozy little apartment at 4134 Seaside Street—there to spend her lonely, loveless hours in her boudoir, lying beside her little Princess phone, 962-7873?"

The prosecuting attorney's voice reached fever pitch as he cross-examined the young male defendant: "You mean to sit there and tell this jury that you had a completely assembled still on your premises, and were not engaged in the illegal production of alcoholic spirits?"

"That's the truth," answered the defendant. "I acquired it as a conversation piece, just like any other antique."

"You'll have to do better than that," sneered the prosecutor. "As far as this court is concerned, the very possession of such equipment is proof of your guilt."

"In that case, you'd better charge me with rape, too," the defendant said.

"Are you confessing to the crime of rape, young man?" interrupted the judge.

"No, Your Honor," answered the defendant, "but I sure as hell have the equipment."

It takes a brave man to admit his mistakes, especially in the middle of a paternity-suit hearing.

The devastating blonde was arrested for prostitution and taken to court. "Have you anything to offer the gentlemen of the jury on your own behalf?" asked the judge.

"Oh, no, Your Honor," she answered. "I've learned my lesson."

When the father discovered that his teen-age daughter had made love with her boyfriend at a wild party, he insisted on having the young man arrested for statutory rape and the case was promptly brought to trial. The first witness was another teen-ager who had attended the festivities. "If you actually witnessed the act," the prosecutor demanded, "why didn't you try to stop the defendant?"

"Well," the testifier admitted, "at the time, it was impossible to tell which of the two would be the defendant."

There is absolutely no truth to the rumor that Christine Jorgensen's mother is writing a book entitled *My Son, the Daughter.*

The attractive and grief-stricken widow had been living in seclusion at the home of her deceased husband's younger brother for several weeks. One evening, when she could no longer control her emotions, she barged into her brother-in-law's study and pleaded, "James, I want you to take off my dress." The brother-in-law did as she requested. "Now," she continued, "take off my slip." He again complied. "And now," she said, with a slight blush, "remove my panties and bra." Once more James obeyed her command.

Then, regaining her composure, she stared directly at the embarrassed young man and boldly announced, "I have only one more request, James. Don't ever let me catch you wearing my things again."

Then there was the transvestite from Yale who wanted to spend his junior year abroad.

Then there was the transvestite sailor who went down to the sea in slips.

When the young career girl consulted a doctor about her diminishing sexuality, she was given a hormone shot and told to call in a week. "Doctor," she wailed over the phone the next week, "my voice has become terribly low."

"That's not too unusual," replied the doctor. "Have you had any other reactions?"

"Yes," she moaned. "I've sprouted hair on my chest."

"My goodness," the doctor gasped. "How far down does it go?"

"All the way to my testicles."

The storm smashed the great ship to pieces. One small boat of survivors found its way to a nearby island and safety. Realizing that they had been blown off the usual steamship route and would probably be on the island for many months before being rescued, the survivors proceeded to set up satisfactory living arrangements. Since the survivors included six women and one man, these "arrangements" were a little unusual.

It was agreed amongst them that rather than fight over the lucky fellow, each girl would take her turn, having him entirely to herself one day each week; and that he would have the seventh day to himself.

Being a normal sort of a guy, our friend threw himself into the situation with a great deal of enthusiasm. The first few weeks, he didn't even bother with his day of rest. As time passed, however, he began looking forward to that one day at the end of each week. Eventually, in fact, it was that day that filled his every thought; he longed to be off the island, to hear a masculine voice again, and to sleep, for days, and days, and days.

One morning, a Saturday, with the week almost at an end, he spotted a small raft on the horizon, and on it a figure. He waved frantically as the raft approached the island, and when it was near enough and he realized that the new arrival was a man, he dashed down the hill to the beach. As the man pulled himself out of the water, our friend threw his arms around him and cried: "Man, you've no idea how glad I am to see you!"

"Well goodness, fellow," swished the new arrival. "I'm gladda see you, too!"

"My God," croaked the weary one, "there go my Sundays!"

Two knights, resplendent in shining armor and mounted on handsome steeds, rode through the forest followed by their meek little page who was huddled uncomfortably on his burro. As they arrived at a strange castle surrounded by the usual moat, one knight shouted the traditional "Tallyho" to inform the castle's proprietors that the travelers desired lodging for the night. The drawbridge was soon lowered and out came a wispy fellow, dressed in flowing robes of many colors. "Well, what can I do for you fellows?" he lisped.

The tired knights, anxious for lodging but taken aback by their limp-wristed host, looked at each other in dismay, then one whispered to the other: "Promise him anything, but give him our page."

Then there was the girl whose boyfriend didn't smoke, drink or swear, and never, ever made a pass at her. He also made his own dresses.

"Is it true that you telegraph flowers anywhere?" the man asked the Western Union operator.

"Of course," she said.

"Wonderful!" he exclaimed. "Send me to New York. I'm a pansy!"

Have you heard about the perverted Aussie who left his wife and returned to Sydney?

Did you hear about the young man who moved to Greenwich Village and turned prematurely gay?

Two garment-district executives were consoling each other with news of how bad their respective businesses had been all year, when the subject of their two sons came up. The first executive shook his head sadly from side to side, exclaiming, "What a no-good son I've got. You really wouldn't believe it. I don't believe it myself. A twenty-thousand-dollar-a-year salary I give him, but you think he pays any attention to the business? He does not. He stays out all night, doesn't come to work until it's time for lunch and then fools around with the models in their dressing room the rest of the day."

"You think that's bad?" the second executive asked. "You should have *my* son. He's so much worse, you couldn't believe it. He also gets a twenty-thousand-dollar-a-year salary, stays out all night, comes to work at noon and spends the rest of the day fooling around with the models in their dressing room."

"So what makes him worse?" asked the first executive.

"You forget," replied the second executive, "I'm in men's clothes."

We've just heard about a pair of hip parents who had their baby christened in Greenwich Village so the little one could have a fairy godfather.

Two Jewish mothers who had lived in the same block in Brooklyn when their children were growing up, but hadn't seen each other in years, happened to meet at a bridge luncheon in a swank hotel in Manhattan. After a tearful embrace, they retired to a corner to chat.

"And how are your two boys, William and Bernard?" the one woman inquired of the other.

"William is an attorney, and a full partner in an important New York law firm," the second woman responded with pride. "And it's *Doctor* Bernard, if you please; with so many patients that even his mother needs an appointment to see her own son in the afternoon! . . . And your son, Herman, how is he?"

The first mother's eyes dropped, but only for a moment.

"Herman is a homosexual," she said.

"That's wonderful!" exclaimed her friend. "And where's his office?"

Two slightly tipsy members of the gay set were sitting sipping cocktails in a bar when an unusually attractive well-built blonde walked by. The first fag didn't even look up, but the second stared in obvious appreciation, emitting a long, low whistle—just loud enough for his companion to hear.

"See here," the first fag said sharply, "you're not thinking of going straight, are you?"

"No, of course not," replied his friend reassuringly, "but when I see something like that go by, I sometimes wish I'd been born a Lesbian."

Then there was the gay fellow who redecorated his bathroom and has *His* and *His* towels.

The succulent career girl had one unhappy trait: She would fall head over heels in love with a different man each week, always with the conviction that her latest beau was *the* man of her dreams, with whom she could live happily ever after. One particularly devastating experience finally convinced her that she had to put an end to this distressing habit. She vowed to spend the next few evenings alone and repaired to her favorite bar to console herself. But, as luck would have it, she encountered a handsome but rather effete stranger, whom she couldn't resist approaching.

"I suppose I could buy you a drink," the young man said, after she sat down next to him. "But I really must tell you that nothing will come of it."

His reserve intrigued her and after several drinks, her attraction to him had grown considerably. In fact, the more the fellow put her off, the more fascinated she became. Here, she thought, was a truly fine young man—who didn't try to take advantage of her like all the rest. Before she knew it, she had invited him to her apartment. "I'm just not the type of person who does that sort of thing," her new friend replied. "But I'll go if you promise to be good."

His hesitance increased her ardor for him all the more. By the time they had reached her apartment, she was irresistibly drawn to him. Once inside, she reclined languorously on the couch and beckoned to him.

"Please," he pleaded. "I told you this couldn't work out."

"But you don't understand," she said. "I want you for my husband."

"That's quite different!" he said enthusiastically. "Send him in!"

"Congratulate me, Pop," said the young man, "I'm in love with a girl."

"Son," observed his dad, "you couldn't have made a better choice."

Then there were the two gay judges who tried each other.

Then there was the gay Manhattanite who moved to Long Island so he could be listed in the Queens directory.

A youthful archeologist was sent to a deserted outpost in the Middle East to assist with an excavation project. "You're going to like it here," a colleague assured him on his arrival. "Friday nights, we get a truckload of booze from the village and have a great time."

"I'm afraid I'm no drinker," the archeologist protested.

The colleague shrugged. "On Saturdays, we bring in a busload of wild girls from the village and have an orgy."

"Gee," the archeologist mused. "I don't think I'd enjoy that at all."

"I say," blurted his colleague. "You're not queer, are you?"

"Of course not," the fellow snapped.

"That's too bad," the colleague said. "You won't like Sunday nights, either."

The draft-board examiners eyed the swishy young man with suspicion. They had orders to watch out for potential draft evaders feigning homosexuality. After subjecting the chap to an extensive physical and psychological examination, one of the board members declared: "Well, fella, it looks to me like you're going to make a good little soldier."

"Fabulous," replied the young man. "When can I meet him?"

To cut down on expenses, the two secretaries decided to vacation together and to share a hotel room. On the first night, one turned to her friend and rested her hand on her shoulder. "There's something about myself I've never told you," she admitted. "I'll be frank—"

"No," her friend interrupted, "*I'll* be Frank."

Then there was the gay tattoo artist who had designs on several of the local sailors.

The family doctor, consulted by the hysterical parents of a pregnant teen-ager, said he positively would not perform an abortion. "But when her time comes, I'll deliver the baby at a private hospital. Then I'll show it to one of my other patients—let's say a woman who's married and who's in for a gall-bladder operation—and tell her there's been a mistake, it wasn't her gall bladder, she was pregnant, and here's the child."

All went as planned; but at the crucial time, there was no available female patient on whom to foist the infant. There was only a male—a priest, in fact. The physician, undaunted, decided to brazen it out. When the man of the cloth awakened from the anesthesia, he was informed that, by a miracle, he had been delivered of an offspring, a boy. Far from being shocked, the good cleric was overjoyed at this evidence of divine intervention and raised the boy as his own.

Years later, as the priest lay dying, he concluded that he must unburden his soul to his son. "I have always told you I was your father, but that is untrue," he confessed, and he told the lad about the "miraculous" incident at the hospital. "So you see, my boy," the priest announced, "I'm not your father. I'm your mother. The bishop is your father."

Rodney, the eldest son of a respectable Boston family, announced to his shocked father that he intended to live openly with his swishy boyfriend on Beacon Hill.

"Damn it, Rodney," the parent responded, "our family came over with John Winthrop and we've never had a scandal such as this."

"I can't help it, Father, I love him."

"But, for God's sake, son—he's Catholic!"

Upon receiving his induction notice, the delicate-looking young man reported to his draft board and confessed that he was a homosexual.

"Queer, huh?" one member grunted. "Do you think you could kill a man?"

"Oh, yes," the fellow giggled, "but it would take me quite a while."

When the Hollywood star announced his plans to vacation in Tangier, his agent told him to be sure to visit a very exclusive brothel there that specialized in unusual sexual practices. On his return, the star called his agent and announced that he'd taken his advice. "It was really quite an experience," he declared. "First the girl told me to strip and lie down on the bed. Then she covered me from head to toe with strawberry jam, sprinkled marshmallows over that, smothered it all with whipped cream and topped it with a handful of almonds and maraschino cherries."

"Fantastic," the agent gasped. "And then she licked it all off?"

"Hell no," the star exclaimed. "It looked so good I ate it myself."

The two elderly farmers were leisurely strolling through a pasture when one stopped and remarked, "Here's where I got my first piece of ass and right over there's where her mother stood."

"Her mother," said his surprised companion. "What did she say?"

"Ba-a-a-a-a," came the reply.

The attractive young coed was filing a report with the campus police on her encounter with an exhibitionist.

"Those nuts always seem to bother the nicest, most innocent girls," one officer said sympathetically. "I'm terribly sorry you were exposed to this experience."

"Oh, that's all right," giggled the undergrad. "It was really no big thing."

The bachelor and his date decided to attend a country-club masquerade ball dressed in a rented cow costume. However, after an hour, they grew tired of their tandem togetherness and he suggested that they slip outside for a breath of fresh air. Still in the costume, the twosome was trotting across a nearby field when the fellow spotted a huge Hereford bull that was preparing to charge. "What are we going to do?" quavered his frightened partner from her posterior position.

"I'm going to eat some grass," the lad croaked as the thundering hooves came closer. "But it sounds like you'd better bend down even farther and brace yourself."

Have you heard about the masochist who had to break a date because he was going to be tied up all night?

A colonel in the Foreign Legion, assuming command of a desert outpost, spied a camel tied up behind the enlisted men's quarters and asked his first lieutenant to explain its presence there. The lieutenant replied that the men, being without female companionship for long periods, had natural urges which required satisfaction, and the camel was used for that purpose. The colonel, being an understanding man, agreed that the camel could remain.

Several weeks later, the colonel himself felt a passionate urge welling up inside him and ordered the camel brought to his room. When the camel arrived, the colonel immediately set upon her with vigor. Having achieved satisfaction, the colonel turned around and discovered, with some embarrassment, that the lieutenant was still standing in the doorway.

"Well," the colonel said, breaking the silence after a moment, "is that the way the men usually do it?"

"Not exactly, sir," the lieutenant replied. "The men ordinarily use her to take them into town."

Then there was the masochist who was starved for affliction.

Two call girls were discussing their experiences of the last few evenings over cocktails when one asked the other, "Say, how did you make out with that eccentric millionaire you met yesterday?"

"He gave me a hundred dollars, but it wasn't worth it," said the second. "He wanted to make love in a coffin."

"No kidding?!" exclaimed her friend. "I'll bet that shook you up pretty good."

"Yeah," she confessed, "but not as much as it did the six pall-bearers."

And then there was the raven-haired sadist who stood up and announced that she could whip any man in the house.

"Darling," she sighed, "love me like you've never loved me before!"

"Not in this state," he replied. "I could get ten years."

After patiently listening to their mother's garbled and mythical version of the facts of life, the precocious first grader said to his younger sister: "Gee, I never thought Dad was the kind of guy who would do it with a stork."

Then there was the unfortunate voyeur who was apprehended at the peek of his career.

Have you heard about the girl who was so ugly that Peeping Toms would reach in and pull down her shades?

Plymouth Colony had fallen on evil days, and Governor Bradford called a meeting to berate the townspeople for their wayward practices. "Terrible deeds are being done," he said. "Men are illicitly knowing their neighbors' wives and daughters; men are having vile relations with other men. And there is bestiality—human beings fornicating with dogs and cats, horses and cows, pigs, sheep, chickens—"

From the back of the room came a voice of disbelieving horror: *"Chickens?"*

Then there was the shoe fetishist who favored Freudian slippers.

Two youths, newly arrived in ancient Crete, were on their way to consult the Delphic oracle when one stopped to admire a rather aristocratic woman who was entering the royal palace. "Come on, Oedipus," his friend sneered. "She's old enough to be your mother."

The Martian landed his saucer in Manhattan, and immediately upon emerging was approached by a panhandler. "Mister," said the man, "can I have a dime?"

The Martian asked, "What's a dime?"

The panhandler thought a minute, then said, "You're right! Can I have a quarter?"

After acquiring enough money from handouts, an inhabitant of the Bowery decided to take his refreshment at one of Wall Street's better drinking establishments.

A financial tycoon seated next to him was visibly appalled at the appearance and odor of the down-and-outer; so much so, in fact, that he turned to the man and pointedly said, " 'Cleanliness is next to godliness'—John Wesley." His words were ignored.

A few minutes later, the financier again intoned loudly, " 'Cleanliness is next to godliness'—John Wesley." Still he was ignored.

Finally, the visibly irritated financier shouted in the man's face: " 'Cleanliness is next to godliness'—John Wesley!"

To which the skid-row denizen calmly replied, " 'Screw you'—Tennessee Williams."

"It must be terrible to be lame," the woman remarked, dropping a quarter into the beggar's hat.

"It sure is, lady," he agreed.

"But wouldn't it be worse to be blind?" she asked.

"Much worse," replied the beggar. "People kept giving me slugs when I was blind."

8
MONEY

"**G**ood heavens, Doctor! What a terrific bill," the patient protested.

"My dear fellow," the doctor replied, "if you knew what an interesting case yours was, and how strongly I was tempted to let it proceed to a post-mortem, you wouldn't complain at a bill three times as big as this."

"**T**hat man made love to me, Judge," said the plaintiff in the breach of promise suit. "He promised to marry me, and then he married another woman. He broke my heart and I want ten thousand dollars."

She got it.

The next case was a damage suit brought by a woman who had been run over by an automobile and had three ribs broken. She was awarded three hundred dollars.

Moral: Don't break their hearts, kick 'em in the ribs.

"**I**'m awfully sorry, miss," said the store clerk, "but this five dollar bill is counterfeit."

"Damn it," she exclaimed, "I've been seduced!"

"**I**'m sorry, George," she said, "I can never learn to love you."

"Gee, that's too bad," said George, "and after I'd saved nearly ten grand, too."

"Give me one more lesson."

Coming home unexpectedly, the husband found his wife in bed with a naked man. He produced a pistol from a dresser drawer and was about to shoot the interloper when his wife pleaded, "Don't, don't! Who do you think bought us that house in the country, that beautiful Cadillac, my sable wrap?"

"Are *you* the man?" asked the husband. The unclothed one nodded. "Then get your clothes on," roared the husband, "you wanna catch cold?"

It was painfully evident to the indignant father that all was not well with his attractive daughter. To his pointed questions, she tearfully admitted that motherhood was approaching and that the wealthy bachelor in the next block was responsible.

With fire in his eyes, the father charged down the street and rang the bachelor's bell. The young man answered the door and readily admitted his guilt.

"Just what do you intend doing about it?" demanded the parent.

The bachelor thought for a moment. "Well," he said, "if it's a girl, I'll give your daughter five thousand dollars. And if it's a boy, I'll give her ten thousand."

"See here," said the father, "if it's a miscarriage, will you give my daughter another chance?"

"All right lady," said the bill collector, "how about the next installment on that couch?"

The lady shrugged. "Better than having to give you money, I guess."

A vice-president at our bank made the sage observation that women without principle draw plenty of interest.

We know a broad-minded miss who will go out with men of any denomination, but prefers those with fifties and hundreds.

A profound philosophy of life is reflected in the reply of a no-longer-wealthy roué who, when asked what he had done with all his money, said: "Part of it went for liquor and fast automobiles, and part of it went for women. The rest I spent foolishly."

A waggish friend of ours observes that money can't buy love, but it can put you in an excellent bargaining position.

After the wealthiest man in the world passed away at a ripe old age, he was mourned on the front pages of newspapers throughout the world. On a mid-Manhattan street corner a short, bespectacled fellow in a rather worn gray-flannel suit seemed particularly broken up by the news. He clutched the paper to his chest and cried unabashedly, "He's dead. He's dead."

"There, there," said the newsdealer, trying his best to console him. "You mustn't carry on like that, sir. We've all got to go sometime. He wasn't related to you, was he?"

"No," sobbed the man. "That's it. That's it."

We've just been informed that the Internal Revenue Department has streamlined its tax form for this year. It goes like this:

(A) How much did you make the last year?

(B) How much have you left?

(C) Send B.

"Something the matter?" asked the bartender of the young, well-dressed customer who sat staring sullenly into his drink.

"Two months ago my grandfather died and left me eighty-five thousand dollars," said the man.

"That doesn't sound like anything to be upset about," said the bartender, polishing a glass. "It should happen to me."

"Yeah," said the sour young man, "but last month an uncle on my mother's side passed away. He left me one hundred fifty thousand dollars."

"So why are you sitting there looking so unhappy?" asked the bartender.

"This month—so far—not a cent."

Two well-dressed, matronly women entered the business office and approached an executive.

"Sir," said one, "we are soliciting funds for the welfare and rehabilitation of wayward women. Would you care to donate?"

"Sorry," replied the exec, "but I contribute directly."

Friend of ours recently made a sizable contribution to the Home for Unwed Mothers. But he says next time he intends to give money.

Men with money to burn have started many a girl playing with fire.

A girl we know has met the rising cost of living by simply selling an extra key to her apartment.

The night-club's hat-check girl was obviously new, and Jack watched in mild amusement as, fumbling frantically to find his coat, she knocked garments off the racks and entangled herself in the hangers. His amusement had changed to fury, however, when a quarter of an hour later the room was a jumble of outerwear and the silly girl had still not found his coat.

"Forget it!" he finally cried in rage. "I'll send somebody for it tomorrow!" And, seething, he strode out into the bitter cold of a snowstorm, clutching the lapels of his suit jacket. The girl ran after him.

"Hey, you cheapskate," she called, "what about my tip?"

Man's greatest labor-saving device is the love of a rich woman.

Affirmation of an ancient proverb comes from a sporty acquaintance of ours who assures us that two heads are indeed better than one, especially when they happen to be on the same coin.

Sam and Al had been partners for many years and they shared and shared alike in almost everything, including the affection of their pliable and rather hot-blooded secretary. One morning Sam came into Al's office extremely upset.

"Al," he moaned, "something terrible has happened. Our secretary is going to have a baby. We are going to be a father."

But Al, who was the calmer of the two, sat his partner down and pointed out that a great many worse things could have happened to them: business could have fallen off, for instance. They agreed that the only thing to do was share and share alike, as they always had. They would see that their secretary got the very best in medical care, they decided, and after the child was born he would want for nothing. A room of his own, fine clothes and the best in schooling; They would set up a trust fund immediately after his birth to guarantee him a college education. The lucky youngster would have two fathers instead of just one.

And before they knew it, the big day had arrived. The two of them paced back and forth in the hospital waiting room, until Sam could stand it no longer.

"I'm too nervous up here," he said. "I'm going to go down and sit in the car. As soon as something happens, you come and tell me."

Al agreed, and in less than an hour he was down on the street wearing a grave expression. It was obvious to Sam, even before his partner spoke, that something was wrong.

"What's the matter?" Sam asked, starting to choke up. "Is it bad news?"

His partner nodded.

"We had twins," Al said, "and mine died."

"**M**y wife is always asking for money," complained a friend of ours. "Last week she wanted two hundred dollars. The day before yesterday she asked me for a hundred and twenty-five dollars. This morning she wanted a hundred and fifty."

"That's crazy," we said. "What does she do with it all?"

"I don't know," said our friend, "I never give her any."

There are more important things than money, but they won't date you if you don't have any.

A girl who says she'll go through anything for a man usually has his bank account in mind.

Silas, a self-made, illiterate millionaire, decided to thwart his ne'er-do-well son by leaving all his money to a small local college. But the son, banking on Silas' strait-laced attitude toward sex, wasn't ready to be counted out.

"Father," he said to the old man one day, "I hope you are aware that at that college—the one you've willed your money—the boys and girls *matriculate* together."

Silas' eyebrows shot up and the son pressed his advantage. "Not only that," he said, "but both boys and girls use the same *curriculum*."

With that the old codger's face darkened and his son leaned forward to whisper, "But worst of all, Father, before a girl can graduate she has to show her *thesis* to the dean."

"That settles it!" roared Silas. "That infernal school won't get a penny from me."

So he left all his money to Harvard.

Many a girl is looking for an older man with a strong will—made out to her.

Detroit's swankiest watering place had rarely seen such excitement as that evening when the suavely dressed young man, attired in cape and dinner jacket, jumped up from his table and proclaimed: "There's five hundred dollars for any lady in this place who'll do it my way." Pandemonium reigned and the crowd stood aghast as the bartender, maître d' and manager forcibly ejected the young fellow. He sat morosely on the curb in front of the lounge, until a beautiful deb-type slipped out of the door, walked over to him and asked if his offer still held. He said it did, and they promptly took a cab to her apartment. There she quickly disrobed, got into bed and, as he lay down beside her, she asked, "Incidentally, just what *is* your way?"

"On credit," he replied.

His last will and testament completed, the old man in the oxygen tent fondly told his son that all his wealth, stocks, bonds, bank account and real estate would be his after the end finally came.

"Dad, Dad," whispered the weeping son, his voice emotion-choked, "I can't tell you how grateful I am . . . how unworthy I am. . . . Is there . . . is there anything I can do for *you*? Anything at all?"

"Well, Son," came the feeble reply, "I'd appreciate it very much if you took your foot off the oxygen hose."

The young executive had taken over a hundred thousand dollars from his company's safe and had lost it playing the stock market; he was certain to be discovered. In addition, his beautiful wife had left him. Down to the river he went, and was just clambering over the bridge railing when a gnarled hand fell upon his arm. He turned and saw an ancient crone in a black cloak with wrinkled face and stringy gray hair. "Don't jump," she rasped. "I'm a witch, and I'll grant you three wishes for a slight consideration."

"I'm beyond help," he replied, and told her his troubles.

"Nothing to it," she said, cackling. "Alakazam! The money is back in the company vault. Alakazam! Your wife is home waiting for you with love in her heart. Alakazam! You now have a personal bank account of two hundred thousand dollars!"

The man, stunned to speechlessness, was finally able to ask, "What—what is the consideration I owe you?"

"You must spend the night making love to me," she smiled tooth-lessly.

The thought of making love to the old crone repulsed him, but it was certainly worth it, he thought. Together they retired to a nearby motel, and in the morning, the distasteful ordeal over, he was dressing to go home when the bat in the bed asked, "Say, sonny, how old are you?"

"I'm forty-two years old," he said. "Why?"

"Ain't you a little old to believe in witches?"

The room was small, misty and dim with pungent incense as the wrinkled gypsy woman looked up from her crystal at the gentleman seated before her. "I will answer any two questions you ask me," said the gypsy, "for fifty dollars."

"Isn't that price rather high?" asked the man.

"Yes, it is," said the gypsy. "Now what is your second question?"

The bleary-eyed, unshaven bum approached a passerby and said, "Mister—could I have $20.10 for a cup of coffee?"

"But," the man protested, "coffee only costs a dime."

"I know," said the bum, "but coffee always makes me sexy."

A fool and his money are soon popular.

"Money doesn't grow on trees," the beauteous showgirl declared as she stooped to adjust her jeweled platinum ankle bracelet, "but some limbs have a way of attracting it!"

In the presence of a client he wished to impress, a high-powered executive flipped on his intercom switch and barked to his secretary: "Miss Jones, get my broker!"

The visitor was duly impressed, until the secretary's voice floated back into the room, loud and clear: "Yes, sir, stock or pawn?"

The newly appointed chairman of the local fund-raising committee decided to call personally at the home of the town's wealthiest
citizen, a man well known for his tightness with a dollar. Remarking on
the impressive economic resources of his host, the committee chairman
pointed out how miserly it would seem if the town's richest man failed
to give a substantial donation to the annual charity drive.

"Since you've gone to so much trouble checking on my assets," the
millionaire retorted, "let me fill you in on some facts you may have
overlooked. I have a ninety-one-year-old mother who has been hospital-
ized for the past five years, a widowed daughter with five young children and no means of support and two brothers who owe the
Government a fortune in back taxes. Now, I think you'll agree, young
man, that charity begins at home."

Ashamed for having misjudged his host, the fund raiser apologized
for his tactlessness and added, "I had no idea that you were saddled with
so many family debts."

"I'm not," replied the millionaire, "but you must be crazy to think
I'd give money to strangers when I won't even help my own relatives."

Then there was the smart cookie who earned money peddling
Girl Scouts.

"Excuse me, sir," the young man said, nervously entering the
living room, where his girlfriend's father was reading the evening paper, "but there's something kind of important that I'd like to ask you.
I was wondering whether—uh—that is, if you'd be willing to, er. . . . "

"Why, of course, my boy," the father exclaimed, jumping to his feet
and shaking the lad's hand vigorously. "I'll give my permission gladly,
because my little girl's happiness is all that matters to me!"

"Permission?" the young man gulped, obviously confused.

"You want to marry my daughter," the father said, "and you have
my blessing. . . ."

"Oh, no, sir," said the boy, "it's nothing like that. It's my car, sir.
A payment was due last Thursday, and unless I can come up with fifty
dollars right away, they're going to repossess it, so I was wondering if
you. . . . "

"Certainly not," the father snapped, returning to the sofa and his
paper. "I hardly know you."

The spirited bidding at Sotheby's in London was halted tempo-
rarily when the auctioneer held up his hand and announced:

"One of the gentlemen in the audience has lost his wallet containing fifteen thousand dollars. He has asked me to tell you that he is offering a reward of five hundred dollars for its immediate return—no questions asked."

There was a brief hush in the hall, then a voice from the back was heard: "Five twenty-five!"

Many girls like the quiet things in life—like the folding of a hundred dollar bill.

A debt-plagued fellow, hopelessly poring over a pile of bills, suddenly shouted: "I'd give a thousand dollars to anyone who would do my worrying for me!"

"You're on," answered his wife. "Where's the thousand?"

"That's your first worry," he replied.

Of course I wouldn't accept money from a perfect stranger," the gold-digger told her girlfriend. "But then, nobody's perfect."

Two old friends, both prosperous businessmen, hadn't seen each other in some time and happened to meet on the beach at Miami. "What brings you here, Jack?" asked one.

"Actually, Fred, a tragedy. My business was burned to the ground, and I'm taking a vacation on part of the $250,000 insurance money."

"What a coincidence," responded Fred. "My business was destroyed by a flood and I got almost a million in insurance."

After a moment of thoughtful silence, Jack leaned close to his friend and whispered: "Tell me, Fred—how do you start a flood?"

A guy with money to burn has a good chance of finding a perfect match.

The wealthy financier was sitting in his study when his eldest son came to him. "Dad," the boy stammered, "I got a girl in trouble and she wants two thousand dollars to keep quiet about it."

The father reluctantly wrote a check for the amount; but just as he finished signing it, his second son burst in with the same bad news, only this time the amount requested was three thousand dollars. While he was writing the second check, his youngest daughter appeared at the door of the study, weeping.

"Daddy," she sobbed uncontrollably, "I think I'm pregnant."

"Aha," the financier exclaimed gleefully. "Now *we* collect."

After stopping his car on a deserted section of country road, the young man turned to his date and made some rather predictable advances. "Just a minute," the girl declared, pushing him away. "I'm really a prostitute and I have to charge you fifty dollars."

After he reluctantly paid her, they made love. Later, the man sat silently at the wheel. "Aren't we leaving?" the girl asked.

"Not quite yet," the fellow said. "I'm really a cabdriver—and the fare back is fifty dollars."

Thomas Gladstone, a stockbroker, received an urgent phone call one afternoon. "My name is Walters," the caller announced. "About two weeks ago, my wife got a crazy idea and started walking the street, asking me to procure customers for her."

"Just a minute," Gladstone protested. "You want Dr. Gladstone the psychiatrist. His name is right below mine in the phone book. Many people dial me by mistake."

"No mistake," came the reply. "I want you to invest all the money we're making."

Encountering a sad-looking man standing on a street corner, the sweet old lady sympathetically walked over to him, pressed a five dollar bill into his palm and said: "Chin up."

Next day, as she passed the same corner, the man walked over to her and gave her twenty dollars. "Thanks for the tip, lady," he said. "He paid twelve to one."

Then there was the compulsive gambler who drove to Las Vegas, pulled up to a parking meter, put a dime in—and lost his car!

When the bookie asked the inveterate horse player the secret of his consistent success, the gambler provided a simple explanation. "I'm just lucky, I guess. I just turn to the racing page, close my eyes and stick a pin in it," he said.

"Lucky!" the bookie exclaimed in disbelief. "How did you pick this four-horse combination?"

"Well," the gambler admitted, "I didn't have a pin, so I used a fork."

Relatives of the late Charles Worthington were gathered to hear the reading of the will, and seated in a far corner was a curvy blonde who had served the last two years as Mr. Worthington's secretary. The lawyer had almost finished and there had been no mention of the very desirable Miss Simpson, who was now perched uneasily on the very edge of her chair, taking in every word.

"And finally," the lawyer read, "to Miss Simpson, my beautiful but unfortunately uncooperative secretary, whom I promised to remember here: Hello, there, Miss Simpson!"

Some girls marry old men for money and spend the rest of their lives looking for a little change.

Two sisters were arguing about the upcoming marriage of their widowed father—a venerable gentleman in his sixties whose wife of forty years had died just a year ago. The bride-to-be was considerably younger than either of the two daughters.

"I really can't understand these May-December marriages," said the first of the sisters. "I can certainly see what December is going to find in May—youth, beauty, freshness, an upbeat attitude toward life—but what on earth is May going to find in December?"

"Christmas," answered the second.

Two playboys were using adjoining booths in the men's room at an exclusive nitery when one of them noticed an appalling absence of tissue. "Hey, George," he called, "hand me some paper, will you?"

A disturbed voice replied: "Gosh, there isn't any in here!"

"Any newspaper lying around?"

"No, don't see any. . . . "

"Do you have an old envelope in your pocket? A letter, maybe? A handbill?"

"Sorry."

"Well, then—have you got two fives for a ten?"

Pitiable is the word for Milton, the manufacturer. He accumulated millions making men's suits, and lost it all making one skirt.

Latest rags-to-riches story—Texas style—concerns a young man from Dallas who inherited five million dollars, and proceeded to run it into a small fortune.

The stranger walked up to a Las Vegas dice table and laid down a thousand dollar bet. He shook the dice, but as he threw them a third cube fell unexpectedly from his sleeve. The house operator was unruffled. He handed back two of the dice and pocketed the third, saying, "OK, roll again. Your point is fifteen."

We've just learned a secret method for returning from Las Vegas with a small fortune: Go with a large fortune.

The compulsive race-track bettor promised to attend church each Sunday with his wife if she would agree not to nag him about the nags the rest of the week. The wife accepted the offer, hoping that this contact with religion might cure her husband of his gambling. On the very next Sunday, the couple were seated side by side in the center of the congregation; the husband seemed to be moved by the service, and he joined in singing the final hymn with such enthusiasm that several parishioners in the nearby pews were visibly impressed. As the couple emerged from the church, the husband acknowledged the smiles with which they were greeted, remarking in a whispered aside to his wife: "I'll bet you didn't expect me to make such an impression! It wouldn't surprise me if they wanted my barroom baritone in the church choir."

"You did very well, dear," his wife remarked, "except for one small thing. It's *Hallelujah*, not Hialeah!"

The Martian landed in Las Vegas and walked into a nearby casino. He passed a slot machine that suddenly whirred noisily, then disgorged a jackpot of silver dollars. The Martian looked closely at the machine and then said: "You know, you're foolish not to stay home with a cold like that."

When she found out that the handsome young millionaire was fond of hunting, Joyce told him she was game.

Limbo dancing was invented by a Scotsman trying to enter a pay toilet.

Card playing can be expensive—but so can any game where you begin by holding hands.

We know a football buff who is such a compulsive gambler that he lost fifty dollars on the last game of the season: twenty-five dollars when the opposing team scored a touchdown from their own fifteen-yard line; and another twenty-five bucks on the Instant Replay.

It was eight A.M. at a Las Vegas gambling palace and two lone bettors were still standing by a dice table awaiting further competition when a lusciously endowed brunette, attired in a suit, happened by. "Although it's quite early in the day," she announced, "I feel lucky this morning. I'd like to roll the dice once for twenty thousand dollars. Would the two of you care to take me up on the wager?"

"Sure, lady," answered one of the men, "we'll take your action."

"I hope you gentlemen won't mind," she then said, "but the only way I can get lucky is to roll the dice without my panties on." So saying, the lissome lovely proceeded to remove her slacks and panties. With a shout of "Momma needs a new pair of pants!" she rolled the dice, gave a squeal of delight and yelled, "I win!" She then picked up her money, her slacks and her underwear and made a hasty exit from the room.

The two men exchanged double-takes and one of them blurted out, "Hey, what did she roll, anyway?"

"How the hell should I know?" snapped the other. "I thought *you* were watching the dice."

A model we know says she's looking for a man who can fill a void in her life—her empty clothes closet.

We know a Texan who is so rich that he has an unlisted phone company.

At the height of the tourist season, a huge Texan replete with diamond-studded cuff links strode up to the desk of one of Miami Beach's most expensive hotels. He was followed by a caravan of bell-hops, all of whom were carrying skis, ice skates and other northern winter-sports gear. The perplexed clerk looked over the entourage and then said to the new guest, "Sorry to have to tell you this, sir, but we never have snow here in Miami."

"That's OK, son," boomed the Texan. "It's comin' with the rest of my luggage!"

Many a modern miss is known by the company that keeps her.

The trouble with being kept is that the rent is always due.

Harry and Fred were playing money golf, ten bucks a hole. After the first, Harry asked Fred how many strokes he had taken. Fred answered five.

"I was home in four," said Harry smiling, "so that's my hole."

When they finished the second, Harry asked the same question.

"Wait a minute," Fred objected. "It's my turn to ask first."

Despite warnings from his guide, an American skiing in Switzerland got separated from his group and fell—uninjured—into a deep crevasse. Several hours later, a rescue party found the yawning pit and, to reassure the stranded skier, shouted down to him, "We're from the Red Cross!"

"Sorry," the imperturbable American echoed back, "I already gave at the office!"

A hitchhiker was picked up by a rich Texas oilman driving a big, bright-colored, richly upholstered, high-powered convertible. As they drove along the open highway, doing well over fifty, the young hitchhiker noticed a pair of very thick glasses on the seat between them.

"Are those glasses yours?" the hitchhiker asked nervously, noting that the Texan was staring intently at the road before him and the speedometer was still climbing.

"Yep," came the reply. "Wouldn't go nowhere without 'em. Cain't hardly see my hand in front of my face when I ain't got 'em on." And to the hitchhiker's dismay, when the Texan turned to talk, he squinted in his passenger's general direction, unable to make him out clearly on the seat beside him. Then sensing the hitchhiker's uneasiness, he added: "Ain't got nothing to fret over, though, sonny. This here windshield is ground to my prescription."

A wag we know once remarked that paying alimony is like pumping gasoline into another man's car.

"Cheer up," the exec advised his recently divorced colleague, "there are plenty of other fish in the sea."

"Maybe so," replied his despondent friend, "but the last one took all my bait."

We've heard of a new low in community standing: a man whose credit rating is so bad his money isn't accepted.

The management of a faltering corporation offered a twenty-five dollar award to those employees who turned in the best suggestions as to how the company could save money. One of the first prizes went to a brilliant young executive who suggested that in the future the award be reduced to ten dollars.

Having spent the entire evening with the pretty young prostitute, the businessman was surprised by the small fee she requested.

"It's not my place to advise you in such matters, my dear," said the executive, "but you're not doing yourself justice and, frankly, I don't know how you manage to get by on payments as small as this."

"Oh, it balances out," the pretty pro said with a smile wiser than her years. "You see, I do a little blackmailing on the side."

His pretty model looked quite despondent, so the photographer asked what was bothering her.

"It's my boyfriend," she explained. "He was wiped out in the stock market—lost all of his money."

"You must feel very sorry for him," remarked the photographer.

"Yes," she replied wistfully, "he'll miss me terribly."

While studying in Paris, the son cabled his wealthy father: "PLEASE SEND $300. AM GOING TO THE COUNTRY TO VISIT A FRENCH COUNT."

Cabled his father in reply: "NOT ANOTHER DIME UNTIL YOU LEARN HOW TO SPELL."

Divorce on grounds of incompatibility usually means either that he has lost his income or she her patability.

9
SHOW
BUSINESS

His lion trainer had quit without notice and the circus manager needed someone to replace him for the next night's show. He put an ad in the local paper and the next morning two applicants showed up outside his office. One was a rather ordinary-looking young man and the other a ravishing, redheaded beauty. Neither one of them looked very much like a lion trainer, but the manager was desperate.

"All right," he said, "here's a whip, and a chair and a gun. Let's see what you can do with Big Leo over there. We'll let you have the first try, miss, but be careful—he's a mean one."

The ravishing redhead strode past the whip, and the chair and the gun and, empty-handed, fearlessly entered the cage.

Big Leo rose, snarling, then came charging across the cage towards her with a ferocious roar. When the lion was almost upon her, the girl threw open her coat. Underneath, she was stark naked. Leo skidded to a stop and crawled the rest of the way on his belly; he nuzzled the girl's feet with his nose, purred and licked her trim ankles.

The astonished circus manager grinned happily and turned to the pop-eyed young man. "Well, young fella," he asked, "think you can top *that?*"

"Yeah," breathed the man. "Just get that stupid lion out of there."

It was the cocktail hour in a swank lounge. Henry, a lingerie manufacturer, recognized the man imbibing next to him as Bud Smiley, well-known TV m.c. Sensing a business opportunity, he introduced himself and his company to the star.

"Listen," he said conspiratorially, "how would you like to plug my product on your show?"

Bud lifted an eyebrow. "That all depends on what's in it for me," he said.

"Tell you what," Henry replied. "I'll send you one of our finest and filmiest negligees. How's that?"

Bud smiled indolently. "That all depends," he repeated, "on what's in it for me."

After a particularly tiring performance, a beautiful New York showgirl returned to her apartment and found a half-dozen handsome admirers waiting there, with naught on their minds but amour. "How sweet of you boys to surprise me like this," she cooed, "but, really, I've had an awfully tough show tonight and I'm simply exhausted. I'm afraid one or two of you will have to go home."

Muster some sympathy for the dilemma of the out-of-work stripteaser: all undressed and no place to show.

We just heard about the human cannonball who wanted to retire from his circus job.

"But you can't quit the show after all these years," moaned the circus director. "Where else can I find a man of your caliber?"

The distraught female patient exclaimed to her psychiatrist: "I have no talent! I can't act! I can't sing! I can't dance! I want to quit show business!"

"Then why don't you?" asked the shrink.

"I can't," she sobbed. "I'm a star!"

We suppose you've heard about the man on the flying trapeze who caught his wife in the act.

We just learned that one of the show girls from the Latin Quarter disappeared last week and hasn't been obscene since.

We enjoyed a luncheon date the other day with a lovely Broadway showgirl who confessed she was unsuccessful in show business until she had her 'no's' fixed.

"It's certainly nice to have someone like you with us this evening," said the night-club comic to the annoying ringside heckler, "and may I be the first to shake you by the throat."

Two chorus cuties were talking things over between shows.

"I've been out with hundreds of men," said the first, "but I haven't let one make love to me."

"Oh," said her friend, "which one was that?"

We know a chorus girl who never votes in an election. She simply doesn't care who gets in.

"Sam," said the agent, "I want you should meet Bubbles LaVerne, a sensational new stripper I have just discovered. She will be a sensation as the feature in your club."

Sam looked the shapely cutie up and down, removed the cigar from his mouth and said: "Well, don't just stand there, sweetheart. Undo something."

A recent independent survey indicates that it's still possible for a young woman with little or no experience to make her way into show business.

We have it on good authority that one of New York's biggest night clubs is going to introduce a new act: a midget stripteaser. She'll entertain the customers who are under the tables.

A director was interviewing a pretty young actress who had just arrived in Hollywood from the East. After the usual questions, he looked her up and down and asked, "Are you a virgin?"

She nodded, then realizing a job might hinge on her answer, she added, "But I'm not a fanatic about it!"

The two television actors feigned friendship, but secretly hated each other's guts, and took great pleasure in giving one another the needle on any and all occasions. This particular evening they met, quite by accident, at a popular bar just off Broadway. The conversation started innocently enough, then one, with sudden inspiration, ran his hand over the other's bald head, and exclaimed: "By God, Fred, that feels just like my wife's *derrière!*"

The other ran his own hand over his head, and nonchalantly retorted: "Well I'll be damned, Jim, so it does, so it does!"

You've undoubtedly heard about the top-salaried movie director who was always trying to make a little extra.

"In my last four shows," complained the Broadway actor, "I've played nothing but heels and cads and egotistical swine."

"Yes, it's a shame," agreed his colleague. "This type-casting is ruining the American stage."

Gina Lottabazooma, the shapely Italian screen siren, was put under contract by a Hollywood studio and brought to the U.S. to make an epic Western.

"I absolutely refuse to play this scene," she exclaimed.

"But Gina," explained the director, "all you have to do is point out the direction the outlaws took when the sheriff and his posse ride up to you."

"I know," said the star, "but have you read the screen action in the script?"

"What do you mean?"

"Look how I'm supposed to point," snapped the star. "It says here that I am to place both hands behind my back, take a deep breath, turn north and say, 'They went thataway!' "

A distinguished Shakespearean actor and an eminent English drama critic were lunching together in a London club when the conversation, as usual, turned to the Bard.

"Tell me," asked the critic of the actor, "is it your opinion that Shakespeare intended us to believe Hamlet had sexual relations with Ophelia?"

"I don't know what Shakespeare intended," said the actor, "but I usually do."

The dazzling movie star was applying for her passport.

"Unmarried?" asked the clerk.

"Occasionally," answered she.

The Hollywood star announced to her press agent that she was about to enter wedlock again, for the fifth time.

"Oh," said the agent. "Against whom?"

A much-married Hollywood leading man was confronted by a pretty brunette at the premiere of his latest picture.

"Don't you remember me?" she enthused. "Three years ago you asked me to marry you."

"Oh, really?" said the blasé actor. "And did you?"

The inroads of television have trebled unemployment among film actors. Take, for example, the movie producer who came home unexpectedly one night and found his wife in the arms of one-time B-movie hero Chester Beefcake.

"Hey!" cried the upset producer. "What are you doing?"

Chester's manly brow knotted in concern. "To tell you the truth," he said earnestly, "not much of anything these days."

Many a starlet has made it to the top because her clothes didn't.

Leon, an unemployed actor, came shuffling dejectedly home after a fruitless day of visiting booking offices. But instead of the quiet comfort he expected, he found his apartment in shambles and Martha, his beautiful young wife, lying on the bed in hysterics. It was obvious that her clothes had literally been torn from her bruised and ravished body.

"Good Lord!" Leon cried. "Martha! What happened?"

"Oh darling!" she sobbed. "I fought and fought, but he. . . ."

"Who did this awful thing? Who? Who was it?"

"He came here looking for you. He said it was very important. Finding me alone and defenseless, he . . . oh. . . ."

"Who?" Leon roared. "Who?"

She hung her head and in a husky voice replied: "Your agent."

"My agent!" Sunlight suddenly flooded Leon's face. "Did he say whether he'd found a part for me?"

Many an actress' career begins when she becomes too big for her sweaters, and ends when she becomes too big for her britches.

While making the rounds of producers' and casting directors' offices, Sally made a successful contact and as a result was offered a speaking role in a feature-length Western.

The first day's script called for her to be thrown from the horse into a clump of cacti. The second day, she had to jump from a cliff, her clothes on fire, into a mountain stream, and swim to shore. On the third day, she was cuffed around by the villain, and the director—a stickler for realism—reshot the scene five times. The fourth day, her boot caught in a stirrup, and a runaway horse dragged her for two miles.

Wearily, she managed to limp to the producer's office.

"Listen," she said hoarsely, "who do I have to sleep with to get *out* of this picture?"

A glamorous actress, whose best days were behind her, began finding herself without male companionship several evenings a week. To help pass the time—and perhaps catch a live one—she decided to attend one of those Hollywood charity meetings. She dozed quietly throughout the opening address, but awoke suddenly to hear the speaker say: "Now let's get out and work like beavers."

The actress nudged the person sitting next to her and whispered, "How do beavers work?"

The answer from the confused lady on her left was, "I'm not too sure, but I think it's with their tails."

The actress jumped to her feet and shouted as loud as she could, "Put me down for three nights a week!"

Two well-known actors were exchanging boasts at Sardi's. "Well, I've been doing all right," said the first one. "During the third act last night, I virtually had the audience glued to their seats."

"Marvelous!" replied the second actor. "Damned clever of you to think of that!"

A shapely Hollywood starlet, about to go for an interview with a producer, was warned by her girlfriend, "Listen, honey, I don't want to upset you, but this guy has a bad reputation with women. If he gets you alone in his office, he's liable to rip the dress right off your back!"

"Thanks for the warning," said the starlet. "I'll go change into an old one."

The director was patiently explaining the scene to the famous Method actor. "You've been on this desert island for twelve years. One morning, you awaken, crawl out of your lean-to and start strolling along the beach. Suddenly you see this beautiful blonde girl lying on the sand beside her discarded life jacket. You rush forward, grab her in your arms and start kissing her."

The actor nodded thoughtfully, then asked, "And what's my motivation?"

After viewing the rushes of a Hollywood hopeful's screen test, the producer was less than enthusiastic: "My dear, it will take an act of Congress to get you into the movies."

The buxom young actress sighed, "That's what I thought—your apartment or mine?"

As the Shakespearean actor slipped off his trousers and prepared to join her in bed, the lady of the evening gave an appreciative whistle at his generous endowment.

"Madam," he cautioned in response, "we have come to bury Caesar —not to praise him."

Hoping to break into films, the aspiring young actress slept with a famous director, who promised to put her name in lights. Sure enough, the very next week there appeared on Sunset Strip a fifty-foot neon sign that flashed, ROBERTA STURGESS IS A PUSHOVER.

Then there was the persistent actress who made it the hard way in Hollywood—she had talent.

The young man took his girl to an open-air theater on their first date. After the first act he found it necessary to excuse himself. He asked the usher where the men's room was located and was told, "Turn left by that big oak tree, go straight ahead about twenty yards, then right another five."

In a few minutes he returned to his seat.

"Has the second act started yet?" he asked his date.

"You ought to know," she said coolly. "You were in it!"

"It was terrible, mother," complained the curvy teen-ager. "I had to change my seat four times at the movies."

"Some man started bothering you?" asked mother.

"Yes," said the girl. "Finally."

The censors of the cinema have never given proper credit to a group probably more responsible than any other for keeping sex out of the movies: ushers.

A local drive-in showed one of the worst movies ever made the other night, but the management reports that the customers loved every minute of it.

"Golly," sighed the shapely coed as she and her date left the drive-in theater, "that certainly was exciting. I wonder if the movie was any good."

As the horror movie was about to reach its terrifying conclusion, the coed began fidgeting in her seat. The man sitting behind her leaned forward and inquired, "Excuse me. Are you feeling hysterical?"

"No," she whispered. "He's feeling mine."

The seventeen-year-old girl had just been told by her physician that she was pregnant. "If only I'd gone to the movies with my parents that night," she lamented.

"Well, why didn't you?" the doctor asked.

"I couldn't," the girl sobbed. "The film was rated X."

They hadn't seen their friend in nearly five years—not since he received a movie contract and went to Hollywood. Now he was back visiting in the Midwestern town where he had lived as a boy.

His friends were pleased to see him and anxious to learn if all the wild stories they had heard about life in Hollywood were really true.

"Nonsense," said the film celebrity. "Hollywood is no different than any other American city. Life out there is normal and well ordered: A movie actress isn't very different from a working housewife in Minneapolis or Milwaukee; a movie director is no more eccentric than the office manager of one of the businesses right here.

"Take my own case: I'm up early every morning, at the studio by eight-fifteen; I work a full, hard day and I'm home every evening by six; dinner, afterwards the evening paper, and I'm into bed before ten.

"Why just the other day, I was saying to my wife: 'George. . . .' "

In Hollywood, when a movie star tells a child a bedtime story, it usually goes like this: "Once upon a time, there was a Mama Bear, a Papa Bear and a Baby Bear by a previous marriage. . . ."

When they speak of anticipating a blessed event in Hollywood, it invariably means the arrival of the divorce papers.

Two young starlets were discussing the remarriage of a well-known Hollywood couple: "I guess," said the one to the other, "it was just another one of those divorces that didn't pan out."

Preparing to fight one another, the two little Hollywood boys were exchanging the eternal taunts.

"My father can beat your father!"

"Oh, yeah?" said the other. "Your father *is* my father!"

We know a luscious young dish who went to Hollywood because she wanted to make love under the stars.

Johnny, a Hollywood youngster, was very proud because he had the most parents at the P.T.A. meeting.

Hollywood marriages are evidently losing their reputation for brevity: We've just heard about a producer who liked one of his wives so well that he decided to hold her over for a second week.

Then there was the cute, but somewhat confused, chick who told the movie producer that she wanted to be a Stollywood harlot.

There's a new jewelry store in Hollywood whose business has suddenly leaped ahead of all the competition. It rents wedding rings.

We know a Hollywood beauty who is an expert housekeeper. Every time she gets divorced, she keeps the house.

Hollywood is the only place we know where you can live happily and get married forever after.

Two sexy young starlets were sipping stingers at Chasen's, in Hollywood.
"You remember that backless, frontless, sideless evening gown I wore to the sneak preview last week?" asked the first.
"Sure," said her friend, "it was a sensation."
"I just found out it's a belt."

When her friends got word that Betty, a beautiful young starlet, had married Homer, an elderly gentleman worth ten million dollars, they all sent her Get Will cards.

Some girls are music lovers. Other can love without it.

On the occasion of Nero's twenty-fifth birthday, he arrived at the Colosseum to find that the Praetorian Guard had prepared a treat for him in the arena. There stood naked virgins, like candles on a cake, tied to poles, burning alive. "Wonderful!" exclaimed the deranged Emperor, "but one of them isn't dead yet. I can see her lips moving. Go quickly and find out what she is saying."
The centurion saluted, and hurried out to the virgin, getting as near the flames as he dared, and listened intently. Then he turned and hurried back to the imperial box. "She is not talking," he reported to Nero, "she is singing."
"Singing?" said the astounded emperor. "Singing what?"
"Happy birthday to you, happy birthday to you. . . ."

Girls are like pianos. When they're not upright, they're grand.

Lots of girls can be had for a song. Unfortunately, it often turns out to be the wedding march.

Then there was the fellow who loved the beautiful cellist—especially when she was on her Bach.

A true music lover has been defined as a man who puts his ear to the keyhole when he hears a girl singing in the tub.

You won't read about it in *After Hours*, but we occasionally get our kicks in a place where the music is so bad that when a waiter drops a tray everybody gets up and starts dancing.

A cool musician was strolling down Broadway when he came upon an old organ grinder playing his beat-up instrument while a monkey did a little dance on the sidewalk and doffed his cap for coins.
"Man," said the musician, stopping to watch, "I don't dig your music, but that crazy kid of yours has got a lot of talent."

Have you heard that catchy little love song that's headed for jukebox fame, titled, *How Can I Miss You If You Won't Go Away?*

Advice to the exhausted: When wine, women and song become too much for you, give up singing.

Whether or not a girl can be had for a song depends on a man's pitch.

The successful young rock singer ordered a very expensive custom-made suit, but was wholly dissatisfied with the finished garment. "I told you to make the pants snug," he angrily remarked to the tailor. "I want them tight enough to show my sex."
"I'm sorry, sir," the tailor protested, "but if they were any tighter, they'd show your religion."

Epitaph for the tombstone of a cool musician: "Man, this cat is really gone."

A good golfer has to break eighty, but a good chorus girl only has to bust thirty-six.

10
MONKEY
BUSINESS

The police were investigating the mysterious death of a prominent businessman who had jumped from a window of his eleventh-story office. His voluptuous private secretary could offer no explanation for the action, but said that her boss had been acting peculiarly ever since she started working for him a month ago.

"After my very first week on the job," she said, "I received a twenty dollar raise. At the end of the second week, he called me into his private office, gave me a lovely black nightie, five pairs of nylon stockings and said, 'These are for a beautiful, efficient secretary.'

"At the end of the third week, he gave me a gorgeous mink stole. Then, this afternoon he called me into his private office again, presented me with this fabulous diamond bracelet and asked me if I would consider making love to him and what it would cost.

"I told him I would and because he had been so nice to me, he could have it for five dollars, although I was charging all the other boys in the office ten. That's when he jumped out the window."

"Who," raged the angry employer, "told you that just because I've kissed you a few times you could loaf around the office and neglect your work?"

"My attorney," cooed his secretary.

One of the airlines recently introduced a special half-fare rate for wives accompanying their husbands on business trips. Anticipating some valuable testimonials, the publicity department of the airline sent out letters to all the wives of businessmen who used the special rates, asking how they enjoyed their trip.

Responses are still pouring in asking "What trip?"

One by one, the vice presidents of a large corporation were called into the boss' office. Then the junior executives were individually summoned. Finally the office boy was brought in.

"I want the truth, Charles," the boss bellowed. "Have you been playing around with my secretary?"

"N-no, sir," the office boy stammered, "I-I'd never do anything like that, sir."

"All right, all right," said the boss, "then *you* fire her."

We like the letter of resignation offered by a charming young secretary who was forced to quit her job because of embarrassing circumstances: "Dear Boss," it began, "I'm getting too big for this job. . . ."

The baby-faced, brown-eyed secretary phoned her mother to inform her: "I'll be late again for dinner tonight, Mom. I made a mistake last night and the boss wants me to do it over again."

"You know," said the gossip-loving office cutie to her lunch companion, "I'd *never* say anything about Margaret unless I could say something good. And, sister, is this *good*. . . ."

One steno observed to another, as the boss' sexy secretary wiggled past the water cooler: "There goes the original good time that was had by all."

"My reason for resigning will soon become apparent," the pretty secretary memoed her boss, "and so will I."

After completing their shopping, two young secretaries were about to drive back to their apartment when one realized that she'd forgotten to stop at the drugstore for birth-control pills. Rushing into the nearest pharmacy, she handed the prescription to the druggist. "Please fill this quickly," she demanded. "I've got someone waiting in the car."

Then there was the clumsy file clerk who dropped her birth-control pills into the Xerox machine. It wouldn't reproduce for a month.

A cute young secretary we know enjoys telling everyone that her boss takes great pleasure in grabbing her by the knee. "But yesterday," she cooed at us over dry Martinis, "he reached a new high."

"Tsk, tsk," said the unhappy executive, "I had to fire my new secretary today."

"How come?" asked the friend. "No experience?"

"None whatever," the exec replied. "I told her to sit down for some dictation and she looked around for a chair."

A young executive we know recently spent three months finding a suitable secretary. He knows it pays to have a good head on your shoulder.

After two years in the New York headquarters of a large advertising agency, the stunning steno was transferred to the company's Chicago office. The morning she reported to her new desk, her boss invited her into his office and said, friendly-like, "I hope you'll be happy working with us, Miss Carson. We'll expect about the same of you here as you've been accustomed to in New York."

"Yes, sir," said she efficiently, "that's what I'd anticipated. Do you mind if I hang my blouse over this chair?"

"I'm so discouraged," said the lovely secretary as she bent down to pick up the papers she had accidentally knocked off her boss' desk. "Everything I do seems to be wrong."

"Oh, really?" said the boss. "What are you doing tonight?"

"Oh, you'll like it here," said the experienced steno to the new girl in the office. "Lots of chances for advances."

"OK, you're hired," said the busy executive, moving around his desk toward the buxom young female. "Now would you like to try for a raise?"

In the race toward matrimony, many a lucky secretary finds herself on the last lap.

Absent-minded is hardly the word for the pretty secretary who left her clothes at the office and took her boss to the cleaner.

An executive friend of ours is so dedicated to his work that he keeps his secretary near his bed in case he gets an idea during the night.

When the struggling stenographer quits struggling, she often discovers that she doesn't have to be a stenographer.

Barry had just opened his law office, and immediately hired three good-looking young stenographers to work for him.

"But how," a visiting friend inquired, eying the three, "do you expect to accomplish anything?"

"Simple," Barry grinned. "By giving two of them the day off."

Some girls ask the boss for advances on next week's salary. Others ask for salary on next week's advances.

Learning that several of his employees were tanking up on no-trace vodka Martinis during lunch hours, a wise company president issued the following memo:

To all employees: If you must drink during lunch, please drink whiskey. It is much better for our customers to know you're drunk than to think you're stupid.

Two successful big-business executives met at a trade convention.

"Tell me," said one, "how's business?"

"Well, you know how it is," replied the other. "My line is like sex. When it's good, it's wonderful—and when it's bad, it's still pretty good!"

The young executive greeted his attractive secretary warmly as he entered the office: "Good morning, Marge," he said, tossing his briefcase on his desk. "I had a dream about you last night."

Flattered, but wishing to appear aloof, she casually inquired, "Oh, did you?"

"No," her boss replied. "I woke up too soon."

A glib young advertising executive took his sophisticated secretary to his luxury apartment on Central Park South, ostensibly for the purpose of dictation. He showed her around and when they came to the bedroom, he quipped, "This is National Sex Week—would you care to contribute?"

She smiled sweetly and replied, "I've already given at the office."

Then there's the fast-rising executive who, on entering his newly decorated office, had his secretary on the carpet because she forgot to order a couch.

It was a wild office party and—in the darkened mail room—a pair of employees was making the most of it. "Oh, Mr. Baxter," the curvy secretary sighed. "You never made love to me like this before. Is it because of the holiday spirit?"

"No," her partner replied, "it's because I'm not Baxter."

During midmorning coffee break, the boss discovered his shapely secretary and a junior executive making love in the storeroom. "How can you explain this?" the boss steamed.

"Well," said the secretary, straightening a nylon, "neither of us likes coffee."

"Any bad habits, Miss Anderson?" asked the young exec, interviewing a shapely secretarial applicant: "Gum-chewing, tardiness, gossiping, chastity?"

The morning after the office Christmas party, the husband woke up with an agonizing hangover. "I feel terrible," he complained.

"You should," said his wife. "You really made a fool of yourself last night."

"What did I do?"

"You got into a quarrel with your boss and he fired you."

"Well, he can go to hell."

"That's exactly what you told him."

"I did?" he said incredulously. "Then screw the old goat!"

"That's just what I did," his wife replied. "You go back to work on Monday."

When the well-molded secretary entered her boss' office one morning, he looked out the window and announced idly, "It's certainly going to be a beautiful day."

"I don't think so," replied the secretary. "The weather forecast is for snow."

"It's not going to snow," contradicted the exec. "I'll lay you twelve to one."

"I'd rather not," she remarked. "That's my lunch hour."

When the pretty secretary failed to appear for the fourth straight day, her suspicious supervisor telephoned her apartment and demanded an explanation.

"I'm very sorry," she sighed breathlessly, "but I won't be in today."

"Well," he conjectured, "you must not be very happy in your present position."

"I'm very happy," she panted. "That's why I'm not coming to work."

Delighted by her good fortune, the statuesque brunette accepted a job as private secretary to a corporation vice-president at a salary of $300 per week. But, arriving for work at nine o'clock the next morning, she was immediately summoned to his office, where she learned that her responsibilities included making love to him. "I guess I knew this would be part of the job," she sighed when they had finished. "But for $300 a week, I really can't object too much."

"Well, here's $3.75 for the past half hour," the executive said. "You're fired."

"Did my wife say anything when you called and said I would be working late at the office?" asked the executive, nuzzling his ravishing secretary.

"The only thing she said," answered the secretary, "was: 'Can I count on it?' "

As the end of the day drew near, the handsome executive summoned the newly hired secretary to his office. "Do you know what time we quit around here?" he asked, glancing at the clock on the wall.

"Sure," the girl nervously giggled. "Whenever somebody knocks on the door."

The handsome president requested that the company psychiatrist further screen the three good-looking girls for the job of private secretary. Deciding to use a standard psychological ploy, the gentleman asked each of the applicants the same question—"How much do two and two make?"

The first young thing, a lovely blonde, whispered "Four"; the second, a smashing brunette, responded with "Twenty-two"; while the third, a shapely redhead, answered, "Four or twenty-two."

The following day, the consultant stopped by the president's office and gave his findings. "The first is solid and reliable," he opined. "The second has a vivid imagination but can't deal too well with reality. And the third is both clever and mature—she being the one I'd suggest we hire. What's your decision?"

"Well," the boss replied, after a moment of deep deliberation, "I think I want the one with the big boobs."

Stunned by the incredible beauty of their new secretary, the two executives resolved to make her adjustment to the firm their personal business. "It's up to us to teach her the difference between right and wrong," said the first.

"Agreed," exclaimed the second, excitedly taking in the girl's generous endowments. "You teach her what's right."

And, of course, you've heard about the wild office Christmas party in a completely automated company—the computer got drunk and tried to undo the electric typewriter's ribbon.

When Harry returned looking tanned and rested, his secretary asked him about his vacation.

"Well," he replied, "a friend of mine invited me up to his hunting lodge—a quiet, secluded place. No night life, no parties, not a woman within a hundred miles."

"Did you enjoy yourself?" she asked.

"Who went?" he said.

We know an executive who is so old that when he chases his secretary around the desk, he can't remember why.

Then there was the fellow who decided to start procrastinating but never got around to it.

> She was "honey chile" in New Orleans,
> The hottest of the bunch;
> But on the old expense account,
> She was gas, cigars and lunch.

Motto seen on the wall of a women's executive club: FAINT HEART NEVER WON FUR, LADY.

"How did you spend the weekend?" asked the pretty brunette secretary of her blonde companion.

"Fishing through the ice," she said.

"Fishing through the ice? Whatever for?"

"Olives."

The two executives had never golfed together before and the first man up took out a new ball, placed it on the tee and proceeded to slice it into the woods to the right of the fairway. Unable to find it in the thick underbrush, he put another new ball on the edge of the fairway and this time he drove it over a fence. Putting a third new ball in position, he then proceeded to hit it into the middle of the lake.

As he was preparing to shoot yet another new golf ball from the edge of the lake, the second executive said to their caddie, "I don't understand why a guy who loses so many continues to shoot a brand-new ball every time."

The caddie shook his head, saying, "Maybe he's never had any used ones."

What must surely be the final version of the traveling salesman's gag has come our way. It concerns a hapless merchant on the move who ran out of gas on a lonely country road, trudged to the nearest farm-house and asked if he could spend the night. The farmer promptly shot him in the head with a shotgun.

We know an insurance salesman who says his greatest successes are with young housewives who aren't adequately covered.

A traveling salesman we know writes passionate love letters to a little farm girl in his territory. Her name is Sarah, but he always starts off his letters with: "Dear Hollyhock. . . ."

We never understood this term of endearment till the other day when we came across this entry in *The Farmer's Almanac*: "HOLLY-HOCK—*Does well in fence corners and behind barns; not so well in beds.*"

"The Related Sale" was the subject of a pep talk given recently by the manager of a certain super-drug store. "For instance, if a customer wants razor blades," he told employees, "ask him how he's fixed for shaving cream and after-shave lotion. That way you can turn a small sale into a bigger one and earn a larger commission."

The youngest clerk was very impressed by the talk and decided to try the technique on his very next customer. This turned out to be a rather embarrassed gentleman who shyly requested a box of Kotex for his wife. Ten minutes later, the manager of the store was amazed to see the customer staggering out loaded down with assorted fishing equipment, tackle, nets, boots and a one-man inflatable life raft. "What happened?!" the manager gasped, and the clerk modestly attributed his success to "The Related Sale."

"Related Sale!" exclaimed the manager. "But all he wanted was a box of—"

"I know. So I said, 'Look, mister, there isn't going to be much doing around your house this weekend. Why don't you take a fishing trip?"

Shed a tear for the unfortunate shoe salesman with a lisp, who got slapped when he asked an adequately proportioned female customer to sit down while he "looked up her thize."

We're sure you've heard about the traveling salesman whose car broke down in a rain storm. He ran to the closest farmhouse and knocked on the door. A grizzled old farmer answered and the salesman pleaded for a place to stay the night.

"I can give ya a room," said the farmer, "but I ain't got no daughter fer ya to sleep with."

"Oh," said the salesman. "Well, how far is it to the next house?"

So then the ubiquitous traveling salesman said to the farmer, "Can you put me up for the night?"

Whereupon the farmer said, "Sure, but you'll have to sleep with my son."

"Good Lord," said the salesman, "I'm in the wrong joke!"

We spotted this ad in the personal column of a large metropolitan daily: "Gentleman who smokes, drinks and carouses wishes to meet lady who smokes, drinks and carouses. Object: smoking, drinking and carousing."

The single-minded dedication required of those who apply themselves to the great advertising game is illustrated by the story of Harry and Joe, Mad Ave types, who met for lunch for the first time in months.

"Where," queried Harry, lifting his lunch and sipping it, "has Charlie Harris been hanging out?"

"Great guns! Haven't you heard? Charlie went to the Great Agency in the Sky."

"You're kidding!"

"Nope. He died last month."

"Good Lord. What did he have?"

"Nothing much," Joe said, reflectively. "A small toothpaste account, and a couple of department stores, but nothing worth going after."

The board members of the Cordial Catsup Company were wowed by the idea their ad agency had come up with for their billboard campaign. It showed a husband-type seated before a delectable steak in a smart restaurant, and a pretty young waitress in a tight-fitting uniform handing him a bottle of catsup.

"This is great," said the prexy of Cordial Catsup, "but remember, our appeal here is to housewives, so let's clean that title up a bit. 'What does she know about your husband that you don't know?' is too suggestive."

A week later the billboards were attracting attention all over the country with the caption: "He gets it downtown—why not give it to him at home?"

Then there was the guy who advertised for a wife and got two hundred replies, most of them from men, who wrote: "You can have mine."

A Mad Ave friend of ours tells of a client who wanted to get his "message" to every married woman in a specific community. The solution to the problem was simple, according to this enterprising publicist: "We just addressed letters to every married man in town and marked them 'Personal.' "

A well-stacked young advertising secretary wore tight knit dresses that showed off her figure, especially when she walked. Her young aggressive boss motioned her into his office one afternoon and closed the door. Pointing to her tightly covered *derrière*, he asked, "Is that for sale?"

"Of course not!" she snapped angrily, blushing furiously.

Unchagrined, he replied quietly, "Then I suggest you quit advertising it."

A monster we know usually eats *things* for lunch, and washes them down with a Coca-Cola. For, as he explains, "Things go better with Coke."

On the first night of her fourth marriage, the still-attractive bride turned to her husband and implored, "*Please*, darling, try to be patient with me in bed—I'm still a virgin."

"A *virgin!*" her mate exclaimed. "But you've been married three times before!"

"I know it's a little hard to believe, but it's the truth," she sighed sadly. "My first husband was a charming alcoholic, but he'd get loaded every night and by bedtime, he'd be dead to the world. My second husband was quite handsome, but on our wedding night, I discovered he was more attracted to my brother than to me. My third husband—the advertising executive—was a persuasive fellow, but he turned out to be a complete captive of his craft."

"What do you mean?" asked her astounded husband.

"Well," she said, "every night, all night long, he'd sit on the edge of the bed, telling me how great it was going to be."

The head of a large advertising firm reluctantly agreed to take on the son of a wealthy former classmate and teach him the ad game. At the first executive meeting the lad attended, a discussion came up about the proper time-slot for a prospective television commercial.

"I'd suggest three o'clock on Sunday," submitted one vice-president.

"Three o'clock on Sunday?" cried the budding executive. "Why *nobody* would be watching then—everybody's out playing polo."

A union official stomped over to an open lot where an excavator was being used. "A hundred men with shovels could be doing that job," he complained to the contractor.

"I agree," the builder retorted, "but why not a thousand men with teaspoons?"

A real-estate man's imperfections
As a lover caused female rejections.
"I'm deflated," he moaned.
"They're erogenous-zoned,
But only for high-rise erections."

When Mr. Kreggemeier returned from Europe, his partner in a men's clothing store hung on his every word. "And I even was in a group that went to the Vatican," reminisced Kreggemeier, "where we were blessed by the Pope."

"The Pope!" exclaimed the other chap. "What does he look like?"

"A very pious man, reverent, spiritual, almost saintly," Kreggemeier answered. "I figure a size thirty-eight, short."

Then there was the crooked crematory operator who sold the ashes to cannibals as Instant People.

And of course you've heard about the pessimistic historian whose latest book has chapter headings that read "World War One," "World War Two" and "Watch This Space."

We know a waggish historian who says that George Washington was the only President who didn't blame the previous Administration for all of his troubles.

11
PLAYBOYS
& PLAYMATES

The prudish old maid found herself seated next to a sophisticated playboy at a formal affair. After a little, rather icy conversation, the lady attempted to dismiss the fellow with, "It's quite obvious, sir, that we do not agree on a single, solitary thing."

The playboy smiled. "Oh, I don't think that's quite true, madam," he said. "If you were to enter a bedroom in which there were two beds, and if, madam, there were a woman in one and a man in the other, in which bed would you sleep?"

"Well," the lady huffed indignantly, "with the woman, of course."

"You see, we agree," the playboy said, laughing. "So would I."

Then there was the playboy who suddenly decided to live a strictly moral life. First, he cut out smoking. Then he cut out liquor. Then he cut out swearing. Then he cut out women.

Now he's cutting out paper dolls.

Many a girl succeeds in keeping the wolf from her door these days by inviting him in.

The young bachelor showed up at the office with a black eye. "What the hell happened to you?" inquired his associates.

"Well," he said, "I was getting dressed this morning when a button came off my fly. I'm all thumbs when it comes to sewing, so I ran in to the married woman in the next apartment and asked her if she'd sew the button on for me."

"Oho," interrupted his friends, "she thought you were getting fresh and pasted you, is that it?"

"No, no. She was very nice about it. Got out her sewing basket and went to work. Sat down in front of me and sewed on the button while

I was standing there. She'd finished it up and was just biting off the thread, when her husband walked in."

Three playboys—English, Arabian and American—were standing on a street corner in Casablanca when a spectacular Oriental beauty walked haughtily by them. "By Jove!" exclaimed the Englishman. "By Allah!" sighed the Arabian. "By tomorrow night," said the American.

A technique perfected by a playboy friend of ours is so unique it deserves a telling.

Quite recently, he had been having difficulty persuading a lovely but stubborn young lady to part with her Victorian moral principles. He tried soft words and soft music; he tried the caveman approach; he tried strong drink. She resisted all these devices. Finally, one Saturday afternoon, he escorted her to an extremely fashionable furrier where he asked to see a collection of their finest mink coats. From these he permitted the girlfriend to choose one costing a cool ten grand.

"I assume you will accept my check," said our friend in a matter-of-fact manner.

The furrier explained that, being Saturday afternoon, the banks were closed and they would be unable to verify his credit until the following Monday. The playboy smiled. "I understand," he said. "Suppose we leave the coat here—I'll drop by Monday and pick it up. Here is my check."

Monday morning when he returned to the store, the furrier said sternly, "I am sorry, sir, but I cannot let you have the mink coat you ordered Saturday. We have called your bank and find that your account will not cover a check of this size."

"Yes, I know that," our friend replied. "I just stopped by to thank you for a wonderful weekend."

We know of an overweight playboy who is unhappy about losing a hundred and five pounds last month. She was a beautiful blonde.

"I'm looking for adventure, excitement, beautiful women," cried the young man to his father as he prepared to leave home. "Don't try to stop me, I'm on my way."

"Who's trying to stop you?" shouted his father. "Take me along."

A popular bachelor attached to the American Embassy in London had just returned from a weekend in the Midlands at a stately country home. When asked by a friend what sort of a time he had had, he replied, "If the soup had been as warm as the wine, and the wine as old as the chicken, and the chicken as tender as the upstairs maid, and the upstairs maid as willing as the duchess, it would have been perfect."

She was, without question, the most beautiful woman he had ever seen in his life. He gulped down the last of his Martini and, without hesitation, walked to where she sat at the end of the bar.

"You must forgive my rudeness," he said, "but when I beheld you sitting here, all wrapped round in white fur, and lights dancing in your hair like stars, I *had* to speak to you. I've never gazed upon such beauty before. I want to lay Manhattan at your feet, buy you jewels, exotic perfumes and a thousand other wondrous things. If you bid me welcome, we will fly this very night to Paris, then on to Venice, Rome, India and finally Egypt for a trip down the Nile."

The young lady was utterly taken with this handsome stranger who stood before her, with bronzed face, hair prematurely graying at the temples, dark suit cut exactly so. She was quite literally speechless and could manage only a breathless "Yes, yes. . . ."

"Then go prepare yourself, my Juliet, my Venus, my Helen of Troy. When you are ready, call me at the number on this card. My Rolls Royce will come for you and take you to my plane."

"Is this your private number at your town house or country estate?" she sighed.

"Well," he said, "it's actually the delicatessen downstairs, but they'll call me."

A bachelor friend of ours defines the ideal wife as a beautiful, sex-starved deaf-mute who owns a liquor store.

One of the most active men-about-town we know was thoroughly upset by the results of a recent medical examination.

"You've set yourself a killing pace with the ladies and it has got to stop," the doctor warned. "You're literally falling apart piece by piece."

The difference between the average man and a playboy is that the average man likes to give a girl a present, while the playboy would rather give her a past.

We know an amorous millionaire who's terribly indiscreet, yet so wealthy that he doesn't give a damn. He begins each letter to his sweethearts, "My Darling, and Gentlemen of the Jury. . . ."

The newspaper account of George's tragic death said: "His friends could give no reason why he should have committed suicide. He was a bachelor."

Spencer, the well-tailored man-about-town, walking ruefully out of court after getting stung by the decision in a paternity suit, was overheard to remark:
"When I make a beaut, it's a mistake."

A recent survey shows that the average young bachelor is more interested in high frequency than high fidelity.

A friend of ours claims to be the world's champ with the chicks, and we're inclined to agree. He let us look at his alphabetical little black book, and the forty-seventh entry was a doll named Annabelle Aarons.

A friend of ours has just told us about a remarkable ploy that's used by an aging and wealthy man-about-town. He dates only the most beautiful girls and confides to each of them that he suffers from a heart condition (not true). Then he takes them home to his magnificent estate, where they are properly dazzled by the quantity and quality of his possessions. He hints at the vast extent of his fortune. Then comes the clincher: he tells each wide-eyed, open-mouthed girl that, by the terms of his will, all his money and possessions go to whomever is with him at the time of his death. Then, so he claims, the girl usually does her level best to kill him with kindness.

Having received a return from a bachelor executive who claimed a dependent son, an income-tax inspector sent the form back with a note saying, "This must be a stenographic error." Back came the report with the added notation: "You're telling me!"

Today's playboy is like a modern cleanser: works fast and leaves no ring.

Enervated by his life's hectic pace, the swinger determined to take a leisurely drive across the country. At first the pastoral sights pleased him, but by the time he got to Kansas, he was dying for some action. Pulling into the only gas station in a small town one Saturday evening, he asked the attendant, "Is there any night life in this town?"

"Not anymore," the native replied. "She moved to Chicago."

A bachelor's goose is seldom cooked in the kitchen.

The newly married couple were entertaining a bachelor neighbor in the den of their suburban home when the conversation turned to sexual morality. "Since you claim to be so liberal," the bachelor challenged the husband, "would you let me kiss your wife's breasts for a thousand dollars?"

Not wishing to seem prudish and needing the extra money, the couple agreed and the wife removed her blouse and bra. Then, pressing his face between her breasts, the chap nestled there for several minutes, until the husband grew impatient to complete the deal. "Go ahead and kiss them," he urged the bachelor.

"I'd love to," the fellow sighed, "but I really can't afford it."

"Forgive me, Father," the embarrassed bachelor told his confessor. "I made love to a beautiful virgin last night."

"That's terrible," the cleric groaned. "Was it Cynthia Goodrich?"

"Please don't ask me that," the fellow pleaded.

"Was it the Carruthers girl?" the man of the cloth prodded him.

"I don't want to answer," he insisted.

"Well, was it Susan Fullerton?" the priest demanded.

"I simply refuse to tell you," the young chap declared firmly.

"All right, my son," the cleric sighed. "For admitting your guilt, you are forgiven, but you'd better see me again next week."

Leaving the church, the fellow met his best friend, who had waited for him outside. "How did your confession go?" the friend inquired.

"Not bad," the bachelor replied. "I got a week off and three new leads."

Most bachelors prefer girls who believe that children should be seen and not had.

A bachelor we know has discovered a new way to get a girl to sleep with him. "I tell her that I'll name her as beneficiary on a fifty thousand-dollar life insurance policy," he declares, "with double indemnity if I ball myself to death."

The four men at the card table were being bothered by an irritating kibitzer. When the troublesome talker stepped into the next room to mix a drink, one of the players suggested, "This next hand let's make up a game nobody ever heard of—he won't know what the hell we're playing and maybe that will shut him up."

When the kibitzer returned, the dealer tore the top two cards in half and gave them to the man on his right: he tore the corners off the next three cards and placed them before the next player, face up; he tore the next five cards in quarters, gave fifteen pieces to the third man, four to himself and put the last piece in the center of the table.

Looking intently at four small pieces of card in his hand, the dealer said, "I have a mingle, so I think I'll bet a dollar."

The second man stared at the pasteboards scattered before him. "I have a snazzle," he announced, "so I'll raise you a dollar."

The third man folded without betting and the fourth, after due deliberation, said, "I've a farfle, so I'll just raise you two dollars."

The kibitzer shook his head slowly from side to side. "You're crazy," he said, "you're never going to beat a mingle and a snazzle with a lousy farfle."

The bountifully endowed young doll was in an embarrassing situation, for her arms were filled with packages and she was wearing a dress that was simply too tight to allow her to step up into the bus for which she had been waiting the last fifteen minutes. A crowd pressed from behind and so she reached back, unobserved she hoped, and attempted to gain some additional freedom by pulling down the zipper at the back of her dress. It didn't seem to help and she still couldn't negotiate the high step, so she reached again for the zipper and additional freedom, but again it was no use. Then from out of the impatient crowd behind her, a young man picked her up and deposited her gently inside the bus.

This, of course, only embarrassed the girl more. "What right have you to pick me up like that?" she gasped. "Why, I don't even know you!"

"Well, miss," the man said, smiling and tipping his hat, "after you pulled my zipper down the second time, I began to feel as though we were pretty good friends."

Sometimes when two's company, three's the result.

A certain small New England town has had exactly the same population figure for the last half-century. This amazing condition is attributed to the fact that every time a baby is born, a man leaves town.

The man who is old enough to know better is always looking for a girl not quite that old.

Then there was the neat fellow who never left his apartment in the morning without having his bed maid.

On impulse, the young man stopped at the flower shop and purchased a dozen roses for his girlfriend. When he presented them to her, she immediately tore off all her clothes and leaped onto the couch. "This will be for the flowers," she announced, stretching languorously.

"Oh, come, now," he replied. "Surely you have a vase somewhere in this apartment."

As Mark fixed himself a Martini to carry him through the ordeal of waiting while Peggy got ready for their date, he could hear her singing in the shower.

"Sorry I'm so late," she finally called out to him, "but I was shopping and lost track of the time." Clutching a large towel about her, she edged into the room. "Would you like to see me in my new dress?" she asked.

Mark took appreciative note of her newly bathed charms straining at the confines of the barely adequate towel.

"I would like," he said with a smile, "nothing better."

While down South on a visit, the young Yankee made a date with a local lovely. When he called for her at her home, she was clad in a low-cut, tight-fitting gown. He remarked, "That's certainly a beautiful dress."

"Sho 'nough?" she said sweetly.

"It sure does," he replied.

"Never put off until tomorrow what you can do today," a wise man once said, "because if you enjoy it today, you can do it again tomorrow."

> "Men *seldom make passes*
> *At girls who wear glasses,"*
> *So Dorothy Parker has said.*
> *She said it quite rightly,*
> *They're very unsightly,*
> *But no one wears glasses to bed.*

A friend of ours gave his favorite playmate a diamond wristwatch and the following night, he reports, he gave her the works.

The best way to approach a woman with a past is with a present.

A polite and rather timid young man, after buying a ladyfriend a pair of gloves as a birthday present, scrivened the following note to be sent along with them:

"I hope you find these a welcome birthday gift, since I noticed— on our last few dates—that you weren't wearing any. They are reversible, so if you get them soiled you can wear them inside out and thus wear them longer without having to wash them. I'm only sorry I cannot be there at your party to watch your smiling face as you try them on."

He left the note with the saleslady, who promptly sent it off with the wrong package: a pair of silk panties.

It's a great life if you weaken enough to enjoy it.

> A *playboy is a cagey guy*
> *Who has a lot of fun.*
> *He samples every pretty wench*
> *And never Mrs. one.*

The difference between men and boys is the cost of their toys.

Men who are getting on in years should console themselves with the thought that when they get too old to set bad examples, they can always start giving advice.

A healthy looking physical-education instructor was having a soft drink at a neighborhood bar, when a devastating brunette approached and made a familiar proposition.

"No, thank you," he said politely. "This might sound strange to you, but I'm keeping myself pure until I meet the girl I love."

"That must be very difficult," the girl sympathized.

"I don't mind," he said, "but it has my wife pretty upset."

A man is old when his dreams about girls are reruns.

A man has reached old age when he can't take "Yes" for an answer.

A man is getting old when he runs out of gas after he runs out of gas.

It's a great life—if your "don'ts" weaken.

> *Breathes there a man with soul so dead,*
> *Who's never to his playmate said:*
> *"To hell with breakfast,*
> *Come back to bed!"*

And, of course, you've heard about the Scotsman who wore a maxikilt. We're not sure if he was just trying to keep up with the styles or bragging.

You've undoubtedly heard about the number of magazines required to fill a baby carriage: a PLAYBOY, a *Mademoiselle*, a few *Liberties* and *Time*.

Many a young tomato has been cultivated by an old rake.

As he approached the haberdashery counter of a large department store, a well-dressed gentleman was greeted by a shapely clerk.

"Good afternoon," she murmured softly, "and what is your desire?"

"My desire," he said, after giving her a long, appreciative look, "is to sweep you into my arms, rush you out of this store and up to my apartment, mix a pitcher of Martinis, put on some soft music and make mad, passionate love to you. But what I *need* is a pair of socks."

A friend of ours who rarely sleeps alone observes knowingly that one good turn usually gets most of the blanket.

Friend of ours says he's read so much about the terrible effects of smoking that he's decided to give up reading.

"**D**arling," seductively sighed the fashion model, "if I didn't wear all these beautiful clothes, would you still think me attractive?"

He smiled, and replied, "Test me."

The golfer confidently eyed the next hole and remarked to his caddy: "This should be good for a long drive and a putt." His swing, however, hit the sod and pushed the ball only a few feet.

"Now," said the caddy, "for a hell of a putt."

Of course you've heard of the playboy baron who went serf riding.

"**I**'d like to buy some gloves for my girlfriend," the young man said, eying the attractive salesgirl, "but I don't know her size."

"Will this help?" she asked sweetly, placing her hand in his.

"Oh, yes," he answered. "Her hands are just slightly smaller than yours."

"Will there be anything else?" the clerk queried as she wrapped the gloves.

"Now that you mention it," he replied, "she also needs a bra and panties. . . ."

"**I**f I had my life to live over again," mused the old gentleman, "I'd make all the same mistakes—but I'd make them sooner."

And then there was the fifty-year-old bachelor who woke up one morning feeling like a twenty year old. But he couldn't find one that early in the day.

"All I need in an apartment," says a bachelor we know, "is enough room to lay my head—and a few close friends."

Then there was the jaded bachelor who finally got married—so that he could join a wife-swapping club.

The couple stepped up to the desk clerk of one of the city's nicer hotels. "I'd like a room and bath for my wife and myself," said the gentleman.

"I'm terribly sorry, sir," said the clerk, "but the only room available doesn't have bathroom facilities."

"Will that be all right with you, dear?" the gentleman asked the young lady at his side.

"Sure, mister," she said.

"If I'm not in bed by ten o'clock," said one female barfly to the other, "I'm going home."

A flashy Mercedes-Benz roared up to the curb, where a cute young miss stood waiting for a taxi.

"Hi," said the gentleman at the wheel. "I'm going west."

"How wonderful," came the cool reply. "Bring me back an orange."

A most attractive redhead, window-shopping on Fifth Avenue, became aware of a well-dressed gentleman following her at a short distance. Somewhat flustered, she accidentally dropped her handbag and he immediately retrieved it for her.

"I dropped that bag accidentally," she said. "I want you to understand that I am not the type of girl you can pick up."

The gentleman smiled and said, "Madam, I am most assuredly not picking you up. I am picking you out."

"Did you pick up any Italian on your vacation?" the secretary asked the honey blonde at the next desk.

"I'll say I did," enthused the honey.

"Let me hear you say some words."

"I didn't learn any words."

Hgh and Ghg, a pair of newly arrived Martians, stood on a New York street corner leering at the traffic light across the way.

"Keep away from her or I'll knock your heads together," said Ghg to Hgh. "I saw her first."

"So what?" Hgh responded. "She winked at *me!*"

Just then the signal changed from GO to STOP. The Martians stalked off disgustedly.

"Women!" Hgh muttered. "If there's anything I can't stand, it's a tease."

She was sweet, she was breathtakingly lovely and she was alone. Most of the men in the cocktail lounge were awed by her beauty, but afraid to approach her. Not so Augie. He downed his drink, straightened his tie and gracefully slid onto the stool next to hers, favoring her with a warm smile.

"You know," he began smoothly, "I hate to see a young girl like you ruin her reputation and destroy her character by hanging around a bar. Let me take you someplace where the atmosphere is quiet and more refined, like my apartment."

The other evening in a bar, a rather shy friend of ours spotted a really remarkably stacked young lady drinking alone a few stools away. He moved over and sat next to her, but was embarrassed about striking up a conversation with a total stranger, so instead, when she ordered her next drink, he ordered another for himself and then paid for both of them. She nodded her thanks, but still he could find no way to begin a conversation. This continued for nearly an hour, and the consumption of four more rounds by the both of them.

Finally, emboldened by the liquor, and aware that the girl seemed to be getting a bit restless and might soon drift away and out of his life, he blurted out, "Do you ever go to bed with men?"

"I never have before," she said, smiling, "but I believe you've talked me into it, you clever, silver-tongued devil, you!"

A man about town who was cruising in his open sports convertible stopped beside an attractive young thing and invited her to take a ride. As she got in, she slyly informed him that she was a witch and could turn him into anything she wished.

"Go ahead and try!" he answered with a smile; she leaned against him and whispered something in his ear. And sure enough, he turned into a motel.

We've heard from our correspondent on the Riviera that there's a dazzling young thing there who's been picked up on the beach so often that she's beginning to grow handles.

Two industrial robots decided to leave their factory to investigate some of the human pleasures they had heard about. After several hours of individual exploration, one noticed the other standing on a corner in front of a mailbox and a fire-alarm box.

"Looks like we're going to get some action," said the new arrival, crossing the street.

"Forget it," answered the other. "The dumpy green one doesn't say a word, and as soon as you touch the red one, she screams her head off."

As two miniskirted coeds were strolling along the wharf one night in San Francisco, they noticed two sailors following them.

"Aren't those sailors out after hours?" one observed.

"I sure hope so," her friend replied.

For five consecutive nights, the young man at the bar witnessed a repeated phenomenon: Attractive girls, alone or in groups of two or three, would wander in and soon be picked up by a funny-looking customer sitting in a corner booth. "I can't understand it," the man grumbled to the bartender after the sixth such incident. "I don't see how that guy does it."

"Me neither, Mac," said the sympathetic barkeep. "I've been watching him for weeks. He's certainly not handsome, he's a lousy dresser and he hardly ever says a word. In fact, he just sits there, licking his eyebrows."

The attractive blonde was standing at a busy intersection waiting to cross the street when she was approached by a handsome young man. "I couldn't help but notice the V that's embroidered on your sweater," he said. "Does it stand for Vassar?"

"No, it stands for virgin," she cooed sweetly, "but it's a very old sweater."

Crazy Charlie, the used-car dealer, was out to break all sales records with his "like new" models. A large sign in his window announced: "A Blonde Free with Each Car."

A delighted young wolf plunked down his cash and, hot with anticipation, drove his newly won blonde out into the country. He parked, gave her a couple of preliminary kisses, and whispered a suggestion in her ear.

She shook her head, smiled, and said, "You got that when you bought this car."

"**H**ere's how," said the playboy, raising his glass.
"Say *when,*" said his date, "I know *how!*"

"**W**ill you have a drink?" the young man asked.
"I don't drink," his date replied.
"May I offer you a cigarette?"
"I don't smoke," she said.
"Would you be interested in going up to my apartment, putting a little mood music on the phonograph, and. . . ." She answered by slapping his face.
"I don't suppose you eat hay either," he said, nursing his jaw.
"Well, hardly," she said icily.
"Just as I thought," he sighed. "Not fit company for man or beast."

A fellow we know is so jaded he has dropped all the subtle preliminaries usually expected by a girl in favor of the direct approach, and we recently overheard the following dialogue with a young lady he had just met at a cocktail party.
"I'm a man of few words. Will you or won't you?"
"Your apartment or mine?" the sophisticated miss responded.
"Well," he said in an exasperated tone, "if there's going to be such a lot of discussion about it, let's forget the whole damn thing."

We approve of this tactful variation on the age-old delicate question: One asks his date for the evening if she'd like to join him for breakfast. Receiving an affirmative reply, he then asks, "Shall I call you or nudge you?"

"**M**y goodness, Mr. Bartholomew," purred the pretty young thing, "I've never met a landlord quite like you before. I wonder if I could pay a few months' rent in advance?"

These days, too many beautiful women are spoiling their attractiveness by using four-letter words—like don't, and can't, and won't.

He'd shown her his etchings, and just about everything else of interest in his apartment and, as Jack poured the last of the Martinis into their glasses, he realized that the moment of truth with Louise had arrived. He decided on the direct verbal attack.
"Tell me," he said smoothly, fingering a lock of her hair, "do you object to making love?"

She turned her lovely eyes up to his. "That's something I've never done," she said.

"Never made love?" cried Jack, appalled at the waste of magnificent raw material.

"No, silly," she said in soft rebuke. "Never objected."

Max the plumber was summoned to a mansion to fix a leak and, discovering a very pretty maid there, he lost no time trying to combine business with pleasure. The girl refused on the grounds that her mistress was home, and she didn't want to be discovered and fired. After several refusals, Max finished the job and returned to his shop.

Next morning his phone rang, and his caller was the maid. In dulcet tones, she informed him that her mistress was out, and asked if he wanted to come over and see her.

"What!" yelled Max. "On my own time?"

While we generally have nothing but contempt for the sassy feminine rejoinder to a forthright masculine proposition, we must express a grudging degree of admiration for the logic displayed by one beautiful chick. The doll in question was being entertained at the apartment of a friend of ours, and at the proper moment he employed the time-honored verbal gambit:

"Come on, baby. Let's live for tonight."

For a moment she considered the prospect happily, but then her limpid blue orbs clouded over, and she replied:

"Yes, but suppose we survive?"

"How about joining me for a cozy weekend in a quiet suburban hotel?" he whispered in the curvaceous lass' ear.

"I'm afraid," she said, "that my awareness of your proclivities in the esoteric aspects of sexual behavior precludes you from such erotic confrontation."

"I don't get it," he said.

"Exactly," she smiled.

"If I refuse to go to bed with you," she whispered, "will you really commit suicide?"

"That," he said grandly, "has been my usual procedure."

"Say when," he said as he poured the drink and snuggled a little bit closer.

"Right after this drink," came the breathless reply.

"**I**'ve heard you're very shy," the young swain murmured reassuringly to his date, as they strolled through the moonlit park. "But you needn't worry about making conversation. I've devised a simple code that eliminates the need for talk: If you nod your head, it means you want me to hold your hand, and if you smile, it means you'd like me to kiss you. Isn't that easy? What do you think of my plan?"

She laughed in his face.

In the midst of one of the wildest parties he'd ever been to, the young man noticed a very prim and pretty girl sitting quietly apart from the rest of the revelers. Approaching her, he introduced himself and said, "I'm afraid you and I don't really fit in with this jaded group. Why don't I take you home?"

"Fine," said the girl, smiling up at him demurely. "Where do you live?"

Having escorted the young lady home from their first date, the rather reserved lad was invited in for a nightcap. As the girl prepared the drinks, the fellow strolled about, a bit ill at ease, admiring her apartment.

"Be careful if you sit on that couch," she cautioned. "If you press down on the arm and pull forward on the seat while pushing against the back cushion, it turns into a bed."

The dazzling young thing was strolling down the street in skin-tight hip-huggers, when a curious bachelor approached and said, "Excuse me, miss, but I can't help asking—how in the world does anyone get into those pants?"

"Well," she replied demurely, "you can start by buying me a drink."

The young couple had met early on New Year's Eve and hit it off quite well as the party progressed. "Sweetheart," he finally said to her, "it's almost midnight—why don't we end the old year with a kiss?"

"If you really want to," replied his striking friend. "Personally, I'd rather go to your place and finish it off with a bang."

As the young Hollywood bachelor sat having coffee with a friend's stunning wife, she announced: "I think I'd better warn you—my husband will be home in an hour."

"But I haven't done anything wrong," responded the bachelor, somewhat surprised.

"I know that," she replied. "But I thought you'd want to know how much time you have—in case you decide to."

While he was struggling with a jammed cigarette machine in the lobby of his hotel, the youthful conventioneer's hand slipped off the knob and his elbow struck a passing girl on the chest.

"I'm terribly sorry," the man said. "But if your heart is as soft as your breast, you'll forgive me."

"Oh, I do," she answered with a warm smile. "And if the rest of you is as hard as your elbow, my room is 613."

"How do you do so well with girls?" the frustrated sophomore asked his roommate.

"You've got to have a gimmick," the roommate responded. "For instance, I've painted a white circle on the dashboard of my car. My dates always ask about it. From there, I turn the conversation to white things in general, then to abstract white things, like virginity; and after that, it's easy to talk them into it."

"That sounds simple enough," the friend agreed. That evening, he painted a white circle on his dashboard before picking up his date.

"That's rather unique—to have a white circle painted on your dash," the girl said, soon after she got into the car.

"Yes, isn't it?" the young fellow replied. "Do you want to screw?"

The lonely executive had spent the whole evening at a cocktail party complaining to an attractive guest about his wife's constant visits to her mother. "She's away again tonight," said the man. "What would you do if you were in my place?"

"Well, honey," his companion cooed, "let's go over to your place and I'll show you."

The buxom country lass had gone to town to do some shopping and, on her way home after dark, encountered one of the neighboring farm boys returning from a day at the market. The two had walked together for a while when the girl said shyly, "I'm almost afraid to be alone with you like this—you might try to take advantage of me."

"Take advantage of you?" the handsome lad gulped. "Here I am, carrying a pitchfork and a chicken in one hand, a washtub in the other and leading a goat. I could hardly take advantage of you."

"Well," she continued, "you could always stick the pitchfork in the ground, tie the goat to it and put the chicken under the washtub, couldn't you?"

The romantic young man sat on the park bench with a first date. He was certain his charming words and manner would win her as they had so many others.

"Some moon out tonight," he cooed.

"There certainly is," she agreed.

"Some really bright stars in the sky."

She nodded.

"Some dew on the grass."

"*Some* do," she said indignantly, "but *I'm* not that sort!"

The evening had been going very well, but now, at the critical moment, the girl wouldn't let the playboy into her apartment. Her excuse was thin: "My roommate's home."

Bitter, her date said, "In other words, I'm supposed to ignore this doormat that says *Welcome?*"

"Of course, silly," she laughed. "There certainly isn't room enough for us on that!"

A lovely southern belle we know is such a slow talker that by the time she got through assuring a friend of ours that she wasn't that kind of girl, she was.

Miss Bradshaw, a comely high school teacher, had saved money for several years and was finally aboard a sleek ocean liner for her long-anticipated trip to Europe. Aboard ship, she wrote:

"Dear Diary: *Monday.* I felt singularly honored this evening. The Captain asked me to dine at his table. *Tuesday.* I spent the entire morning on the bridge with the Captain. *Wednesday.* The Captain made proposals to me unbecoming an officer and a gentleman. *Thursday.* Tonight the Captain threatened to sink the ship if I do not give in to his indecent proposals. *Friday.* This afternoon I saved sixteen hundred lives."

A sweet young school teacher who had always been virtuous was invited to go for a ride in the country with the gym instructor, whom she admired. Under a tree on the bank of a quiet lake, she struggled with her conscience and with the gym instructor and finally gave in to the latter. Sobbing uncontrollably, she asked her seducer, "How can I ever face my students again, knowing I have sinned twice?"

"Twice?" asked the young man, confused.

"Why, yes," said the sweet teacher, wiping a tear from her eye, "you're going to do it again, aren't you?"

It's hard to keep a good girl down—but lots of fun trying.

An interloper at a meeting of the Society of Mayflower Descendants put the august group in a bit of a tizzy when he responded, "Actually, I'm descended from a long line my mother once heard."

If Dorothy Parker will forgive us, it is our observation that men often make passes at girls who drain glasses.

The long-shanked, ash-blonde Hollywood starlet was grappling with the producer in his Laurel Canyon home for a full half-hour. Finally, with a supreme effort, she picked herself up off the couch, straightened her stockings, brushed the hair off her forehead, looked him straight in the eye and said, "Flirt."

A girl who finds it possible to resist every attempt made to seduce her should be going out with stronger men.

A wealthy young American was wandering through the Montmartre section of Paris when he came upon a lovely French miss who looked for all the world like Brigitte Bardot.

"Could I buy you a drink?" he asked, by way of striking up a conversation.

"No thank you," she said, "I don't drink."

"What about a little dinner with me in my room?"

"No, I don't believe that would be proper," she said.

Having had no success with the subtler approaches, the young man pressed directly to the point: "I am charmed by your refreshing beauty, *mademoiselle,* and will give you anything your heart desires if you will spend the night with me."

"Oh, no, no, *monsieur,* I could never do a thing like that."

"Tell me," the young man said, laughing, "don't you ever do anything the slightest bit improper?"

"Oui," said the French girl, "I tell lies."

We know a girl who hates losing her heart to a man, but who loves having him search for it.

When a girl is invited to a man's apartment to see his etchings, it's usually not a standing invitation.

Fred's convertible glided to a halt on the edge of a lonely country road.

"I suppose," said his pretty but reluctant date, "you're going to pull the old 'out of gas' routine."

"No," said Fred, "I'm going to pull the 'here after' routine. . . ."

"The 'here after' routine—what's that?" she wanted to know.

"If you're not here after what I'm here after, then you're going to be here after I'm gone."

The best kind of girl is the one who says stop only when she sends a telegram.

A friend of ours, who blows second sax in a chic society orchestra, was taking a break at the bar one evening and overheard the following conversation:

"First, I'm going to buy you a few drinks and get you a little tight," said the guy aggressively.

"Oh no you're not," said the girl.

"Then I'll take you to dinner and ply you with a few more drinks."

"Oh no you're not."

"Then I'll take you to my apartment and keep serving you drinks."

"Oh no you're not."

"Then I'm going to make violent, passionate love to you."

"Oh no, you're not!"

"And I'm not going to take any precautions either!" said the guy.

"Oh yes you are!!" said the girl.

Then there was the fellow who got badly scratched up fighting for his girl's honor. She wanted to keep it.

After repeatedly warding off her date's amorous advances during the evening, the pretty young thing decided to put her foot down: "See here," she shouted indignantly. "This is positively the last time I'm going to tell you 'no.' "

"Splendid!" exclaimed her date. "Now we can start making some progress."

A man will often take a girl to some retreat in order to make advances.

Joan had invited her younger sister, Nancy, to leave her country home and come to the city for a weekend to see how the urban half lived. She also arranged for a friend of hers named Bill to take Nancy out for a night on the town.

After a pleasant dinner and a show, Bill and Nancy went to Bill's apartment for a nightcap. They talked and listened to soft music for a pleasant interlude; then Bill suggested that they retire to the bedroom.

"Oh, no," Nancy protested. "I don't think my sister would like it."

"Nonsense," said Bill, as he gently took her arm. "She loves it."

The shy young man and his shapely date were parked under a romantic moon. Placing his hand on her thigh, he whispered, "I love you."

With a deep sigh, the girl replied, "A little higher."

"I love you," came the higher-pitched reply.

The inexperienced young man had heard that a good way to arouse sexual desire in a girl who proved impervious to the more usual forms of wooing was to forthrightly place her hand on his organ. Having parked with a date for more than an hour in the local lovers' lane, with nothing to show for it but some sisterly kisses, he decided to try this new technique. The response was instantaneous: The girl berated him with the longest stream of invectives he'd ever heard. Stunned, he tried to reply, but she refused to listen, insisting, instead, that he take her home at once.

As he pulled up in front of her house, she again started shouting imprecations. Finally, out of breath, she demanded: "Well, do you have anything to say for yourself ?!"

"Yes, I have," was his pained reply. "Please let go."

12
ON THE ROAD

Overheard in a fashionable sports-car salon: "This model has a top speed of a hundred and fifty-five miles per hour, and she'll stop on a dime."

"What happens then?"

"A small putty knife emerges and scrapes you gently off the windshield."

A cool friend informs us that the best way to cut off a cat's tail is to repossess his Jaguar.

The car sped off the highway, went through the guardrail, rolled down a cliff, bounced off a tree and finally shuddered to a stop. A passing motorist, who had witnessed the entire accident, helped the miraculously unharmed driver out of the wreck.

"Good lord, mister," he gasped, "are you drunk?!"

"Of course," said the man, brushing the dirt from his suit-front. "What the hell you think I am—a stunt driver?"

A used-car dealer of our acquaintance informs us that, to cope with the cynical attitudes of present-day buyers, the little old lady who drove only on Sundays has been replaced in the standard sales pitch by a nymphomaniac who only used the back seat.

If, as the scientists say, sex is such a driving force, why is so much of it nowadays found parked?

A friend of ours who is a nut on classic automobiles bought a car a few weeks ago that runs entirely on electricity, and he paid ten thousand dollars for it—five thousand for the car and five thousand for the extension cord.

"I take the next turn, don't I?" asked the driver of the car. The muffled reply from the back seat: "Like hell you do!"

The convertible glided silently to a stop on a lonely country road. "Out of gas," he said, with a sly smile.

"Yes, I thought you might be," said his date, as she opened her purse and pulled out a small hip flask.

"Say, you *are* a swinger," he said. "What do you have in there— Scotch or bourbon?"

"Gasoline," she replied.

We've just heard about a new club called AAA-AA for people who are being driven to drink.

In a whiskey it's age, in a cigarette it's taste, and in a sports car it's impossible.

Then there was the karate expert who rolled down his car window to signal for a left turn—and chopped a Volkswagen in half.

We know a superstitious sports-car enthusiast who, upon hearing that Saint Christopher had been decanonized, immediately switched to a Ralph Nader medal.

The highway patrolman stopped a speeding car and, noticing the motorist's inebriated condition, delivered a stern lecture on the dangers of drunken driving. "Do you realize that you were going over seventy miles an hour?" the officer demanded.

"I know," the driver explained. "I want to get home before I have an accident."

A taxi driver was cruising for a fare when a pregnant woman, crossing against a red light, walked right in front of his cab. He slammed on the brakes and yelled indignantly out the window, "You better watch out, lady, or you'll get knocked *down*, too."

Did you ever notice what *motel* spells backwards?

We know a modern Cinderella who, at the stroke of midnight, turns into a motel.

The angry woman's voice made the hotel manager wince. "I'm up here in room 1510," she ranted over the phone, "and I want you to know there is a man walking around in his room across the way with not one stitch of clothes on and his shades are up and it's a shocking way to run a hotel."

"I'll send the house detective up right away, madam," the manager assured her, and motioned for his minion of the law to scoot upstairs and see what the hassle was about.

The detective entered the woman's room, peered across the way, and said, "You're right, madam, the gentleman hasn't any clothes on, but his window sill covers him from the waist down no matter where he is in his room."

"Indeed?" yelped the lady. "Stand on the bed! Stand on the bed!"

The house detective had been told to check the guest's luggage in room 1013 for any property belonging to the hotel.

"Did you find any towels in his suitcase?" asked the manager.

"Not a one," replied the detective, "but I found a chambermaid in his grip."

The hotel reservations clerk opened the telegram and read: " DO YOU HAVE ANY ACCOMMODATIONS WHERE I CAN PUT UP WITH MY WIFE?"

The proprietor of a combination dude ranch and resort hotel, the Westward Ho, found his business, which had been slow, suddenly booming after he hired a new bus driver to meet all incoming trains. Curious as to how the man managed to bring in so much new business, the owner questioned him about it.

"Ah really don't know," answered the driver, a gentleman just up from the Deep South. "When that train comes chuggin' in, all ah do is hollah, 'Free bus to the Westward Ho House' and they all come pilin' in."

We just heard about the expensive new Miami Beach hotel that's so exclusive Room Service has an unlisted number.

Some of the best bedtime stories can be found in motel registers.

The young man-about-town enjoyed luxury but didn't always have the means to buy it, and so he huffily walked out of the Miami Beach hotel when he found out the charges for room, meals and golf privileges were fifty dollars a day. He registered across the street at an equally elegant hotel, where the rates were only ten dollars. The following morning he went down to the hotel's golf course and asked Scotty, the pro, to sell him a couple of golf balls. "Sure," said Scotty. "That'll be twenty-five dollars apiece."

"What?" screamed the bachelor. "In the hotel across the street they only charge a dollar a ball!"

"Naturally," replied the pro. "Over there they get you by the rooms."

The two couples were enjoying their vacation together at a resort hotel. They were in the middle of a game of Scrabble in the lobby when a thunderstorm cut off the hotel's electricity, leaving little to do but retire to their rooms. Will was a rather devout chap, so before getting into bed with his companion, he said his prayers. As he got under the covers, the lights suddenly went on and he discovered he was in the wrong room. He instantly jumped up and started to dash for the hallway. "It's too late," called the girl from the bed, "my guy doesn't pray."

The house detective, hearing odd noises from the room of a female guest, knocked on the door and inquired sternly, "Are you entertaining in there?"

"Just a minute," came the reply, "and I'll ask him."

The Texas oil millionaire, an old-time wildcatter who had been so busy making money all his life that he'd never had time to learn to read and write, took the pen from the hotel clerk and signed the register with an X. Then, after a thoughtful glance at the blonde he had picked up in a nearby cocktail lounge, he drew a circle around the X.

"I've had people sign their name with an X before," remarked the curious clerk, "but what's the circle for?"

"Shucks, sonny," retorted the oilman, "when a man checks into a strange hotel with a gal he's just met, y'all can't expect him to use his right name."

After checking into the large motel complex, the self-styled evangelist read in his room for several hours, then sauntered over to the bar, where he struck up a conversation with the pretty hatcheck girl. After she had finished working, they shared a few drinks and then retired to his room. But when the evangelist began removing her blouse, she seemed to have second thoughts. "Are you sure this is all right?" she asked. "I mean, you're a holy man."

"My dear," he replied, "it is written in the Bible."

She took him at his word, and the two spent a very pleasant night together. The next morning, however, as the girl was preparing to leave, she said: "You know, I don't remember the part of the Bible you mentioned last night. Could you show it to me?"

In response, the evangelist took the Gideon Bible from the night stand, opened the cover and pointed to the flyleaf, on which someone had inscribed: "The hatcheck girl screws."

During her first visit to Las Vegas, the inexperienced and frustrated young schoolteacher readily succumbed to the advances of the first man she met—a bellboy. Following their frenzied lovemaking, she breathed in his ear: "Wouldn't it be more discreet if you got me a room where the door would stay closed?"

"Yes, ma'am," he said. "But this isn't your room—it's the elevator."

From Florida we hear that the stillness of the wee morning hours in one of Miami's most fashionable hotels was broken recently by a bellhop who ran up and down the corridors, screaming at the top of his voice: "The hotel's on fire, cha cha cha!"

If all the world loves a lover, why do they have hotel detectives?

The forgetful professor had left his umbrella in his hotel room when checking out; he missed it on the way to the train station and, still having time to spare, he hurried back. He found the room and was about to ask a passing chambermaid to open it for him, when he became aware of voices within and realized that in the brief time since his departure, the room had been let to new occupants.

"Whose little baby are you?" asked a youthful male voice from behind the door, and the question was followed by the sound of kisses and a girlish giggle.

"Your little baby," said the youthful female voice.

"And whose little hands are these?" asked the boy.

"Your little hands," responded the girl, with more giggles and more kisses following.

"And whose little feet are these?" More kisses and giggles of delight. "And whose little knees . . . and whose little. . . ."

"When you get to an umbrella," said the professor through the door, "it's mine!"

Most major cities have a "Dial-a-prayer" number for anyone requiring religious reassurance in the form of a brief, prerecorded sermon. Now there's talk of establishing a similar number for atheists. When you dial it, no one answers.

The prudish landlady suspected that her comely new boarder was breaking the no-men-upstairs rule of the dwelling. Finally, the busybody stormed up to the young thing's room, banged on the door and called out, "Miss Reynolds, are you entertaining gentlemen in your room?"

"I must be," was the giggled reply. "They all keep coming back for more."

A wealthy gentleman was badly bitten by bugs while riding on a certain railway line. Arriving at his destination, he wrote the company an indignant letter and received a prompt reply. It was, said the letter, the first complaint the company had ever had of this nature. Inquiry had failed to reveal any explanation for this unprecedented occurrence. Nevertheless, a number of new precautions were being taken to make absolutely certain such an unfortunate incident never happened again. The letter was signed by a high official of the railway.

The gentleman was well satisfied with this reply and was returning it to its envelope when a slip of paper fell out onto the floor. The hastily scribbled note on it read: "Send this guy the bug letter."

While visiting our country, a lovely French maiden found herself out of money just as her visa expired. Unable to pay her passage back to France, she was in despair until an enterprising sailor made her a sporting proposition. "My ship is sailing tonight," he said. "I'll smuggle you aboard, hide you down in the hold and provide you with a mattress, blankets and food. All it will cost you is a little love."

The girl consented and late that night the sailor snuck her on board his vessel. Twice each day, thereafter, the sailor smuggled a large tray of food below decks, took his pleasure with the little French stowaway and departed. The days turned into weeks and the weeks might have turned into months, if the captain hadn't noticed the sailor carrying food below one evening and followed him. After witnessing this unique bit of barter, he waited until the sailor had departed and then confronted the girl, demanding an explanation. She told him the whole story. "Hmm," mused the captain. "A clever arrangement, and I must say I admire that young seaman's ingenuity. However, miss, I feel it is only fair to tell you that this is the Staten Island Ferry."

Then there were the two honeymooners who wanted to fly United, but the stewardess wouldn't let them.

The mother got on the train with her six children and when the conductor came by for her tickets, she explained, "Those two are twelve and have to pay full fare, but these two are eight and the other two six-and-a-half, so they only pay half rate."

The conductor scratched his head and as he punched her tickets, he said: "Excuse me for asking, madam, but do you get two every time?"

"Oh, no," she said. "Sometimes we don't get any at all."

A friend of ours who travels by plane a good deal says that his pet peeve is the good-looking airline stewardess who straps him in his seat and then asks, "Is there anything you'd like?"

Many a man who thinks he's going on a maiden voyage with a girl finds out later from her lawyer that it was a shakedown cruise.

When a smart girl travels by train, she gives the boys in the club car a wide berth.

In the new jet planes, you know you're moving faster than sound when the stewardess slaps your face before you can get a word out.

The three hundred passengers on the first fully-automatic rocket plane flight from New York to Paris were aboard and belted in, and the great machine had whooshed aloft and into flight, when a voice came over the loudspeaker, in measured tones of infinite assurance:

"Ladies and gentlemen, there is no crew on this aircraft, but there is nothing to worry about. Automation will fly you to Paris in perfect safety at a speed of twenty-five hundred miles per hour. Everything has been tested and retested so exhaustively for your safety that there is not the slightest chance anything can go wrong . . . go wrong . . . go wrong . . . go wrong. . . ."

Our favorite airline stewardess is the one who says, "Coffee, tea or me?"

"Your fare, young lady," said the handsome train conductor.
She smiled at him sweetly, "You're not so bad yourself."

The pretty young thing approached the ship's steward. "Can you tell me where I might find the captain?" she asked.
"The captain is forward, miss," he replied.
"That's all right," she said, giggling. "This is a pleasure cruise, isn't it?"

There's a wonderful new French airline that is almost completely automated. You push a button and out comes your seat belt. You push a button on the seat belt and out comes your pillow. You push a button on your pillow and out comes the hostess. You push a button on the hostess and out come your teeth.

During the frantic rush hour on a New York subway train, a lecherous old man pressed close to a pretty young lady and whispered in her ear:

"You know, you're rather a tasty morsel."

"And do you know," she replied angrily, "that it's impolite to eat with your hands?"

The cheery voice of the stewardess came over the airplane's intercom: "Good afternoon, ladies and gentlemen, this is your stewardess, Miss Hotchkiss. I have some bad news and some good news to report.

"First the bad news. Your pilot and copilot are both drunk. There's been a malfunction in the radio and we've lost contact with the field. We're three hundred miles off course and expect to run into some heavy turbulence over the Rocky Mountains. And it appears that we have an insufficient fuel supply to reach an alternate airport.

"And now for the good news. We're making very good time."

A young man on a very crowded bus put his hand on the shoulder of an attractive girl sitting next to him. "Couldn't you find a more suitable place for your hand?" asked the young girl sharply.

"I'm sure I could," he replied, "but I get off at the next stop."

After he entered a packed subway train, the young man was crushed against a shapely blonde. Several stations later, as he started to get off, she kicked him in the shin. "What the hell did you do that for?" he asked.

"Next time," the indignant girl whispered, "don't start something you can't finish."

While dancing with a dapper Englishman, the American girl's brooch became unfastened and slid down the back of her gown.

She told her escort about it and asked him to retrieve the lost article. Somewhat embarrassed, but determined to please, he reached cautiously down the back of her gown. After a moment, he said, "Awfully sorry, but I can't seem to locate it."

"Try further down," she advised. He did, beginning to blush. Still no brooch. "Down still further," she ordered.

Looking around and discovering that he was being watched by every couple on the dance floor, the Englishman blushed even deeper and whispered, "I feel a perfect ass."

"*Never mind that!*" she snapped. "Just get the brooch!"

Lord Cramsfedder was startled out of his sleep by his trusted valet, Gordon.

"Oh, M'lord, there's a bounder in congress with her Ladyship," announced the servant.

Lord Cramsfedder leaped out of his bed, hastily slipped into his robe and grabbed his fowling piece from the mantle. Together they proceeded upstairs on tip-toes, and cautiously pushed open the door to Her Ladyship's boudoir. The situation was immediately obvious. The outraged husband lifted the weapon, aimed carefully and blasted away with both barrels.

When the smoke had cleared, Gordon looked in. "Oh, sir," he cried out, his voice filled with admiration, "a sportsman ever, you got him on the rise."

The visiting American was quite upset by his sudden drop in popularity. During his first two weeks in England, he had been invited everywhere, feted and entertained. Now, quite suddenly, his phone no longer jingled and no invitations crowded his mailbox. Perplexed, he called his friend, Reginald.

"Reggie, you can speak frankly with me, what's happened? I'm being virtually ostracized."

"Well, old boy," Reggie replied, "you'll remember that fox hunt you went on last weekend? Here in England it's customary to cry '*Tally ho!*' when you sight the fox—not, I'm afraid, 'There goes the little son of a bitch!' "

At breakfast one morning Lady Cribblesfram suggested to His Lordship that since their son, Reginald, was fast approaching manhood, someone should be telling him "about the birds and bees."

Lord Cribblesfram did not welcome discussion on matters so delicate, but he recognized a father's duty and so, that evening after dinner, he summoned his son to his study.

"Er . . . ahem . . . Reginald," he began uneasily, "Lady Cribblesfram and I both feel it is time you and I had a man-to-man talk on the subject of . . . uh . . . the birds and bees."

"Yes, pater," said Reginald brightly.

"Son, do you remember our trip to Paris last summer?"

"Yes, sir."

"And do you remember our visit to the Folies Bergère?"

"I do, pater."

"You will then, perhaps, remember our drinking with the two lovely ladies from the Folies?"

"I do, indeed, pater."

"And afterward, you remember our taking them to our hotel and what we did there?"

"Yes, sir."

"Well, son," said Lord Cribblesfram, wiping the perspiration from his brow, "it's very much like that with the birds and bees, too."

Lord Chesterfield made this rather wry commentary on *la grande passion*: *(1.)* The enjoyment is quite temporary. *(2.)* The cost is quite exorbitant. *(3.)* And the position is simply ridiculous.

Three Frenchmen were discussing the meaning of the word *savoir-faire*. The first explained, "If you come home and discover your wife in another man's arms and you say, 'Excuse me,' that's *savoir-faire*."

"No, no," said another who was slightly older and more experienced, "that's not quite right. If you come home and find your wife in another man's arms and you say, 'Excuse me, proceed,' that's *savoir-faire!*"

The third Frenchman was still older and wiser, and he said, with a smile, "I'm afraid neither of you really understands the full meaning of the word. If you come home and discover your wife in the arms of another man and you say, 'Excuse me, proceed,' and he proceeds, then *he* has *savoir-faire*."

The French executive was travelling home by rail from a Paris business conference. As he pulled aside the curtains of his berth, he discovered two beautiful girls there. A glance at their tickets told him that the girls were in the wrong car. Distressed, the beauties flashed their most melting smiles and asked if they might stay where they were.

"My dear ladies," explained the executive, "I am a married man, a pillar of my community, and scandal has never touched me. *One* of you," he concluded, "will have to leave."

Three French boys, ages eight, ten and twelve, were walking together down a Paris street and, passing an open window where a young bride and groom were consummating their marriage, stopped to watch. "Observe!" said the eight year old. "That lady and gentleman are fighting!"

"You are mistaken," said the ten year old, both older and more sophisticated than his comrade. "They are making love."

"*Oui,*" said the twelve year old. "And badly."

There was a young lady from France,
Who decided to just "take a chance."
For an hour or so,
She just "let herself go."
And now all her sisters are aunts.

With the world of Paris passing by their outdoor café, Gaston was explaining to Pierre the plot of *Lolita*, which he had just finished reading.

"It is an amazing book," Gaston said to his worldly friend. "It tells of a love affair between a middle-aged man and a twelve year old."

"*Ah!*" exclaimed Pierre. "A twelve-year-old *what?*"

A pair of good friends, Frenchmen both, were strolling down the Champs-Élysées one balmy afternoon when they spied two women approaching.

"*Sacré bleu,* Pierre," cried out the one in dismay. "Here come my wife and my mistress walking toward us arm in arm!"

"*Mon Dieu,* Henri," cried out the second. "I was about to say the very same thing!"

In Paris, everybody dates until the *oui* hours.

Two French *bons vivants* were relaxing over an after-dinner drink, following an especially enjoyable meal, when one, knowing of his friend's true appreciation for the grape, asked his dining companion, "*Dites-moi,* Paul, I am sure you would have no difficulty in eliminating song from your life, but what would you forgo if you were forced to choose between women and wine?"

Paul paused to inhale the bouquet of his cognac, then replied, "That, *mon ami,* would depend on their respective vintages."

For weeks the young man had answered correctly all the questions asked him on a television quiz show. His subject was lovemaking, and for his final question and a grand prize of a hundred thousand dollars he was allowed to call in an expert from France. The jackpot question was: If you had been a king during the first fifty years of the Babylonian Empire, which three parts of your bride's anatomy would you have been expected to kiss on your wedding night?

The contestant snapped off the first two answers without hesitation —"Her lips and her neck." When it came to choosing the third and final most kissable part of a new Babylonian queen, however, he turned to the Frenchman for help.

"*Mais,* do not ask me," said the expert. "I have been wrong twice already!"

The wealthy Frenchman's beautiful wife had died, and while the husband stoically controlled his grief throughout the funeral proceedings, the wife's lover sobbed loudly and made an open display of his loss. The husband observed this demonstration patiently and then, when the services were over, walked over to the younger man, put his arm around him and said sympathetically, "Don't be so upset, *mon ami.* I plan to marry again."

Two young French boys were talking about sex on their way home from the cinema when the younger member of the duo suddenly exclaimed, "As far as I can tell, *mon ami,* sex is just a big pain in the *derrière.*"

"*Quel dommage!*" sighed his older confrere. "You're doing it wrong."

A New York police captain was vacationing in Paris and decided to stop by the local *sûreté* office and spend the day acquainting himself with the latest in French crime-fighting techniques. After indulging in the usual amount of shoptalk with one of the French detectives assigned to welcome visiting law-enforcement officials, the New York cop asked, "What would you say is the most successful technique used by your country's police department?"

"Well, *monsieur,*" the Frenchman mused, "in France we 'ave ze saying '*Cherchez la femme,*' which in English means 'Find ze woman.' "

Not very impressed with this rather romantic bit of Gallic philosophizing, the New Yorker demanded, "Do you mean to sit there and tell me that you actually catch more crooks by merely chasing after women?"

"*Mais non, capitaine,*" came the reply. "But we 'ave ze happiest police force in all of Europe."

A noted French physician maintains that if a man consumes a glass of brandy after dinner each evening for twelve hundred months, he will live to be a hundred years old.

During a recent expedition into the wildest part of darkest Africa, a group of explorers came upon a village of primitive savages.

In an attempt to make friends, the leader of the explorers tried to tell the natives what it was like in the civilized, outside world.

"Out there," he said, "we love our fellow man."

To this, the natives gave a ringing cry of *"Huzzanga!"*

Encouraged by this, the explorer continued: "We treat others as we would want them to treat us!"

"Huzzanga!" exclaimed the natives, with much enthusiasm.

"We are peaceful!" said the explorer.

"Huzzanga!" cried the natives.

With a tear running down his cheek, the explorer ended his fine speech: "We come to you as friends, as brothers. So trust us. Open your arms to us, your houses, your hearts. What do you say?"

The air shook with one long, mighty "HUZZANGA!"

Greatly pleased by the reception, the leader of the explorers then began talking with the natives' chief.

"I see that you have cattle here," he said. "They are a species with which I'm unfamiliar. May I inspect them?"

"Certainly, come this way," said the chief. "But be careful not to step in the *huzzanga.*"

The bearded Cuban was describing his country to a U.S. women's club.

"Our most popular sport is bullfighting," he declared.

One matron, obviously upset at the thought of so bloody a spectacle, asked, "But isn't it revolting?"

"No," said the Cuban, smiling, "that is our second most popular sport."

The newly arrived Asian diplomat was being given a thorough tour of Washington nightlife by his State Department escort. After watching a group of young couples in a discothèque, the escort said, "I don't imagine you've ever seen anything quite like this in your country. Do you know what they're doing?"

"Yes," said the diplomat. "But why are they standing up?"

Seeing the sights of New York City via the Fifth Avenue bus, a very prim young lady was scandalized to hear an obviously newly immigrated man saying to an attentive companion:

"Emma coma first, I coma next, two assa coma together, I coma again, two assa coma together again, I coma once-a-more, pee-pee twice, then I coma for the lasta time."

The young lady was crimson-faced when he finished, and then, noticing a policeman seated nearby, she whispered to him, "Aren't you going to arrest that terrible old man?"

The policeman stared at her, genuinely bewildered, and said, "For spelling Mississippi?"

A Chinese Communist diplomat was having more than his share of troubles fielding questions thrown at him by a British newsman. "Next thing you'll be telling me," said the columnist, "is that China has elections."

The Oriental nodded gravely as he replied: "Ah, yes—you have analyzed China's biggest ploblem—too many elections evely night."

One of our foreign correspondents swears that he heard the following station break in Israel: "This is Radio Tel Aviv, 1500 on your AM dial, but for you, 1498."

When he arrived in Vietnam in the early 1960's, the American intelligence officer was surprised to see a Vietnamese riding a donkey —while his wife, loaded down with bundles, trudged along behind. Upset at the lack of chivalry, he approached the man and asked: "Why do you ride while your poor wife walks behind?"

"Custom," grunted the man, jogging past.

A few years later, the officer was visiting the same village and spied the man again—he was still riding the donkey, but now his wife preceded him down the road.

"You probably don't remember me," said the officer, "but you told me a few years ago that your wife walked behind you because of custom. But now I see she's in front. Why the change?"

"Land mines," came the reply.

You certainly have to hand it to the American woman, which is why so many guys prefer European girls.

The well-traveled executive returned from his trip to Italy and called a friend in New York to meet him for lunch. "Did you do anything exciting over there?" the friend asked.

"Oh, you know the old saying," the exec shrugged. "When in Rome, do as the Romans do."

"Well, exactly what did you *do?*" the friend persisted.

"What else?" the businessman replied. "I seduced an American schoolteacher."

An Italian cabdriver was telling a passenger that only real men like himself drive taxis in Rome. "We use our left hand for signals and our right to wave at women," he proclaimed.

His passenger finally asked, "But how do you steer?"

"I told you," the cabby shouted, "only *real* men drive taxis in Rome."

Then there was the Polynesian nymphomaniac who was always longing for Samoa.

Historians at the Aztec pyramids in Mexico have finally deciphered the last words of the famous emperor Montezuma, found inscribed upon an ancient scroll: "Will someone tell those damned Marines to stop singing in the halls?"

"Certainly, America has its problems," the pompous politician roared. "But we're still the only people in the world who are free to criticize our courts, our Congress and our President."

"That's what you think," the foreign diplomat retorted. "People all over the world are criticizing your courts, your Congress and your President."

It was her first trip to Hawaii and the middle-aged matron had noticed that several of her fellow passengers did not pronounce the island name as she had previously assumed it should be pronounced. Anxious not to offend the natives of our fiftieth state, she decided to approach the first islander she saw and said: "Excuse me, sir, but I wonder if you could tell me if it is pronounced Ha*w*aii or Ha*v*aii?"

"Havaii," the man responded.

"Thank you very much," said the grateful tourist.
"You're velcome!" said the man.

Then there was the Eskimo girl who spent the night with her boyfriend and next morning found she was six months pregnant.

In what they thought was a great propaganda coup, the Russian government sent an order to an American rubber company for a thousand gross of contraceptives, eighteen inches long and eight inches in circumference. The company filled the order, but countering propaganda with propaganda, labeled each container: MEDIUM.

A South American republic under a new regime decided its troops needed special uniforms. A tailor was called in and shown the design—fuchsia trousers, crimson boots, snow-white caps and orange jackets with gold epaulets.

"Is this to be the uniform for the president's palace guard?" inquired the admiring tailor.

"No," barked the officer in charge. "It's for the secret police."

"But how can you tell a Viet Cong from a patriotic South Vietnamese?" the nervous private asked the seasoned sergeant.

"Simple," the sergeant drawled. "You just holler, 'To hell with Ho Chi Minh!' and see how he reacts."

A few days later, while visiting the company hospital, the sergeant saw the private lying in a bed, badly battered. "What happened to you?" the sergeant asked. "Didn't you remember to do what I told you?"

"Sure I did," the private answered weakly. "I saw this guy coming out of the brush and I yelled, 'To hell with Ho Chi Minh!'"

"And what happened?"

"He yelled back, 'To hell with L. B. J.!'—and while we were standing in the middle of the clearing shaking hands, a tank ran over us."

The Alaskan miners were whooping it up in a Fairbanks bar and kidding a visiting Texan about his state now being the *second* biggest in the Union.

"Texas may no longer be the biggest state," said the Lone Star oilman, "but it's still the toughest!"

"Toughest?!" cried one of the miners, almost beside himself with laughter. "Why, up here in Alaska we don't consider a man a man unless he can down a fifth of whiskey in one pull at the bottle, wrestle a grizzly

bear with his bare hands and rape an Eskimo woman, all in one night!"

"There's nothing to that," said the oilman. "Any Texan worthy of the name could do that!" Whereupon, a wager was made on whether or not this particular Texan could prove himself by these prescribed Alaskan standards. He took a full fifth of whiskey and downed it without considerable trouble.

"All right," he said, "where do I find me a grizzly bear?"

The miners explained that the mountains surrounding the town were full of bears and that he would have no trouble finding one, so the Texan stalked out into the night, and the Alaskans returned to their drinking and merrymaking, convinced they had seen the last of their new acquaintance. But two hours later, lo and behold, the Texan came staggering back into the bar. His clothes were in shreds and his body a mass of bloody cuts and bruises. For a moment no one spoke, then the Texan said: "All right, now where's the Eskimo woman you want me to wrestle?"

13
WINING
& DINING

"How many beers does it take to make you dizzy?" he asked. "Four or five," she retorted, "and don't call me dizzy!"

The girl sitting daintily on the bar stool was luscious, shapely and tempting. Naturally, she aroused the interest of the playboy at the other end of the bar. He smiled at her. Then he winked. When this failed, he tried out his best leer. Just then the bartender—two hundred pounds of muscle with a hairy chest—leaned over the bar and said, "Look, Buster: that there's my wife. So cut the funny business, understand?"

Replied the flustered playboy: "Funny business? I don't know what you're talking about. I just dropped in for a cool drink. Give me a piece of beer."

A drunk and his inebriated friend were sitting at a bar.
"Do you know what time it is?" asked the drunk.
"Sure," said the friend.
"Thanks," said the drunk.

The connoisseur sat down at the bar and ordered a Martini. "Very dry," he insisted. "Twenty parts gin to one part vermouth."

"All right, sir," said the bartender. "Shall I twist a bit of lemon peel over it?"

"My good man, when I want lemonade, I'll ask for it."

Maybe you heard about the drunk who was staggering through the park and saw a young athlete practicing pushups. "Washamatter, Mac?" inquired the lush. "Lose your girl?"

We know a freeloving secretary who says that two Martinis usually make her feel like a new man.

The big city sporting houses were hard hit by the housing shortage. One of them became so crowded on busy nights that it was obliged to entertain some of its customers on the roof. On one such evening, a client and his charming hostess became so excited they fell off the top of the building. Still locked in love's embrace, they landed on the street with a thud, barely missing a passing drunk.

The drunk staggered up to the sporting house door and knocked loud and long.

"Beat it," said the Madam, through a slot in the door. "We don't allow no drunks in here."

"I don't wanna come in," said the drunk. "Jush wanted to tell ya your sign fell down."

It was a large, lavish dinner party and many important dignitaries and members of society were there.

"I suppose I mustn't offer you wine," said the hostess to the guest of honor seated on her right. "Aren't you the chairman of the Temperance League?"

"Oh, no," replied her guest with a smile, "I'm the head of the Anti-Vice League."

"Oh, of course," said the embarrassed hostess, "I knew there was something I shouldn't offer you."

One of our favorite bartenders told us about a very proper Englishman who came into his place a couple of weeks ago. The fellow sat down at the bar, but didn't order. The bartender, an unusually friendly guy, asked him if he couldn't fix him a drink, on the house.

The Englishman shook his head. "Tried liquor once," he said. "Didn't like it."

The bartender then offered the Englishman a cigarette.

"No thank you," he said. "Tried tobacco once. Didn't like it."

Still trying to be friendly, the bartender asked the Englishman if he would like to join a couple of friends seated at the bar in a few hands of poker.

The Englishman shook his head. "Tried gambling once. Didn't like it. I wouldn't be sitting in this place at all, but I promised my son I would meet him here."

"I see," said the bartender. "Your only child, I assume."

The switchboard operator in a swank New York hotel received a call at a little past two in the morning from a somewhat inebriated man who wanted to know what time the hotel bar opened.

"At nine A.M., sir," she replied.

At three-thirty A.M. the phone rang again and the same man, this time obviously feeling no pain, asked the same question.

"Not until nine A.M.," she said a second time.

At five-fifteen A.M. the switchboard operator received still another call from the same guy, now completely stoned. Once again he asked the same question.

More than a little irritated, she snapped, "I told you, sir, you'll have to wait until nine A.M. to get in the bar."

"*Get in*, hell," croaked the drunk, "I want to get *out* of the damn place!"

A table of improper measures we came upon the other day informs us that it takes two pints to make one cavort.

A friend has described a pink elephant as a beast of bourbon.

The two buddies had been out drinking for hours when their money finally ran out.

"I have an idea," croaked Al. "Lesh go over to my housh and borrow shum money from my wife."

The two of them reeled into Al's living room, snapped on the light, and, lo and behold, there was Al's wife making love on the sofa to another man. This state of affairs considerably unnerved Al's friend but didn't seem to affect the husband. "Shay, dear, you have any money for your ever lovin' hushban?" he asked. "Yes, yes," she snapped, "take my purse from the mantel and, for Pete's sake, turn off those lights." Outside they examined the purse, and Al proudly announced, "There's enough here for a pint for you and a pint for me. Pretty good eh, old buddy?" "But, Al," protested his friend somewhat sobered by the spectacle he'd just witnessed, "what about that fellow back there with your wife?" "The hell with him," replied Al, "let him buy his own pint."

The young man was determined to win his girl that evening.

"I have loved you more than you will ever know," he said.

"So I was right," she exclaimed, slapping him across the face. "You *did* take advantage of me last Saturday night when I was drunk!"

The wife of a friend of ours purchased a rather large grandfather clock at an auction and then sent her unhappy husband to pay for it and carry the damn thing home. To make matters worse, the husband had been to a formal dinner earlier in the evening and was still wearing his full dress suit. He was having some difficulty with the unwieldy mechanism even before he met the drunk staggering in the opposite direction. They collided and the husband fell backward to the sidewalk, the clock on top of him.

"Why in blazes don't you watch where you're going!" the angry husband demanded.

The drunk shook his head dazedly, looked at the man in the full dress suit and at the grandfather clock that lay across him.

"Why don't you wear a wrish watch like everybody elsh?" he inquired.

Two inebriated gentlemen stood at the bar near closing time.

"I've an idea," said one, "lesh have one more drink and then go find us shum girls."

"Naw," replied the other. "I've got more than I can handle at home."

"Great," replied the idea man, "then lesh have one more drink and go up to your place."

A rather inebriated fellow on a bus was tearing up a newspaper into tiny pieces and throwing them out the window.

"Excuse me," said the woman sitting next to him, "but would you mind explaining why you're tearing up that paper and throwing the pieces out the window?"

"It scares away the elephants," said the drunk.

"I don't see any elephants," said the woman, smiling.

"Effective isn't it?" said the drunk.

After gunning his Mercedes the wrong way down a one-way street, the rather inebriated young man was asked where he thought he was going by an inquisitive police officer.

"I'm not really sure," confessed the drunk, "but wherever it is, I must be late, because everybody seems to be coming back already."

The father, passing through his son's college town late one evening on a business trip, thought he would pay his boy a surprise visit.

Arriving at the lad's fraternity house, dad rapped loudly on the door. After several minutes of knocking, a sleepy voice drifted down from a second floor window, "Waddyah want?"

"Does Ramsey Duncan live here?" asked the father.

"Yeah," replied the voice. "Dump him on the front porch."

A man-about-bistros we know assures us that he has no trouble leaping out of bed as soon as the first ray of sunshine enters his window. Of course, he adds, his window faces west.

We know a bartender who says that water is a fine drink if taken with the right spirit.

Quaffing at his favorite bar one afternoon, the gentleman was particularly struck by the odd behavior of a man three stools down. As fast as the bartender could serve him, he was tossing off hookers of bourbon. Becoming alarmed, the gentleman moved over to the compulsive imbiber and asked, "What kind of a way is that to drink good bourbon?"

"It's the only way I can drink it since my accident," the man replied, throwing down two more shots in fast order.

"What kind of an accident was that?"

The man guzzled another one, shuddered and then answered, "I once knocked over a drink with my elbow."

We were somewhat startled the other evening to spot an obviously sozzled gentleman feeling his way around and around a lamppost and muttering, "S'no use, I'm walled in."

"Are you sure this is your house?" the cop asked the thoroughly sozzled gentleman.

"Shertainly," said the drunk, "and if you'll jush open the door f 'me, I'll prove it to you.

"You shee that piano?" the drunk began. "Thash mine. You shee that television set? Thash mine, too. Follow me, follow me."

The police officer followed as he shakily negotiated the stairs to the second floor. The drunk pushed open the first door they came to.

"Thish ish my bedroom," he announced. "Shee that bed? Thash my bed. Shee that woman lying in the bed? Thash my wife. An' shee that guy lying next to her?"

"Yeah," said the cop suspiciously.

"Thash *me!*"

As the cop helped the bruised and battered bibber up from the pavement in front of the bar, he asked, "Can you describe the man who hit you?"

"Oh, yes," said the drunk. "That's just what I was doing when he hit me."

"What's that drink you're mixing?" the stranger asked the bartender in the exotic Caribbean bar.

"I call this a rum dandy," said the bartender.

"What's in it?" asked the stranger.

"Sugar, milk and rum," said the barkeep.

"Is it good?" asked the stranger.

"Sure," said the bartender. "The sugar gives you pep, the milk gives you energy."

"And the rum?" asked the stranger.

"Ideas about what to do with all that pep and energy."

He offered her a Scotch and sofa, and she reclined.

The six fraternity men came weaving out of the off-campus gin mill and started to crowd themselves into the Volkswagen for the rollicking ride back home. One of them, obviously the house president, took charge of the situation. "Herbie," he said, "you drive. You're too drunk to sing."

Staggering into his apartment, the bibber deposited himself in his bed and fell asleep. A half hour later he was awakened by a knock on the door. Wearily he struggled out of bed and, stumbling over almost every piece of furniture in the room, made his way to the door and opened it. Standing there was his drinking companion of an hour before.

"Gee, I'm sorry I woke you up, Joe," said the companion.

"Oh, that's all right," said Joe. "I had to answer the door anyway."

Harry stepped out of his office building and bumped into a group of his advertising-agency friends.

"Join us for lunch, Harry boy?" asked one of them.

"Sorry," was the answer. "I'm on the wagon."

A man who looked like a high-powered business executive began to drop in at Milton's Bar regularly, and his order was always the same: two Martinis. After several weeks of this, Milton asked him why he didn't order a double instead of always ordering two singles.

"It's a sentimental thing," the customer answered. "A very dear friend of mine died a few weeks ago, and before his death he asked that when I drink, I have one for him, too."

A week later, the customer came in and ordered only one Martini.

"How about your dead buddy?" Milton asked. "Why only one Martini today?"

"This is my buddy's drink," the man said as he gulped the Martini down. "I'm on the wagon."

These days the necessities of life cost you about three times what they used to, and half the time you find they aren't even fit to drink.

Upon leaving a hotel bar one evening, an executive friend of ours noticed a drunk sitting on the edge of a potted palm in the lobby, crying like a baby. Because our friend had had a couple himself that night and was feeling rather sorry for his fellow man, he asked the inebriated one what the trouble was.

"I did a terrible thing tonight," sniffled the drunk. "I sold my wife to a guy for a bottle of Scotch."

"That is terrible," said our friend, too much under the weather to muster any real indignation. "And now that she's gone, you wish you had her back."

"Thas right," said the drunk, still sniffling.

"You're sorry you sold her, because you realize too late that you love her," sympathized our friend.

"No, no," said the drunk. "I wish I had her back because I'm thirsty again."

A gravedigger, thoroughly absorbed in his work, dug a pit so deep one afternoon that he couldn't climb out when he had finished. Come nightfall and evening's chill, his predicament became more uncomfortable. He shouted for help and at last attracted the attention of a drunk staggering by.

"Get me out of here," the digger pleaded. *"I'm cold!"*

The inebriated one peered into the open grave and finally spotted the shivering digger in the darkness.

"Well, no wonder you're cold, buddy," said the drunk, kicking some of the loose sod into the hole. "You haven't got any dirt on you."

Some people have no respect for age unless it's bottled.

A castaway was washed ashore after many days on the open sea. The island on which he landed was populated by savage cannibals who tied him, dazed and exhausted, to a thick stake. They then proceeded to cut his arms with their spears and drink his blood.

This continued for several days until the castaway could stand no more. He yelled for the cannibal king and declared, "You can kill me if you want to, but this torture with the spears has got to stop. Dammit, I'm tired of being stuck for the drinks."

Discovering too late that a watermelon spiked with vodka had accidentally been served to a luncheon meeting of local ministers, the restaurant's owner waited nervously for the clerics' reaction.

"Quick, man," he whispered to his waiter, "what did they say?"

"Nothing," said the waiter. "They were all too busy slipping the seeds into their pockets."

As soon as most women have a drink or two, they start looking for a chaser.

Having wandered helplessly into a blinding snowstorm, Sam, a notorious drinker, was greatly relieved to see a sturdy Saint Bernard dog bounding toward him with a keg of brandy strapped to his collar.

"At last," cried Sam, "man's best friend—and a great big dog, too!"

The voluptuous blonde was chatting with her handsome escort in a posh restaurant when their waiter, stumbling as he brought their drinks, dumped a Martini on the rocks down the back of the blonde's dress. She sprang to her feet with a shriek, dashed wildly around the table, then galloped wriggling from the room followed by her distraught boyfriend. A man seated on the other side of the room with a date of his own beckoned to the waiter and said, "We'll have *two* of whatever *she* was drinking."

A friend of ours has come up with the David and Goliath cocktail —a small one and you're stoned.

"I hate to go golfing with any of the executives from my own agency," complained the advertising prexy, while relaxing with his fourth Scotch and soda at the clubhouse bar. "Every time I yell 'Fore' they chime in with—he's a jolly good fellow!"

The large, burly man approached the bartender and said, "I see by the sign in your window that you're looking for a bouncer. Has the job been filled yet?"

"Not yet," said the bartender. "Have you had any experience?"

"No," the man admitted, "but watch this!" He walked over to a loudmouthed drunk at the back of the room, lifted him off his feet, and threw him sprawling out into the street. Then, returning to the bar, he said, "How's that?"

"Great!" admitted the bartender. "But you'll have to ask the boss about the job. I only work here."

"Fine," said the burly man. "Where is he?"
"Just coming back in the front door."

A modern motto explaining the gentle art of conquest: Ply now, Play Later.

An irate *carabiniere* was in the process of arresting an inebriated young Roman who decided to take a nap in the middle of the Via Veneto. "It's my duty to warn you," he said sternly, "that anything you say will be held against you."
"Sophia Loren," whispered the drunk, and passed out.

Passing a cemetery in the wee hours of the morning, a drunk noticed a sign that read, RING THE BELL FOR THE CARETAKER. He did just that, and a sleepy-eyed man staggered to the gate. "What do you want at this hour?" the man demanded.
The drunk looked the caretaker over for a minute and then retorted, "I want to know why you can't ring the damn bell yourself!"

Some girls are discreet up to a point, and some are discreet up to a pint.

Two drunks wandered into a zoo and as they staggered past a lion's cage, the king of beasts let out a terrific roar.

"C'mon, let's get out of here," said the first drunk.

"You go ahead if you want to," replied his more inebriated cohort. "I'm gonna stay for the movie!"

The inebriated university professor staggered into the bar and asked the bartender for a dry Martinus.

"Beg your pardon, sir," the bartender replied, "but do you mean a Martini?"

"Now see here, my good man," exclaimed the ninety-proof prof. "If I want two, I'll ask for them."

A millionaire we know has filled his swimming pool with Martinis. He claims it's impossible to drown, since the deeper you sink, the higher you get.

"Happy New Year, everybody!" the drunk shouted as he staggered into a small neighborhood bar.

"For your information, buddy," said the somewhat irritated bartender, "today is the first of April."

"April!" exclaimed the bewildered bibber. "Why, my wife will kill me for being out on a bender this long."

It was almost midnight and the attractive, well-stacked woman had been standing at the bus stop for over half an hour, obviously several Martinis past her limit, when up drove a personable-appearing chap with an offer of transportation home. Sliding into the seat beside him, the inebriated miss managed to mumble her address, then slumped drowsily against the fellow's shoulder. Responding to the opportunity, the driver wrapped his free arm around his pretty passenger and pressed her closer to him, proceeding with as personal an appraisal of the terrain as possible without taking his eyes off the road, or his other hand off the wheel.

At first she seemed oblivious to what was going on, but then she came to life, exclaiming, "Man, you're passionate!"

Quite naturally flattered by this apparent reference to his romantic technique, he attempted to take further liberties and was promptly greeted with a stinging slap across the face. Stopping the car abruptly, he turned to her angrily and said: "Look, lady, on the one hand you tell me how passionate I am and with the other you smack me. Why don't you make up your mind?"

"I don't know what you're talkin' about, mishter," came the slurred reply, "but all I was referring to was my house—I said you're pashin' it!"

A new organization has been formed, called Athletics Anonymous. When you get the urge to play golf, baseball or any other game involving physical activity, they send someone over to drink with you until the urge passes.

A pair of intoxicated pals were seated in their favorite bar imbibing their favorite libation.

"I think I'll have a bite to eat," said the first inebriated fellow. Whereupon, he plucked the olive from his Martini and ate it.

"Ah," said his sozzled companion, "that calls for an after-dinner drink!"

A pair of inebriated strangers struck up a friendly conversation at a bar and the subject soon got around to sex, as it usually does.

"Say," said the first fellow, smirking, "have you ever been so drunk that you kissed a woman on the navel?"

With a mighty effort, the second sot propped himself up and said, "Drunker."

One of our favorite drinks is a French eggnog—two egg yolks, two teaspoons of sugar and four jiggers of cognac in a tall, warm lass.

The young man stepped up to the bar and ordered a Manhattan. The bartender returned shortly with the drink, in which floated a piece of parsley.

"What's that?" he asked, pointing to the glass.

"A Manhattan," replied the bartender. "Isn't that what you ordered?"

"Well, yes," said the young man. "But what's *that?*" He pointed to the parsley.

"Oh, that," explained the bartender, "that's Central Park."

The elegantly dressed gentleman entered the sumptuously appointed cocktail lounge. After surveying the many patrons gathered there, he motioned for silence and called, "Bartender, I'd like the opportunity of buying a drink for everyone in the place."

After a brief pause, he added, "And please have one yourself." This generosity was hailed and toasted by one and all.

After downing his own drink and bidding everyone adieu, the fine fellow started for the door. His progress was interrupted by the slightly embarrassed bartender. "I hate to bother you, sir," he began, "but the tab comes to two hundred dollars. . . ."

"So what are you bothering me for? I don't have as much as a penny," replied the gentleman.

Realizing that a cruel hoax had been perpetrated upon him, the enraged bartender seized the brash fellow, beat him sharply about the head and shoulders and threw him into the street.

The following afternoon, the bartender was amazed to see the same man come into the lounge. The deadbeat stopped and motioned once again for silence. As a hush fell over the crowd, he snapped his fingers and shouted, "Bartender, drinks for everyone. That is, everyone but *you*—I've seen the way you act when you get a drink in you."

Storming into the frontier saloon, the fervid temperance evangelist boomed: "Repent, you vile sinners! Drinking that noxious fluid will send you all to hell. Join with me—all of you who want to go to heaven stand on this side."

All but one drunk staggered to his side. To the holdout, the evangelist shouted: "Don't you want to go to heaven?"

"No, I don't," replied the drunk.

"You mean to tell me that you don't want to go to heaven when you die?" asked the astonished evangelist.

"Oh," the drunk replied, "when I *die*. I thought you were making up a load right now."

The libidinous miss listened patiently as her married sister extolled the benefits of the quiet life. "That's not for me," she playfully commented. "I once tried to give up drinking, smoking and sex—and it was the longest twenty minutes I ever spent."

Never pour black coffee into an intoxicated person. If you do, you'll wind up with a wide-awake drunk on your hands.

A well-dressed but obviously inebriated gentleman stumbled up to a policeman at a busy downtown intersection and voiced a thick-tongued complaint. "Somebody stole my car, officer," he announced groggily. "I had it right here on the end of my ignition key."

"We'll go right to the station and report it," the patrolman replied, amused at the fellow's drunken condition. "But I think you should zip your trousers before we leave."

"Oh, my God," blubbered the drunk, noticing his open fly. "Somebody's stole my girl, too."

Don't drink when you drive. You might hit a bump and spill it.

A well-dressed gentleman seated at the bar was quietly guzzling Martinis. After finishing each one, he carefully ate the glass and arranged the stems in a neat row. The ninth time this occurred, the bartender could stand it no longer and commented to another customer, "There's a guy who's absolutely nuts."

"He sure is," agreed the other man. "The stems are the best part."

An acquaintance of ours has discovered a sure-fire way to avoid a hangover—keep drinking.

Several members of a temperance league approached a ninety-year-old teetotaler for a testimonial declaring that his longevity was due to a life of abstention from alcohol. The old gentleman said he would be pleased to sign such a statement and was in the process of making his mark when sounds of a riotous party came from an adjacent room. "My God, what's that?" gasped one of the visitors.

"Oh, that's just my dad," the teetotaler laughed. "He's probably getting drunk again."

"Just look at me," declared the robust oldtimer. "I don't smoke, drink or chase women and tomorrow I'll celebrate my eightieth birthday."

"You will?" asked a curious friend. "How?"

A new housekeeper, accused of helping herself to the master's liquor when he was absent, waxed indignant. "I'll have you know, sir," she declared hotly, "that I come from honest English parents."

"I'm not concerned with your English parents," countered the master. "What's worrying me is your Scotch extraction."

A fat man was seated on his front steps drinking a can of beer when a busybody spinster from down the street began to berate him for his appearance.

"What a disgusting sight," she said. "If that belly was on a woman, I'd swear she was pregnant."

To which the man simply smiled and replied, "Madam, it *was* and she *is*."

He did not drink, or smoke, or swear,
His morals were not bad;
Nor did he live a century—
He only felt he had.

At the inquest the coroner gently asked the widow if she could remember her late husband's last words.

"Yes," she replied. "He said, 'I don't see how they make a profit out of this stuff at a dollar and a quarter a fifth.' "

It was Tracy's first crossing, and he was assigned to a table with a suave Frenchman. The first night out, the Frenchman rose, bowed slightly, and said, *"Bon appétit."*

Tracy got to his feet, bowed and said, "Tracy."

The following morning, at breakfast, then at lunch and again at dinner, the ceremony was repeated and Tracy found his politeness wearing a little thin. "It's beginning to annoy me," he told a companion in the lounge. "Same thing over and over: he tells me his name, *Bon appétit*, I tell him mine and we do it all over again at the next meal."

His companion, a bit more worldly than Tracy, laughed. "He's not introducing himself. *Bon appétit* is French for 'good appetite.' He's hoping that you enjoy your meal."

Tracy felt pretty silly. The next morning when he appeared at breakfast, the Frenchman was already seated. Tracy bowed and said, *"Bon appétit."* Whereupon the Frenchman jumped up, bowed and answered, "Tracy."

They made an engaging-looking couple in the swank restaurant: Prentiss—handsome, graying, obviously well to do, and young Margaret —ravishing, delectable and obviously hungry.

"Tell me, my dear," he asked indulgently, "what would you like?"

She scanned the menu with an experienced eye.

"To begin," she said, "you may bring me a champagne cocktail, then a dozen oysters on the half shell and a tureen of turtle soup. As entrees I'll have the filet of English sole followed by the pheasant under glass. Baked potato with sour cream and chives, plus an à la carte order of asparagus would be nice, too. And I'll have French dressing on the salad. For dessert I'd like a great big double order of chocolate ripple ice cream, some blueberry pie and a cup of coffee. That should do it."

Somewhat taken aback, Prentiss nevertheless managed a smile as he asked, "Do you eat this well at home?"

Margaret favored him with a lazy grin.

"No," she said. "But then, nobody at home wants to sleep with me."

A gourmet friend of ours advises that when preparing a dish for bedtime, champagne makes the best tenderizer.

Two cannibals were chatting over lunch. One said, "You know, I just can't stand my mother-in-law."

"Forget about her," the other replied, "just eat the noodles!"

14
BOYS & GIRLS TOGETHER

A business friend was trying to convince us the other day that sex is so popular because it's centrally located.

The mother entered the darkened room unexpectedly and found daughter and boyfriend in passionate embrace on the sofa.

"Well—I never!" exclaimed mother.

"But, mother, you must have!" said daughter.

We've just received the results of a survey conducted to ascertain the various reasons men get out of bed in the middle of the night. According to the report, 2% are motivated by a desire to visit the bathroom and 3% have an urge to raid the refrigerator.

The other 95% get up to go home.

Everyone was surprised when fastidious, virginal Percy lispingly announced his intention to wed. "What, *you*, Percy?" was the amazed reaction. Some skeptics made bets that he wouldn't go through with it, but Percy fooled them. He even went on a honeymoon. Upon his return, one of the losers bitingly asked, "Well, is your wife pregnant?"

"I certainly hope so," said Percy with great sincerity. "I wouldn't want to go through *that* again!"

A socially prominent dowager from Boston was visiting friends in New York and a dinner party was held in her honor. She was seated next to another, younger woman, and began discussing the relative merits of Boston society.

"In Boston," she said, "we place all our emphasis on good breeding."

"In New York we think it's a lot of fun, too," agreed the other woman, "but we also manage to foster other interests."

The opera singer Giovanni Rotondo, star of the Metropolitan during its Golden Age, is credited with making the following common-sense statement: "It is not wise to make love in the morning—you never know whom you'll meet later in the day."

"Your Honor," said the husband suing for divorce, "my wife beats me."
"And just how often does she beat you?" queried the judge.
"She beats me every time, Your Honor."

Our tireless Research Department, after extensive house-to-house canvassing, has come up with the three best things in life: a Martini before and a nap after.

"How is it I find you making love to my daughter?" stormed the outraged father. "I ask you, young man, how is it?!"
"Why, just great, sir," replied the calm young man, "just great!"

The expectant father paced the hospital waiting room.
"Say, this is our first child," he said to the relaxed veteran slouched in the corner reading a newspaper. "How long do you have to wait, after the baby is born, before you can—uh—resume marital relations with your wife?"
"Well, that depends," said the seasoned sire, "on whether she's in a ward or a private room."

He held her close against him, a warm glow of satisfaction covering them both.
"Am I the first man you've ever made love to?" he asked.
She studied him reflectively. "You might be," she said. "Your face looks very familiar."

The moon shone silver on the waters of the lake, and the waves beating on the shore were hardly equal in intensity to the waves of passion nearby. One ardent couple pulled apart long enough for the young man to whisper, "Darling, am I the first man to make love to you?"
Her tone, when she answered, was irritable. "Of course you are," she said. "I don't know why you men always ask the same ridiculous question."

"You can never tell about men," the sophisticated miss advised her younger sister. "Either they're so slow you want to scream, or so fast you have to."

His apartment was his living quarters and laboratory combined, Sam, the brilliant young inventor, explained to his friend as he showed him around the premises. With an uncharacteristic flourish, he drew back the velvet curtains enclosing a cozy alcove. There, stretched out on a divan, was a dazzling blonde, as nubile and as nude as any the visitor had ever seen. In her hand she held a glass, empty except for two ice cubes.

"This is my latest and greatest invention," the genius beamed proudly. "I call it instant sex. You just add Scotch."

To most modern writers, sex is a novel idea.

Sally and Hortense were busy, in the age-old manner of secretaries on their lunch hour, gabbing and gobbling at the same time. The subject was men, and strangely enough it was Hortense, the plainer of the two, who was doing the talking.

"I tell you, Sally," she said excitedly, her eyes sparkling, "he's the only guy in my whole life who's made me feel this way. Oh, the touch of his hand, the sound of his voice, the—"

"You certainly sound pretty far gone on him," Sally interrupted amusedly.

"Oh yes," said Hortense brightly. "This time it's the real thing—*sex.*"

The 6:07 commuter's train was quite late in leaving for its exurban destination, and Hank and Mack were enjoying their wait in the station bar. They had, in fact, been drinking long enough to have reached the stage of semimaudlin confession about their sex life.

"You know," Hank said, "I never had any relations with my wife at all before we were married. Did you?"

Mack reflected with what, under the circumstances, was admirable sobriety. "Gee," he finally said, "I dunno. What was her maiden name?"

Chivalry has changed from the days of Sir Walter Raleigh, but contrary to rumor, it hasn't died out altogether: A man will still lay his coat at the feet of a pretty girl; the difference is that nowadays it's intended to keep her back from getting dirty.

Making love to a woman too many times is like scratching a place that doesn't itch any more.

Girls believe in love at first sight; men believe in it at first opportunity.

They moved apart as Frank lit their cigarettes; then she snuggled close to him again and pulled the bedsheets up around their chins.

"Darling," she cooed, "how many others were there before me?"

After a few minutes of silence, she said, with a slight pout: "Well, I'm still waiting!"

"Well," he replied, puffing thoughtfully, "I'm still counting."

A wise man has observed that people who live in glass houses shouldn't.

A small group of scientists had spent an enlightening week on Mars, comparing life there with our own.

"Tell me," one Earth scientist asked his Martian counterpart, "just how do you reproduce the species here on this planet?"

"I shall be pleased to demonstrate," replied the leader of the Martian group, and he called forth a voluptuous Martian beauty with three heads. They then engaged their tentacles for a few moments, and almost at once a small pouch began to form on the female's back; it grew, and within little more than a minute, it opened up very much like a blooming flower and a small Martian dropped out, as fully developed as the adults, but much smaller, and began scampering about the room.

Once the Earth scientists had recovered from this unexpected experience, they attempted to explain how procreation differs in our world. The Martians insisted upon being shown, and after unsuccessful attempts to dissuade them, the chief scientist of the expedition finally agreed. Choosing a comely scientific aide from the group, he took her to a cot in the corner of the room and there proceeded to make love to her in a manner to which we here on Earth are more accustomed.

The Martians examined the couple from every angle, and when they were finished, their leader said, "That was certainly unusual and I must say, interesting, but where is the baby—or was the demonstration a failure?"

"It is difficult to say," replied the Earth scientist. "We cannot tell at once. But if the contact was successful, then the baby will arrive in approximately nine months."

"*Nine months!*" exclaimed the Martian. "Amazing. But tell us then,

Doctor, if the Earth child will not be born for nine months, why were you in such a hurry there at the end?"

"**W**asn't it lovely out there on the lake?" the young man said to his date as they were returning from the canoe ride.

With a happy sigh she replied, "It's lovely anyplace."

We know a nearsighted girl who can't tell her friends until they're on top of her.

> *Mary had a little sheep,*
> *And with the sheep she went to sleep.*
> *The sheep turned out to be a ram—*
> *Mary had a little lamb.*

We don't for a minute believe it, but we have a friend who insists that he recently met a girl who is so naïve that when he asked her if she knew the difference between a Caesar salad and sexual intercourse she said she had no idea.

"Did you explain it to her?" we asked.

"Hell no," said our friend. "But I have lunch with her every day."

Harry had proudly demonstrated his new ultracompact sports car to his date of the evening and had spun the little wonder to a halt on a lonely country road. After a considerable amount of amorous preliminaries, his girl coyly jumped out of the car and headed for a mossy spot nearby. Noticing that Harry wasn't following, she turned and said, "Hurry and get out of the car before I get out of the mood."

Harry struggled for a minute, then mournfully said, "Until I get out of the mood I *can't* get out of the car!"

A famed, but particularly succinct, psychiatrist had been invited to address an international conclave of his fellows on the subject of sex. When the day for his speech came, the amphitheater was packed and scores of reporters sat waiting at the press desk as the great, solemn man strode to the podium. A hush fell over the crowd as he adjusted his glasses and sipped a bit of water. Then he looked up and said in a firm, clear voice, "Gentlemen, it gives me great pleasure" . . . and sat down.

Boasting Sam, one of the worst braggarts who ever bent a bar rail, was loudly lamenting that his doctor had ordered him to give up half of his sex life.

"Which half are you going to give up?" asked a weary listener. "Talking about it or thinking about it?"

"Do you smoke after sex?" the gentleman asked.

"I really don't know," the sophisticated lady replied. "I've never looked to see."

Any girl who believes that the way to a man's heart is through his stomach is obviously setting her standards too high.

People who live in glass houses should ball in the basement.

When Ali, the sheik's most devoted eunuch, died unexpectedly in the middle of the night, the potentate's teen-aged son asked his father how this unhappy event had come to pass.

"My son," said the sheik, "Ali's death teaches us a valuable lesson. Last night, upon retiring, I commanded him to hasten to my harem and select for my pleasure the one most beautiful among the hundred houris waiting there. He returned with surprising swiftness with a ravishing brunette, but this tasty morsel merely whetted my appetite for further amour, so I summoned Ali again and told him to fetch forth the most sensual female of the harem. This time he returned even more quickly—though the harem is a considerable distance from my quarters, as you know—with a female whose hair was red as flame, with a passion to match.

"This erotic creature further increased my desire and I instructed Ali to have the most innocent maiden he could find brought to my bedchamber; he reappeared soon after, short of breath and perspiring from his efforts in my behalf, with a honey blonde who was the very image of innocence.

"So it went throughout most of the night—with a fourth, fifth, sixth and seventh—faithful Ali scurrying back and forth between harem and bedchamber again, and again, and again, and again, until he dropped dead at my feet. . . ."

"And what is the valuable lesson to be learned from all this?" the perplexed son of the potentate wanted to know.

"There's no harm in sex," said the sheik with a wise smile; "it's the running after it that can kill you!"

The model climbed up the ladder,
As Titian, the painter, had bade her.
Till her position, to Titian,
Suggested coition.
So he climbed up the ladder and had her.

Shortly after his spaceship landed on the moon, the astronaut debarked and began exploring the strange new terrain. He had walked for only fifteen minutes when he came upon a lovely young moon girl, who was busily stirring an empty pot with a stick.

"Hi," he said, introducing himself, "I'm an astronaut here to discover things about the moon."

The moon girl stopped stirring long enough to throw him quite a pleasant smile. "How nice it is that you are formed just like our moon men," she observed. Throwing off her clothes, she asked, "And am I structured as are earth women?"

"Yes, you are," answered the now-excited astronaut. "But tell me, why do you stir that pot?"

"I'm making a baby," she said. And sure enough, a few minutes later, a baby appeared in the pot.

"Now would you like to see how we make babies on earth?" asked the astronaut. The girl agreed and the astronaut proceeded with his passionate demonstration.

"That was enjoyable," she said afterward, "but where is the baby?"

"Oh, that takes nine months," explained the astronaut.

"Nine months?" she asked. "Then why did you stop stirring?"

The strapping Australian farm boy on his first visit to Melbourne explained to a streetwalker he'd just met, "Ma run off when I was just a little critter, so there weren't no one to raise me 'ceptin' Pa. He taught me most of what I need to know, but he said I'd have to come to the city to learn about women, so I'd be obliged if you'd teach me that."

The sympathetic prostitute took the farm boy to her apartment. She told him to get undressed and then she went into an adjoining room and changed from her street clothes into a filmy black negligee. When she returned, she found all of her furniture stacked against the walls, the carpet rolled back and the young man stripped and squatting in the middle of the bare floor.

"What's going on here?" she demanded.

The young man explained, "I don't know how it is with a woman, but I figured if it's anything like kangaroos, we'd be needing plenty of room."

A philosophical friend of ours points out that at cocktail parties the men usually stand around getting stiff, and the women are usually tight, but when they get home they frequently find that neither is either.

As Sunday approached, the middle-aged minister grew slightly desperate, for he could think of no suitable subject for his sermon. When his wife suggested that he be original and preach on water-skiing, he decided he would do it.

Sunday came and the minister's wife—ill with a virus—remained at home. As the minister drove to church, his doubts about parables found in water-skiing increased. Finally, he decided to abandon the subject entirely, and instead, delivered a brilliant extemporaneous sermon on sex.

Later in the week, a matron of the church met the minister's wife in the supermarket and complimented her on her husband's magnificent talk.

"Where on earth did he ever get all that information?" she asked. "He seemed so positive and sure of himself."

"I'm sure I don't know," the minister's wife replied. "He only tried it twice and fell off both times."

A bachelor friend tells us the only thing better than the sleep of the just is the sleep of the just-after.

Awakening the morning after the orgy, the god of war was stretching sleepily when he noticed a lovely Valkyrie standing in the doorway.

"Good morning," he said. "I'm Thor."

"*You're* thor?" she replied. "*I'm* tho thor I can hardly pith."

Never make love on an empty stomach," admonishes a playboy we know. "Take her out to dinner first."

"I'm beat," confessed the pretty career girl to her friend. "Last night I didn't fall asleep until after three."

"No wonder you're tired," her friend replied. "Twice is usually all I need."

A young man drove his date into the Hollywood hills in search of a suitable spot for a sexual interlude. They got out of the car, but the girl had reservations about making love in the open, so the boy suggested they crawl under the car, where no one could possibly see them. They were locked in passionate embrace when an authoritative voice demanded to know what the hell they thought they were doing.

Without looking up, the young man answered, "Fixing the transmission."

"Oh, yeah," snapped the cop. "Well, you'd better fix your brakes, too. Your car is at the bottom of the hill."

"It's really true," exclaimed the satisfied miss to the man beside her. "Nice guys finish last."

"Isn't the moon lovely?" she sighed.

"If you say so," answered her date. "Personally, I'm in no position to say."

The distinguished-looking gentleman asked the department-store floorwalker where one might purchase some personal stationery. He was directed to the notions department on the third floor, but in the crowded elevator he became confused and got off on the fourth floor by mistake. Approaching a sexy salesgirl standing near the elevator doors, he said, "Excuse me, miss, but do you have notions?"

"Sure," she replied, blinking her big eyes suggestively, "but I try to suppress them until after five o'clock."

"No, no, you don't understand," he stammered. "I mean to say, do you keep stationery?"

"Right up until the end," replied the salesgirl, "and then I just go all to pieces."

"Mother," the sweet young thing asked, "remember when you told me the way to a man's heart was through his stomach?"

"Yes, dear," the mother answered.

"Well," the girl went on, "last night I found a new route."

A Chicago salesman on a business trip to Boston had a few hours to kill before catching a plane home. Remembering an old friend's advice to try some broiled scrod, a favorite fish in Boston, he hopped into a cab and asked the driver: "Say, do you know where I could get scrod around here?"

"Pal," replied the cabby, "I've heard that question a thousand times, but this is the first time in the pluperfect subjunctive."

In an English-lit course on D. H. Lawrence, the professor requested an attractive but not overly bright coed to explain the difference between fornication and adultery.

"Well," she stammered, "I've tried them both, and they seem about the same."

After several unsuccessful advances, the bachelor asked his alluring but standoffish date: "Do you shrink from making love?"

"If I did," she sighed, "I'd be a midget."

"Am I the first man who ever asked you to make love with him?" inquired the bachelor.

"Yes," answered his attractive date. "All the others did it without asking."

A waggish friend of ours explains that the difference between being hard up, and down and out, is about two minutes.

Unable to manage his rebellious girlfriend, the young man asked his father how he had dealt with similar problems. "Well, son," the father frankly replied, "every time your mother began to act up, I'd take down her pants and spank her."

"I tried that," said the boy, "but by the time I get my girl's pants down, I'm not mad at her anymore."

The captain of the football team walked into the athletic office to see the coach. "Would you like to tell me your problem?" the pretty student receptionist asked. "I'll need the information for your school record."

"It's rather embarrassing," the athlete stammered. "You see, I have a very large and almost constant erection."

"Well, the coach is very busy today," she cooed, "but maybe I can squeeze you in."

Then there was the zealous fellow who recruited girls for the sexual revolution and then spent the first three weeks drilling the platoon.

Having been rudely awakened by screams in the night, the husband turned groggily to his wife and mumbled, "What's that noise?"

"It sounds like the woman next door is having a fit," she replied.

"Yeah," he agreed, "and a tight one, at that."

Upon taking a seat at the bar, the exec noticed that each stool had a number painted on it. Sitting next to him was a rather depressed-looking gentleman and an attractive blonde who was obviously enjoying herself. The newcomer turned toward the unhappy fellow and asked if he knew the purpose of the numbers.

"Sure," answered the chap. "Every half hour, the bartender spins a wheel and whoever has the winning seat gets to go upstairs for the wild sex orgy they have up there."

"That's terrific!" exclaimed the surprised customer. "Have you won?"

"Not yet," shot back the man, "but my date has—four times in a row."

The sign on the church lawn announced in bold letters: IF TIRED OF SIN, COME IN.

Under it, written in lipstick, was the message: "If not, call Park 4-6898."

"Is it a sin to have sexual relations before receiving Communion?" the young woman asked her pastor.

"Only if you block the aisle," he replied.

The newly ordained young priest asked his monsignor a favor: Would the older and more experienced man audition the young man's handling of confessions, and give him a candid critique? The monsignor agreed, and at the end of the day called the priest to give his verdict.

"Quite good, on the whole," he said. "But I do have a suggestion. I'd have preferred to hear a few more 'Tsk! Tsk! Tsk!' and fewer 'Oh, wows!'"

A young man met his ex-wife at a party and after a few drinks, he suggested that they have another try at marriage.

"Over my dead body," she sneered.

He downed his drink, and replied, "I see you haven't changed a bit."

On an isolated stretch of beach near Cannes, a beautiful French girl threw herself into the sea and drowned despite a young man's attempt to save her. The man dragged the half-nude body ashore and left it on the sand while he went to notify the authorities. Upon his return, he was horrified to see a man making love to the corpse.

"Monsieur, monsieur," he shouted, "that woman is dead, that woman is dead!"

"Sacré bleu," exclaimed the man, springing up. "I thought she was an American girl."

"I love you terribly," said the girl.

"You certainly do," agreed her boyfriend.

The divorce court was attentive as the wealthy woman complained to the judge that her husband had left her bed and board. When she had finished, the husband rose to his feet and coolly replied: "A slight correction, Your Honor. I left her bed—bored."

While making love to his wife, Carl discovered he couldn't concentrate. Though they'd been married only a few years, he reflected unhappily, their lovemaking had become infrequent and essentially joyless. Then quite suddenly, alarmed, he cried: "What happened? Did I hurt you?"

"No," said his surprised wife. "Why do you ask?"

"No reason, really," he replied with a sigh. "It was just that, for one moment there, I thought you moved."

The learned judge looked down from the bench at the young man who was suing his wife for divorce.

"Your Honor," the young man said, "I just can't live with my wife anymore. She's a hobosexual."

"Just one moment," interrupted the judge. "Don't you mean homosexual?"

"No, your Honor," replied the man. "I mean hobosexual. You see, my wife's a bum lay."

"Oh, darling," she purred, turning over in bed, "I love you in the worst way."

"I know," he replied, "but maybe you'll get better if we keep practicing!"

By the middle of his senior year, the worldly collegian had dated most of the girls on campus. One day, while seated in the student union, he looked up and saw the captain of the football team coming toward him, an angry scowl on his face.

"I hear you went out with Susan Fremont," the huge fellow boomed, doubling up his fists. "Did you score with her?"

The sophisticated chap hesitated for a moment and then answered, "Yes, once."

"Well, I'm her new boyfriend," the gridiron giant announced, "and I don't dig that at all."

"Come to think of it," the senior mused, "I didn't either."

An elderly gentleman visited his doctor with the complaint that he believed he was becoming impotent.

"When did you first become aware of this problem?" the doctor asked.

The old gentleman replied, "Yesterday afternoon, twice last night and again this morning."

When a French Lady Representative managed to close all the brothels in France after the war, they promptly opened up again as private clubs. Shortly afterward an elderly gentleman, unaware of the change, knocked at the door of one of the "clubs." Having been instructed to maintain the impression that he was working for a private club, the doorman first asked: "Active member?"

"I hope so," the old man replied.

An elderly playboy we know has catalogued the three stages of a man's life: Tri-Weekly, Try Weekly, Try Weakly.

A recently deposed Eastern potentate (who shall remain unnamed) was known for his prowess in the harem—often entertaining no less than a dozen wives per night. Shorn of his crown and possessions, he was seeking employment and was overjoyed when an American theatrical agent signed him up to perform these same feats at certain choice and private showings. The contract was signed, bookings were scheduled and twelve delectable beauties hired for the premiere. The box-office was sold out. The audience waited eagerly, for they had paid ten dollars per ticket to see the fabulous potentate. A symphony orchestra struck up an overture, the lights dimmed, the curtains parted and the dozen lovelies were revealed, reclining on couches. The potentate stepped briskly out from the wings, bowed to the audience, then proceeded. Naturally, after such a build-up, the audience was disappointed when the great man fell flat on his face after taking pleasure with only four of the beauties. They howled for their money back, and the theatrical agent regretfully had to comply. Later, he went backstage and wailed to the potentate, "I'm ruined! How could you do this to me? What happened?"

The potentate shook his head sadly. "I don't understand it," he said. "Everything went smoothly this afternoon at dress rehearsal."

Two shapely stenographers were standing on a crowded subway. One asked the other: "That man behind me—is he good looking?"

"Well," was the answer, "he's young."

The first girl nodded. *"That* I know."

After the age of forty-five, a man's get up and go is likely to have got up and gone.

The new American ambassador to the Far Eastern country called on the Emperor to present his credentials. During his official visit, he was disturbed by the presence of a number of comely, near-nude maidens wandering about the palace, but hoping to restrict the conversation to matters of state, he asked, "Your Highness, when was the last time you had an election here?"

"Ah," said the Emperor with a smile and a sly wink, "just befo' blekfast."

The aging playboy should find some satisfaction in the know-ledge that though he's not as good as he once was, he's as good once as he once was.

An old man, walking down the street, saw a small boy sitting on the curb crying. He stopped and asked, "Little boy, why are you cry-ing?"

The little boy said, "I'm crying because I can't do what the big boys do." So the old man sat down alongside of him and cried, too.

Two young men seated in a restaurant were watching a cus-tomer busily disposing of a plate of oysters on the half-shell. One of the young men remarked to his friend: "Did you ever hear that business about raw oysters being good for a man's virility?"

"Yes, why?" the friend replied.

"Well, take it from me, that's a lot of foolishness. I ate a dozen of them the other night and only nine worked."

Friend Bob Willoughby finally took his long-dreamed-of trip to *la belle* France. When he returned, after a two months' visit, we asked him about it.

"Wonderful," he sighed, "especially Paris. My only regret is that I couldn't have made the trip twenty years ago."

"When Paris was really Paris, eh?" we said.

"No," said Bob, a little sadly. "When Willoughby was really Wil-loughby."

"I really don't know what you see in him, my dear," said the pony-tailed model to her lunch companion. "He's just an everyday sort of man."

"Gee," was the response, "what more could a girl ask for?"

Everyone in the smart night club was amazed by the old gentle-man, obviously pushing seventy, tossing off Manhattans and cavorting around the dance floor like a twenty year old. Finally, curiosity got the best of the cigarette girl.

"I beg your pardon, sir," she said, "but I'm amazed to see a gentle-man of your age living it up like a youngster. Tell me, are all of your faculties unimpaired?"

The old fellow looked up at the girl sadly and shook his head. "Not all, I'm afraid," he said. "Just last evening I went nightclubbing with a girlfriend—we drank and danced all night and finally rolled into her place about two A.M. We went to bed immediately and I was asleep almost as soon as my head hit the pillow. I woke around three-thirty and nudged my girl. 'Why George,' she said in surprise, 'we did that just fifteen minutes ago.'

"So you see," the old boy said sadly, "my memory is beginning to fail me."

Precisely nine months after the young couple were married, the wife was rushed to the hospital with an urgent call from the stork. Shortly after her arrival, the doctor came out of the delivery room and told the husband he was the father of a bouncing baby boy.

The new father consulted his watch, and said, "Well, nature certainly is precise. It's exactly seven o'clock."

Twenty minutes later, the doctor came out again, all smiles. "Congratulations again," he said. "You're also the father of a baby girl."

"Yessir, doc," came the father's reply, "right to the minute." Then, glancing at his watch, he added, "Well, I guess I'll go out and have a drink. There isn't another one due until ten-thirty."

Imagine the dismay felt by the aging Don Juan who finds himself Don after Juan.

In keeping with all self-respecting vehicles owned by traveling salesmen, Ed's car broke down in the middle of a blizzard, and he trudged to a nearby farmhouse. The farmer, being up in his lines, said: "We're short of beds, but you can sleep with my daughter." She proved to be eighteen, sloe-eyed and a strapping figure of healthy young womanhood. So they went to bed. And shortly, Ed made a pass at the daughter.

"Stop that!" she said. "I'll call my father." He desisted. But half an hour later he made another attempt.

"Uh, stop . . . that," she said. "I'll call my father." But she moved closer to him, so he made a third try. This time, no protest, no threat. Just as Ed, satisfied, was about to drowse off, she tugged at his pajama sleeve.

"Could we do that again?" she asked. Ed obliged, and this time fell asleep, only to be awakened by the tug at his sleeve.

"Again?" And again Ed obliged. But when his sleep was once more rudely interrupted by the tugging at his pajama sleeve, Ed indignantly pulled it away from her and mumbled, "Stop that! Or I'll call your father."

O'Mally hurried to church one morning to see his priest. "Father," he said excitedly, "I made love ten times last night!"

"O'Mally, I'm surprised at you," the priest replied sternly. "Is the woman married?"

"Oh yes, Father, she's my wife."

"But you don't have to come to confession if you make love to your wife."

"I know—but I just had to tell *somebody.*"

After rushing into a drugstore, the nervous young man was obviously embarrassed when a prim, middle-aged woman asked if she could serve him.

"N-no," he stammered, "I'd rather see the druggist."

"I'm the druggist," she responded cheerfully. "What can I do for you?"

"Oh . . . well, uh, it's nothing important," he said, and turned to leave.

"Young man," said the woman, "my sister and I have been running this drugstore for nearly thirty years. There is nothing you can tell us that will embarrass us."

"Well, all right," he said. "I have this awful sexual hunger that nothing will appease. No matter how many times I make love, I still want to make love again. Is there anything you can give me for it?"

"Just a moment," said the little lady, "I'll have to discuss this with my sister."

A few minutes later she returned. "The best we can offer," she said, "is two hundred dollars a week and a half-interest in the business."

A pretty but curious young American tourist found herself in conversation with a ruggedly handsome, middle-aged Scot at a cocktail party. "Excuse my bluntness," she said, "but is anything worn under your kilt?"

"Nay, lassie," he replied with a grin. "It's as good as it ever was."

Having been married to each other for forty of their sixty years, a sophisticated couple decided on separate vacations. After reveling for two months in the island paradise of Hawaii, the old gent made a rather lengthy phone call to the far shores of Miami, where his wife had decided to vacation:

"I'm having a great time," he said. "I met the most fabulous thirty-year-old blonde and we're really swinging." After a pause, a matronly voice aimed at Honolulu replied: "Well, darling, I'm having a great time, too. I met a thirty-year-old man who has been squiring me all over town and I can assure you I'm certainly enjoying myself more than you are."

"How do you figure that?" he responded in an irritated tone.

"Simple mathematics, my dear," she purred. "Thirty goes into sixty more times than sixty goes into thirty."

ONE HUNDRED DOLLARS TO ANY MAN WHO CAN MAKE LOVE TO ONE OF OUR GIRLS TEN TIMES IN SUCCESSION read the sign on a wall in the hall of the brothel. A sailor who had just returned from ten months at sea decided to accept the challenge. Picking himself a particularly appetizing, pleasantly plump brunette as a partner, he started strong, but began to falter after the seventh performance. When the somewhat sated gob asked the girl what the count was, she said, "That's five times, sailor." Realizing that the girl was lying to keep him from winning the wager, he became furious and refused to continue until he was given an honest count.

At that point the house madam entered to investigate the shouts of outrage, and she managed to soothe the sailor by agreeing that he must be satisfied with the scoring.

"There's only one fair way to settle this, deary," she said. "We'll simply start the count over from the beginning."

A new potency pill developed for men has only one drawback—if it's swallowed too slowly, the user winds up with a stiff neck.

"I won't say I'm getting old," the aging duffer told his golfing partner, "but lately my sex drive's turned into a putt."

Then there was the aging playwright who, no matter how hard he tried, could never get beyond the first act.

"I went to a Chinese abortionist," the rueful receptionist confided to a friend. "Everything worked out fine, but thirty minutes later, I was pregnant again."

According to a middle-aged soothsayer we know, anyone who can still do at sixty what he did at twenty probably wasn't doing much at twenty.

The precocious teen-ager returned late from school one afternoon and confessed to his mother that he made love to his girlfriend on the way home. "I'm disappointed in you," his mother scolded. "But for telling the truth, you may go to the corner for a milk shake."

The next day, the boy came home late again, and this time he confessed to making love to one of the neighbors' wives. "Well, at least you're still honest," he was told, and again he was rewarded with a milk shake.

On the third day, the boy strode into the house and proudly announced to both of his parents that he had stayed after school to make love to his teacher. As his mother began to scold him, the father picked up a frying pan, "Don't hit him," she pleaded. "At least he told the truth."

"Hit him, hell," his father exclaimed. "I'm going to cook him a steak. How long do you expect him to keep this up on those lousy milk shakes?"

An attractive young buyer for a department store was having coffee with her assistant and complaining about her fiancé's extraordinary sexual appetites. "I barely have the strength to come to work in the morning," she murmured. "And now that he's on his vacation, things will probably get worse."

"How long is he off?" the assistant inquired.

"It varies," she replied. "But usually it's just long enough to smoke a cigarette."

And, of course, you've heard about the eighty-year-old man accused of rape but later acquitted because the evidence wouldn't stand up in court.

Two elderly gentlemen, whose active days were behind them but whose wild-oats memories were not forgotten, were amusing themselves at the bar of a cocktail lounge by watching two young men ply their dates with Martinis and lengthy conversation.

"These young bucks today just don't know how it's done," said one. "Why in our day we would have had those girls in the buggy and out in the moonlight by this time."

"Yes," agreed his companion. "They sure don't make 'em like they used to."

It wasn't long after the town grocer gave his beautiful teen-age daughter a job as clerk in his store that the local wolves began dropping by almost daily with requests for items stocked on the highest shelves, since each time the pretty little thing had to climb up a ladder to fill their orders, they were assured a spectacular view. Being as naïve as she was attractive, the daughter didn't catch on; she tried rearranging the stock a few times, but no matter how she planned it, her male customers always seemed to ask for the items she put at the top. One day an elderly gent happened to enter the store while a contingent of these young cads was sending the poor girl up and down the ladder, each one in turn ordering a loaf of raisin bread from the top shelf. Hoping to save herself an additional trip while still aloft on her eighth successive climb to the same height, the girl called down to the senior citizen, "Is yours raisin, too?"

"Nope," said the old-timer. "But it's twitchin' a mite."

An elderly French playboy entered the door of his favorite sporting house and asked the Madam if he might have an audience with Renée.

"Alas, *monsieur*," replied the Madam, "Renée is visiting her dear Mother in Provence. Would you care to see Musette?"

The old gentleman smiled. "No, thank you, *chère madame,* I will return another day. When do you expect Renée to be back?"

"Saturday next," said the Madam. "Your devotion is to be admired. But can you not find diversion in the company of Clothilde? Or Gaby? Or the lively Yvette?"

To each suggestion, the old man shook his head. Curious, the Madam asked, "Renée is, of course, charming, but what does she possess that the other girls do not?"

"Patience, *chère madame,*" he replied, "patience."

Pouring out his troubles to his great and good friend over a couple of triple Martinis, Brad had to confess that things weren't going too well at home.

"My wife and I just don't hit it off at night," he was saying to Bart. "I hate to admit it, but I'm afraid I just don't know how to make her happy."

"Hell, boy," said Bart, "there's really nothing to it. Let me give you some advice. At bedtime, switch on a new Sinatra platter, turn all the lights low and spray some perfume around the room. Next tell your wife to get into her sheerest nightie; then make sure you raise the bottom window."

"Then what do I do?" asked Brad.

"Just whistle."

"Whistle?"

"That's right. I'll be waiting outside the window. When I hear you whistle, I'll come right up and finish the job."

Trouble with being the best man at a wedding is that you don't get a chance to prove it.

The haze and warmth of the summer evening added to the atmosphere of passion on the small lake, deserted except for a canoe drifting lazily on its surface. In it, clasped in close embrace, lay George and Marilyn, gazing into each other's eyes and murmuring the special phrases of lovers.

With a delicious silken rustle that set the canoe to gently rocking, she pressed herself still closer to him.

"Georgie," she sighed, "will you love me always?"

"Of course, my darling," he whispered tenderly. "Which way would you like me to try first?"

Sue lay sprawled in sweet exhaustion on the bed, wearing a red ribbon in her bright blonde hair. Beside her, wearing not even a ribbon, Mark slowly lit two cigarettes and passed one to her. For a long moment, smoke and silence hung in the air. Then:

"My mother always told me to be good," Sue said with a little smile. "Was I?"

Conversation at the club had turned to sex and the techniques thereof.

"But should I talk to my wife while making love?" asked newlywed Fred.

"Certainly," counseled an older member, "if you happen to be near a phone."

All girls are born good. Experience makes them better.

"How did this accident occur?" asked the doctor.

"Well," explained the patient, "I was making love to my girl on the living-room rug when, all of a sudden, the chandelier came crashing down on us."

"Fortunately, you've only sustained some minor lacerations on your buttocks," the doctor said. "I think you're a very lucky man."

"You said it, doc," exclaimed the man. "A minute sooner and it could have fractured my skull."

Then there was the single-minded miss who finally got fed up with her shy boyfriend's fumbling advances and decided to put him in her place.

We know a passionate young girl who was barred from the beach when the lifeguard saw her going down for the third time.

"I'd like to buy some body make-up for my girlfriend," the young lawyer told the clerk at the cosmetics counter.

"Certainly, sir," the clerk remarked. "What color would you like?"

"Never mind the color," the attorney said. "What flavors do you have?"

"My so-called liberal mother is really such a prude," the high school cheerleader sadly told her locker partner. "She said that I could only pet with my dates if they didn't touch me below the waist."

"Oh, that's too bad," her schoolmate commiserated. "What do you intend to do about it?"

"Well," the cheerleader giggled, "the first thing I'm going to do is learn to stand on my head."

Stepping off the bandstand at a psychedelic *discothèque*, the long-haired drummer approached a miniskirted chick and asked if she'd like to join him for a steak dinner. "No, I'm a vegetarian," she confided. "Vegetables are the only thing I eat."

"Well, then, let's go to my pad," he offered. "I'm a humanitarian."

After trying to fix a flat tire during a raging blizzard, the young man jumped back into the car with his date and began rubbing his nearly frozen hands. "Let me warm them for you," she offered, placing his hands between her thighs.

When his fingers had thawed out, the chap rushed back to continue working on the tire, but he quickly returned again, complaining that his hands were numb with cold. As he reached under her skirt, she slid forward and whispered ecstatically, "Darling, aren't your ears cold, too?"

We know a fellow who complains that this winter has been so cold it takes him forty-five minutes to get his girlfriend started.

Then there was the little boy who, after happening by his parents' open bedroom door one night, wondered why he had gotten a spanking for sucking his thumb.

We know a cinema buff who's very excited by current trends in films—the hero still gets the girl in the end, but he's never sure which end it will be.

Then there was the basketball player who was so tall that his girlfriend had to go up on him.

Upon applying for admission to one of the most exclusive country clubs in New England, the rather reserved, unimpressive looking young man was notified that he must play a round of golf with the club officers as a prerequisite to his acceptance.

On the appointed afternoon, he met them on the first tee equipped with a hockey stick, a croquet mallet and a billiard cue. The officers looked him over incredulously, but nevertheless proceeded to tee off. To their dismay, the young man coolly drove three hundred and ten yards with the hockey stick, gracefully arched his second shot to the green with the croquet mallet, and sank a twenty-foot putt with the billiard cue.

After soundly drubbing the baffled officers with a sub-par sixty-eight, the applicant retired with them to the club bar. There he ordered a Scotch and soda, and when it arrived, he mixed the drink himself by tossing the contents of the shot glass over his shoulder into the waiting soda behind him on the bar. This further display of the young man's incredible physical coordination was too much for the officers of the club.

"You're miraculous," they exclaimed. "What's the story behind these fantastic talents of yours?"

"All my life," the man explained, "physical activity of any sort has been child's play for me. To overcome the boredom that has resulted from my monotonous mastery of everything, I try to do almost everything in the most difficult way possible. Thus, I play tennis with a Ping-Pong paddle, Ping-Pong with a tennis racket, and so on."

"Wait a minute," interrupted one of the club officers. "If it's true, as you say, that you do everything physical in the most difficult manner possible, I have one question. . . ."

"I know," said the talented young man, smiling. "Everyone asks me the same thing and I don't mind telling you. Standing up . . . in a hammock."

We know a cautious man who, upon discovering that his gorgeous date had forgotten to take the pill, decided to give her a tongue-lashing.

The pretty patient nervously asked the doctor to perform an unusual operation—the removal of a large chunk of green wax from her navel. Looking up from the ticklish task, the physician asked, "How did this happen?"

"Well, you see, doctor," the girl said, "my boyfriend likes to eat by candlelight."

The shapely coed was undressing for the night when she noticed a puzzled look on her roommate's face. "Do you know there's the impression of a large M on your stomach?" the roommate asked.

"My fiancé's in town this weekend," confided the young thing, "and he likes to make love with his football-letter sweater on."

"Which school does he attend, Michigan or Minnesota?" questioned her friend.

"Neither," giggled the first girl. "He goes to Wisconsin."

A married friend of ours comments that the only thing worse than coming home with lipstick on your collar is being caught with leg make-up on your ears.

15
ANIMALS

The circus was finishing its final performance in the country town when one of its zebras had a stroke. The local veterinarian prescribed a few weeks' rest for the beast, so the circus owner made arrangements to board it at a nearby farm.

The zebra took to the new life immediately and spent the first day meeting all the animals of the barnyard.

He came across a chicken and said, "I'm a zebra, who are you?"

"I'm a chicken," said the chicken.

"What do you do?" asked the zebra.

"I scratch around and lay eggs," said the chicken.

Moving on, the zebra found a cow. He introduced himself saying, "I'm a zebra. Who are you?"

"I'm a cow," said the cow.

"What do you do?" asked the zebra.

"I graze in the field and give milk," said the cow.

The zebra met a bull next. "I'm a zebra," he said. "Who are you?"

"I'm a bull," said the bull.

"And what do you do?" asked the zebra.

"What do I do!" snorted the bull, pawing at the turf with a forefoot. "Why you silly looking ass—take off your pajamas and I'll show you!"

The old bull's active days were over, but the kindly farmer permitted him to stay on in the pasture with the cows. Of course, the farmer also turned a young bull loose in the field and the newcomer went to work immediately. Seeing this, the old bull began snorting and pawing the ground with his hoof.

"You're wasting your time," said the farmer. "You're too old for that sort of thing now."

"I know," said the bull, "but I can show him I'm not a cow, can't I?"

The old maid bought herself a parrot to brighten her lonely hours. The parrot's name was Bobby, and he was a charming bird, with but one small fault. Whenever the mild-mannered lady had company in, Bobby would cut loose with a number of obscene expressions he'd picked up from his previous owner, a retired madam.

The lady discussed this problem with her pastor, and after witnessing a particularly purple display, the good man suggested, "This parrot needs company. Get him interested in another of his species, and he'll soon forget his sinful past.

"I, myself, have a parrot. Her name is Sarah and she is an unusually devout bird. She *prays* constantly. Let me bring her with me the next time I call. We'll keep them together a few days—I'm certain her religious background will have a marked influence on this fellow's character."

Thus, the next time the pastor called, he brought his parrot, and the two birds were placed in a single cage. They spent the first couple of minutes hopping about and sizing one another up, then Bobby spoke:

"I go for you, sweetie," he whistled. "How about you and me shacking up?!"

"You betcha, big boy," said Sarah. "Whatcha think I've been *praying* for!"

A performing octopus could play the piano, the zither and the piccolo, and his trainer wanted him to add the bagpipe to his accomplishments. With this in mind, a bagpipe was placed in the octopus' room and the trainer awaited results.

Hours passed, but no bagpipe music was heard. Since the talented octopus usually learned quickly, the trainer was disturbed. Opening the door the next morning, he asked the octopus, "Have you learned to play that thing yet?"

"*Play it?*" retorted the octopus. "I've been trying to *lay* it all night!"

Two small mice were crouched under a table in the chorus girls' dressing room of a big Broadway show.

"Wow," exclaimed the first mouse, "have you ever seen so many gorgeous legs in your life?"

"Means nothing to me," said the second. "I'm a titmouse."

Perhaps you've heard of the impecunious snake who was so poor he didn't have a pit to hiss in.

Of course, you've heard the definition of an emasculated dinosaur: A colossal fossil with a docile tassel.

The beautiful young lady strolled through the zoo, and finally stopped in front of the monkey island. Mystified as to the whereabouts of the animals, she queried the keeper, "Where are all the monkeys today?"

"They're back in the cave, Miss, it's the mating season."

"Will they come out if I throw them some peanuts?"

The keeper scratched his head. "I don't know, Miss. Would you?"

The little old lady rushed into the taxidermist and unwrapped a package containing two recently deceased monkeys. Her instructions to the proprietor were delivered in a welter of tears.

"Favorite pets ... (blubber, sob) ... caught cold ... (moan) ... don't see how I'll live without them . . . (weep, sob) . . . want to have them stuffed . . . (blubber, blubber)!"

"Of course, Madam," said the proprietor in an understanding voice, "and would you care to have them mounted?"

"Oh, no," she sobbed, "just shaking hands. They were just close friends."

A pink elephant, a green kangaroo and two yellow snakes strolled up to the bar.

"You're a little early, boys," said the bartender, "he ain't here yet."

A kangaroo hopped into one of the better midtown Manhattan bars and requested a Martini, dry. The bartender had never seen a kangaroo outside the zoo, but he complied with the request.

"How much?" asked the kangaroo.

"A dollar and a half," said the bartender.

As the marsupial downed the drink, the bartender remarked, "I've never seen a kangaroo in here before."

"No," said the kangaroo, "and at these prices, you're not likely to again."

When we asked a zoologist friend of ours how porcupines have sex, we were told, "Carefully, very carefully."

Marvin the Nature Lover spied a grasshopper hopping in the grass, and in a mood for communing with nature rare even among full-fledged Nature Lovers, he spoke to the grasshopper, saying: "Hello, friend grasshopper. Did you know they've named a drink after you?"

"Really?" replied the grasshopper, obviously pleased. "They've named a drink Fred?"

Screams of delight piercing the air attested to the fact that Harry's tomcat was indeed the cat's meow. But, after numerous complaints from the neighbors, Harry sadly agreed to allow a veterinarian to render the cat fit to guard a sultan's harem.

"I'll bet," ventured one of Harry's neighbors weeks later, "that that ex-tom of yours just lies on the hearth now and gets fat."

"No," said Harry, "he still goes out. But now he goes along as a consultant."

Attend now to a fable that proves that lasting fame is not always built upon success: Once upon a time, two boll weevils from the Deep South traveled to New York, there to seek their fortune. Upon arriving, the first boll weevil got a job as a ringmaster in a small flea circus. As time went by, he moved to bigger and better flea circuses until he became internationally renowned as a flea-circus impresario. The other boll weevil, however, was unable to find any employment and, as time passed, he faded into total obscurity.

That was fifty years ago. But today, do you suppose anyone remembers that boll weevil who was once impresario of the world's greatest flea circuses? No! But we do remember the other one—the one who was a failure—for, even today, we refer to him as "the lesser of two weevils."

The new rooster caused a great stir in the barnyard. From resplendent comb to defiant spurs, he was the picture of young bantamhood. Almost immediately upon his arrival, he was greeted by an elderly rooster who took him behind the barn and whispered in his ear: "Young fellow, I'm long past my prime. All I want now is to live out my remaining days in peace and solitude. So you take over right now as ruler of the roost with my blessings."

The newcomer did just that. He went about his squirely duties as only a young rooster could. After several days, however, the elder rooster again took the young champion behind the barn.

"Kid," he whispered, "the hens have been after me for giving up my position so easily. So why don't we have a race—say, ten laps around the farmhouse? The winner becomes undisputed keeper of the henhouse, and then the hens will stop nagging me."

The young rooster, with only contempt for his elder's athletic ability, quickly agreed. Surprisingly, the older one jumped off to an early lead. His younger counterpart, weakened by the activities of the previous week, was never quite able to overtake him. As they rounded the barn for the fourth time, the elder rooster still maintained a formidable lead.

Suddenly, a shotgun blast rang out. The young rooster fell in the dust, his plumage riddled with buckshot.

"Dammit, Emmy," said the farmer. "That's the last rooster we buy from Ferguson. Four of 'em this month, and every one's been queer."

When a newly bought rooster died after only three weeks on the job, the farmer was determined that the replacement would last a while longer, and so, before putting the rooster into the hen coop, he dosed it heavily with vitamins and pep pills. The instant the bird was released, it charged into the coop and serviced every one of the hens therein. Then, before the farmer could stop it, it flew into the adjoining coop and proceeded to do the same for the geese. At this point, the farmer gave up and went back to the house, shaking his head and muttering, "He'll never last out the day." Sure enough, around sunset the farmer was crossing the yard, and there lay the rooster, legs aloft, flat on its back, with two hungry buzzards slowly circling above his supine body. "Damn it!" groaned the farmer. "Now I've got to buy me *another* new rooster!" At which point the rooster opened one eye, winked and, pointing at the nearing buzzards, said, *"Shh!"*

Loping down a Manhattan street, the boxer stopped and wagged his tail in friendly greeting at a Russian wolfhound, likewise unencumbered by collar or leash.

"How do you like America?" he asked.

"Well, it's different from my homeland," said the wolfhound. "In

Russia I eat bones dipped in vodka and caviar. In Russia I have my own doghouse made of rare Siberian woods. In Russia I sleep on a rug made of thick warm ermine."

"Then why did you come to America?"

"I like to bark once in a while."

The little white-haired spinster was rocking on her front porch with her tomcat at her feet when a good fairy suddenly appeared and offered her three wishes.

"Aw, go on," the little old lady said disbelievingly. "If you can grant wishes, let's see you turn this rocking chair into a pile of gold."

A wave of the good fairy's wand and the spinster found herself atop a pile of pure gold. Her face lighting up, she asked: "I get two more wishes?"

"Yes," the good fairy assured her. "Anything your heart desires."

"Then make me into a beautiful, voluptuous young girl," she ordered. Another wave of the wand and her wish was granted.

"Now," she said, "make my faithful old cat into a tall, dark and handsome young man."

The good fairy waved her wand and disappeared as the third wish came true and a muscular swain stood where the tomcat had just been sleeping.

The young man approached the once-old lady, took her in his arms and murmured gently: "Now aren't you sorry you sent me to the vet?"

"If you're looking for a really unusual pet," said the shop owner, "this cage contains a giant Crunch Bird. Its powerful beak and claws are capable of completely demolishing almost anything."

"How horrible," said the woman customer.

"Not at all," the pet-shop owner replied, "for the bird is remarkably well behaved and completely obedient. It is only when he is given a direct command, such as 'Crunch Bird, the chair,' or 'Crunch Bird, the table,' that he attacks and destroys the thing that was named."

"Could he destroy a television set?" the woman asked, with new interest.

"Console or table model. Color or black-and-white. If the Crunch Bird was given the command he would turn any set into a pile of metal scrap, wires and tubes in a few seconds."

"I want him!" the woman exclaimed. "I don't care what he costs, I want him!"

When the woman returned home, she found her husband in his usual spot—directly in front of the television set. No amount of coaxing could draw him away. Her once-loving spouse had lost all interest in sex, in conversation, in everything except TV. But things will be different from now on, she thought, opening the Crunch Bird's cage.

"What sort of pet did you buy?" her husband asked, without looking up from the set. "A poodle, a parakeet, or what . . . ?"

"I bought a Crunch Bird," she replied, preparing to give the one command that would smash her electronic rival into a million pieces.

"Crunch Bird, my ass," said her husband.

The boor tapped on the sleeping parakeet's cage and said, "Hey, birdie, can you talk?"

"Sure," said the bird, "can you fly?"

"No!" cried the girl centipede crossing her legs, "a thousand times, no!"

A Broadway bookie was given a parrot in lieu of cash payment. The bird's vocabulary included choice phrases in English, French, Spanish and German. Sensing a winner, the bookie hauled the bird off to his favorite bar.

"Speaks four languages," he said to the bartender, who snorted in disbelief. "Wanna bet this bird can speak four languages?" the bookie challenged.

Annoyed, the bartender finally agreed to a ten-dollar wager. The bookie turned to the parrot and said, *"Parlez-vous français?"* There was no response.

Nor was there any reply to the question in English, Spanish or German. The bartender picked up the bookie's sawbuck from the bar and went about his business.

On the street, the bookie glared at the bird. "You fink!" he exclaimed. "I've got ten bucks riding on you and you clam up on me. I oughta strangle you!"

"Don't be a jerk," the parrot replied. "Just think of the odds you'll get tomorrow."

Complaining of the distance between campus buildings, the veterinarian's daughter wrote home for money to buy a bicycle. But by the time the money arrived, she'd changed her mind and bought a monkey instead. After a few weeks, the animal began losing its hair. Hoping her father might know a cure, she wrote: "All the hair is falling off my monkey—what shall I do?"

Two days later came the terse directive: "Sell the bicycle."

"Grrr," said the wolf, leaping at Little Red Ridinghood. "I'm going to eat you."

"For God's sake," Red replied. "Doesn't anybody screw anymore?"

A man walked into the local pub with a frog atop his head. The startled bartender asked, "Hey, where did you get that?"

The frog croaked, "Would you believe it started out as a wart on my ass?"

During camouflage training in Louisiana, a private disguised as a tree trunk had made a sudden move that was spotted by a visiting general.

"You simpleton!" the officer barked. "Don't you know that by jumping and yelling the way you did, you could have endangered the lives of the entire company?"

"Yes, sir," the soldier answered apologetically. "But, if I may say so, I did stand still when a flock of pigeons used me for target practice. And I never moved a muscle when a large dog peed on my lower branches. But when two squirrels ran up my pants leg and I heard the bigger say, 'Let's eat one now and save the other until winter'—that did it."

Desperate for work, the young man took a job at the zoo masquerading as a gorilla, to replace the prize animal who had died. The fellow launched into his act with gusto, screaming at the top of his lungs and swinging madly from the bars. The crowd applauded wildly. Inspired, he grabbed a bar and went sailing over the top of his cage into an adjoining pen occupied by four fierce lions. As the animals approached him, the chap screamed, "Help, they're going to kill me."

"Shut up, stupid," whispered one of the lions, "or we'll all lose our jobs."

A newlywed couple established a household routine that included having sexual relations each evening at five-fifteen. After several weeks, the bride contracted the flu and received an injection that killed all but three germs. The trio of survivors frantically discussed how they might escape. "I'm moving to the tip of her ear," said the first. "They'll never get me there."

Thinking for a moment, the second bug chirped, "I'm going to the tip of her toe!"

"You guys do what you want," retorted the third, "but when that old five-fifteen pulls out tonight, I'm going to be on it."

Two lovers interested in spiritualism and reincarnation vowed that if either died, the one remaining would try to contact the partner in the other world exactly thirty days after the tragedy. As luck would have it, a few weeks later the young man perished in the wreck of his new sports car, and true to her word, his bereaved sweetheart attempted to contact him in the spirit world exactly thirty days later. She lay on her bed in the darkness and called out, "John, John, this is Martha. Do you hear me, John?"

A ghostly voice answered her. "Yes, Martha, this is John. I hear you."

Then his newly bereaved asked: "Oh, John, what is it like where you are?"

"It's beautiful, Martha. There are azure skies, a soft breeze and quiet beauty sweeping the horizon."

She exclaimed, "It sounds beautiful. What do you do all day?"

"Well, Martha, we are all up before sunrise, eat breakfast and then it's nothing but sex until noon. After lunch, we nap until two and then make love until five. After dinner there's more of the same until midnight when we go to sleep to get ready for the next morning."

Martha was somewhat taken aback. "But, John," she exclaimed, "is that really what heaven is like?"

"Heaven? I'm not in heaven, Martha!"

"Where are you, then?"

"I'm a jack rabbit in Arizona!"

Anna sat on an ant hill at a picnic with most unfortunate results. She asked her sister to send a telegram to their mother and tell her what had happened. The sister, faced with the problem of telling the tale in a way acceptable to Western Union and having only enough money for a six-word wire, came up with this message: "ANACIN HOSPITAL ADAMANT BITTER ASININE PLACES."

An ingenious artist-friend of ours recently gave us a foolproof method for sculpting an elephant: "First, you get a huge block of granite; then you chip away everything that doesn't look like an elephant."

During a wild party at a friend's country estate, the attractive city girl strolled outdoors for some air. Happening onto a grassy field, she lay down to watch the stars.

She was almost asleep when a cow, searching for clover, carefully stepped over her. Groggily, she raised her head and said: "One at a time, boys, one at a time."

A girlfriend of ours entered a crossword-puzzle contest and missed first prize by just two letters. The problem, she said, was to find a four letter word, ending in *i-t*, to describe what is commonly found on the floors of bird cages. She was sure she had it, but the judges didn't care for her solution. Seems the correct answer was *grit*.

16
FIGURES
& FIGLEAVES

You might say that a girl has reached the awkward age when she is too old to count on her fingers and too young to count on her legs.

On a windy street corner, a shapely miss held tightly to her hat with both hands while her skirt billowed higher and higher about her legs. In response to the amused glances of two masculine passersby, she explained with refreshing candor: "What you are looking at is twenty-three years old, gentlemen; what I'm hanging onto is brand new."

Engineers are continually surprised to find that girls with the most streamlined shapes offer the most resistance.

An attractive young lady was having difficulty keeping her skirt down about her shapely legs while awaiting a bus on a windy street corner. She was aware of a man watching her discomfort with considerable interest and she addressed him in an irritated voice: "It is obvious, sir, that you are no gentleman."

With appreciation in his voice, the man replied, "It's obvious that you're not either."

For every girl who has the curves, there are a dozen men who have the angles.

"I was a 97-pound weakling," the man said to his drinking companion, "and whenever I went to the beach with my girl, this 197-pound bully came over and kicked sand in my face. So I took this weight-lifting course I read about and in a little while I weighed 197 pounds."

"So what happened?" his friend wanted to know.

"I went to the beach with my girl and a 257-pound bully kicked sand in my face."

We really don't believe the nasty rumor floating around that Vikki Dougan's fame is spreading.

At the risk of differing with Dorothy Parker, a friend of ours insists that men often make passes at girls who wear glasses. It really depends on their frames.

Mike had just moved into his apartment and decided he should get acquainted with his across-the-hall neighbor. When the door was opened he was pleasantly surprised to be confronted by a young damsel considerably more than passing fair, and considerably less than fully clad. Though justifiably flustered by this smiling apparition, Mike nevertheless managed a remark singularly appropriate to the occasion:

"Hi, I'm your new sugar across the hall—can I borrow a cup of neighbor?"

Nothing keeps a girl on the straight and narrow more than being built that way.

A girl with an hourglass figure can often make grown men feel like playing in the sand.

A stunningly stacked blonde walked into a dress shop, and asked the manager, "I wonder if I might try on that blue dress in the window?"

"Go right ahead," he said. "It might help business."

With due respect to old Charlie Darwin, although man has learned through evolution to walk in an upright posture, his eyes still swing from limb to limb.

It's usually a girl's geography that determines her history.

A middle-aged executive was becoming increasingly irritated by the constant ribbing he received at the hands of junior employees who couldn't resist making fun of his baldness. One morning, a particularly brash trainee had the gall to run his hand across the older man's pate while loudly exclaiming, "Feels just like my wife's ass!"

With a look of genuine curiosity, the aging exec also felt his gleaming pate. "You're right," he said, "so it does, so it does."

It's easy to lie with a straight face, but it's nicer to lie with a curved body.

A career girl's mind moves her ahead, while a chorus girl's mind moves her behind.

An American on a business trip to Glasgow entered a restaurant and asked the waitress what the specialty was. "Roast and rice," the Scottish miss replied in a heavy brogue.
"You certainly do roll your Rs," the visitor observed.
"I suppose," she giggled, beginning to blush, "but only when I wear high heels."

Shapely limbs help many a girl to branch out.

When a girl says she's got a boyish figure, it's usually straight from the shoulder.

Recent statistics indicate that 70% of the women with breast cancer attribute it to men who smoke.

A young man was out on a first date with a rather flat-chested girl. The evening ended on the sofa in the young lady's parlor. The boy put his arm around her and made a few preliminary passes.
The girl stiffened indignantly. "Here, here!" she exclaimed.
"Where, where?" he replied.

As Sam the fruit man reminded us the other day, the apple of the average playboy's eye is usually the prettiest peach with the biggest pear.

The incident took place on the boat deck of the S.S. United States the first day at sea. A well-stacked young morsel, out for a stroll, bumped into an officer as both rounded a corner. They drew back, apologized, stepped forward and bumped again. A third try produced the same results. This time the officer courteously tipped his cap and said, "Just once more, miss—and then I really must go."

A sweater girl is one who knows that it's possible for a man to concentrate on two things at once.

Charlie entered the airlines ticket office in a rush, but did a double-take almost immediately: The girl behind the ticket counter was as magnificently endowed with feminine equipment as any girl he could ever remember seeing. What's more, she was clad in a gown whose diving neckline barely observed the boundaries of decorum. And to cap matters, she was evidently unaware of his presence, for she bent low over notations she was making. Finally, she looked up and saw him.

"Oh! What can I do for you, sir?" she cried gaily, taking a deep breath.

Charlie heard his own breath hissing in his ears, like steam, but tried manfully to master the situation. He did, after all, need two tickets to Pittsburgh.

"—Uh—" he began, distractedly, "give me two pickets to—"

An undemanding friend of ours defines a well-balanced girl as one with an empty head and a full sweater.

Everybody thought the Miss Albuquerque beauty contest was going to be a hotly contested affair, but Susan walked away with first place with nary a dissenting vote. Turned out she was the only one of the contestants who could get all those letters across her chest.

It has recently been brought to our attention that a definite parallel exists between a Martini and a woman's breasts. One is not enough, and three are too many.

On a recent TV quiz show, a contestant was asked to give the first names of people having the last name of Wilkinson, with a prize of five hundred dollars for each he could name.

"Well," he said, "there's 'Bud' Wilkinson, football coach at Oklahoma University."

"That's one," said the m.c.

"Then," continued the contestant, "there's June Wilkinson."

"Correct," said the m.c. "That makes three. . . . "

Nothing is more wasted than a smile on the face of a girl with a forty-inch bust.

Being troubled with coughing spells, a teen-age girl was taken by her mother to see a doctor. He explained that the girl's chest must be examined for a proper diagnosis. Placing his stethoscope above her heart, he said, "Big breaths."

"Yeth," she replied proudly. "And I'm only thixteen!"

The maître d'hotel at the Ritz was interviewing waiters for an important society banquet to be held in the hotel that night. There were very few applicants for the jobs and time was running short. One applicant named Angelo, when asked where he had previously worked as a waiter, gave Harry's Hash House as a reference. The maître d' reluctantly engaged Angelo, with a word of warning to mind his manners, for *this* is the Ritz.

During the banquet, after serving the turtle soup, Angelo noticed that the bosom of an attractive young debutante had fallen out of her low-cut gown into her plate of soup. Quick as a flash, Angelo jumped forward, seized the lady's bosom and, after drying it with a table napkin, slipped it back into her gown.

As he was returning to the kitchen to serve the next course, the maître d' seized him by the arm and furiously denounced him as a clumsy oaf.

"But what was I to do?" Angelo cried. "I couldn't very well just leave it out there lying in the soup."

"Well of course not!" the maître d' said, stiffening noticeably. "But when an incident such as that occurs at the Ritz, one uses a warmed serving spoon!"

The theatrical agent, trying to sell a new strip act to a nightclub manager, was raving about the girl's unbelievable 72-26-40 figure. "What kind of a dance does she do?" the manager asked, duly impressed by the description of the girl's dimensions.

"Well, she doesn't actually dance at all," the agent replied. "She just crawls out onto the stage and tries to stand up!"

The best gift for the girl who has everything is a topless bathing suit to show it off.

Then there was the guy who explained why he wasn't interested in visiting a topless bar: "If you've seen two, you've seen them all."

We knew a guy whose feet were so big that even when he danced with Raquel Welch he stepped on her toes.

A very plain nurse was telling a voluptuous co-worker about the sailor who was a patient in Ward Ten. "He's tattooed," she confided (and her voice dropped low), "in a very *intimate* place!"

"You mean—" gasped the beautiful nurse.

"Yes! Isn't that odd? There's actually a *word* tattooed there. The word 'swan.'"

"This I've got to see," exclaimed the voluptuous one, and she hurried off to Ward Ten. Half an hour later, she returned. "You were right," she said, "he *is* tattooed there. But you were wrong about the word. It's 'Saskatchewan'!"

"What part of the human body," asked the anatomy professor, "is harder than steel?" Nobody in the class volunteered the information, so he looked in the direction of a sweet coed and asked, "Can you tell me, Miss Riley?"

She blushed a deep scarlet and lowered her eyes, murmuring, "Oh, *please* don't ask me to answer that, professor!"

Crisply, he said, "The answer is the tissue of the nails. And you, Miss Riley," he added with a sigh, "are an optimist."

Three female members of an exclusive country club walked into the women's shower room and were shocked to see the lower part of a man's anatomy behind the door of one of the shower stalls. "Well!" said one of the ladies, "that certainly isn't *my* husband!" The second one added, "He isn't mine, either." .

And the third, the youngest of the three, said, "Hell, he isn't even a member of the club."

Peters was the university's star fullback. A few days before the big game, he injured his leg during a practice scrimmage and was told he would be unable to play in the game of the year. The college paper planned to announce the sad news with the headline, "Team Will Play Without Peters."

However, the Dean caught this bit of college humor before the paper went to press and ordered the editor to change it or be kicked off the paper. The editor complied, and Saturday morning the paper hit the campus with the headline, "Team Will Play With Peters Out."

Little Mitchell hurt his finger and ran crying to his mother. She kissed it and said, "There, that will make it feel better."

A few minutes later, Mitchell scratched his forehead. His mother took care of the wound, then once more kissed the spot and sent her little man out to play.

In half an hour Mitchell was back again. This time one of his friends had kicked him in a more intimate region; he came in screaming wildly and pointing to the spot.

"Damn it," said his mother, "you're getting more like your father every day."

The psychiatrist was holding a group consultation with three young mothers and their small children. "You all have obsessions," he told them. To the first one, he said, "Your obsession is eating. Why, you've even named your little girl Candy." The second, he said, was obsessed by money. "Again, it manifests itself in your child's name, Penny." At this point, the third mother arose and, taking her little boy by the hand, whispered, "Let's go, Peter."

> There was a young fellow named Lancelot
> Whom the neighbors all looked on askance a lot.
> For whenever he'd pass
> A presentable lass,
> The front of his pants would advance a lot.

The Dean of Women at a prominent Eastern college was introducing a visiting politician to the student convocation. In her sweetest tones of admiration, she said, "I couldn't begin to tell you all of the Senator's accomplishments, but as an indication you'll be interested to know that he has a nine-inch *Who's Who*."

A beachcomber of twenty-five had been shipwrecked on a desert island since the age of six. One day, while in search of food, he stumbled across a beautifully sensuous female lying on the beach nearly naked;

she'd been washed ashore from another shipwreck just that morning. After they got over their initial surprise at seeing each other, the girl wanted to know how long he had been alone on this barren bit of land.

"Almost twenty years," he said.

"Twenty years!" she exclaimed. "But how ever did you survive?"

"Oh, I fish, dig for clams and gather berries and coconuts," he replied.

"And what do you do for sex?" she asked.

"What's that?" He looked puzzled.

Whereupon the bold maiden pulled the innocent beachcomber down onto the sand beside her and proceeded to demonstrate. After they had finished, she asked how he had enjoyed it.

"Great!" was the reply. "But look what it did to my clam digger!"

The busy Park Avenue veterinarian impatiently assured the well-dressed lady with the schnauzer dog that there was nothing wrong with the animal's hearing. "There's just too much hair around the dog's ears," he said. "Get some hair remover and he'll be all right."

She purchased a bottle of depilatory at a nearby pharmacy, and the clerk instructed her to use it at full strength for leg hair and to dilute it by half for underarms. "Thanks," said the woman with a puzzled frown, "but I want to use this on my schnauzer."

"Oh," said the clerk, somewhat taken aback. "Well, in that case you'd best use it at one-third strength . . . and . . . uh, I wouldn't advise bike riding for a while!"

The stunning coed was stunned herself when the biology professor asked her, "What part of the human anatomy enlarges to about ten times its normal size during periods of emotion or excitement?"

"I-I refuse to answer that question," the girl stammered, as she shyly avoided looking at her male classmates sitting nearby. One of them was called upon next and he correctly answered, "The pupil of the eye."

"Miss Rogers," said the professor, "your refusal to answer my question makes three things evident. First, you didn't study last night's assignment. Second, you have a dirty mind. And third," concluded the professor, "I'm afraid marriage is going to be a tremendous disappointment for you."

Taking a shortcut through a graveyard on their way home, the fellow and the girl began to feel the eerie mood of the place.

"Scary, ain't it!" said the youth, putting his arm protectively around the girl.

"Yes, isn't it!" said the girl.

"Weird, ain't it!" said the fellow, holding her closer.

"Yes, isn't it!"

"Gruesome, ain't it!"

"Yes, hasn't it!"

His first day in the Army, the recruit was issued a comb, and then the company barber shaved off all his hair. The second day he was issued a toothbrush, and then the dentist pulled all his teeth. The third day he was issued an athletic supporter, and he went A.W.O.L.

"Why do you have to buy such expensive brassieres?" the irate husband snapped as he looked over his wife's latest department-store bills. "You certainly don't have much to put in them."

"If that's the way you figure," she replied sardonically, "then you haven't needed a new pair of shorts in years!"

"Floors, please," said the hotel elevator operator, and a young man at the back of the car called out, "Ballroom, please."

At which the pretty young thing in front of him turned and said, "Oh, I'm sorry, I didn't realize I was crowding you."

The student nurse was beautiful, dedicated and dumb. Her bedside manner included mishaps with hypodermic needle, rectal thermometer and bedpan; but she was determined to devote herself to the sick and suffering, and she wasn't discouraged by disparaging individuals who suggested she might be better suited for spreading discomfort than alleviating it.

On one particular afternoon, the doctor in charge of the ward left our neophyte Nightingale to care for a middle-aged executive, secure in the knowledge that this man's affliction was uncomfortable but minor, and the treatment prescribed was too simple to be misunderstood. But a few minutes later, the doctor was shocked to see his patient running down the hall, white hospital robe billowing out behind him, howling at the top of his lungs, with the nurse chasing after him carrying a basin of steaming water.

"No, no, Miss Smith!" exclaimed the doctor, as the pair rushed past him. "I told you to prick his boil!"

The handsome ad exec and his date entered a restaurant and were seated near the center of the floor. A pretty waitress, observing that the man had forgotton to zip his trousers, scribbled a message on her order pad, left it at his table and scurried away.

Unfolding the note, the man read: "Sir, I'm sure you don't know it, but your fly is unzipped and you're exposing yourself. I will go back to the kitchen and knock some trays off a shelf. The noise will distract everyone and you'll have a chance to adjust your trousers.

"P.S. I love you."

After meeting at a *discothèque,* the young couple repaired to a local lovers' lane, where they proceeded to cement their new relationship. Having freed her of blouse and bra, he was helping remove the rest of her clothing when a police car drove by.

"Fuzz," he whispered excitedly.

"What did you expect," she replied, "a ponytail?"

Reminiscing with her girlfriend about their childhood, the sweet young thing asked, "Did you ever play with jacks?"

"Oh, yes," her friend replied. "And with Tommy's, Bill's and Freddy's."

"For several weeks," the distraught factory worker confided to his psychiatrist, "I was obsessed with the idea of putting my organ in the pickle slicer. The thought kept me awake nights. When I finally fell asleep, I would dream about it. I couldn't work effectively. All I could do was stare at the pickle slicer and daydream. Finally, I couldn't con-

trol my passion. During lunch hour yesterday, I stayed in the factory
and fulfilled my desire."

"My God!" gasped the psychiatrist. "What happened?"

"The foreman came back from lunch early," said the worker, "saw
what was going on and fired me on the spot."

"What happened to the pickle slicer?"

"Of course," the worker responded, "she was fired, too."

The two career girls were discussing plans for their forthcoming
vacations. "I don't know about you," bubbled one enthusiastically, "but
I'm going to Monaco for the Grand Prix."

"I'm afraid you're in for an awful letdown," remarked her friend.
"For one thing, that's not even the way it's pronounced."

Strolling through London's Soho district, the young Cockney
noticed an attractive girl furiously struggling to hold down her micro-
skirt in the brisk wind. Tipping his hat, he said: "Airy, ain't it?"

"What the 'ell did you expect?" she replied. "Feathers?"

"Do you really think I can be a star?" cooed the young actress,
snuggling closer to the famous producer. "I certainly do," replied the
showman. "You're already starting to make it big."

In the darkness of the all-but-empty theater balcony, the couple
embraced so passionately that the man's toupee slid from his head.
Groping to find it in the darkness, he reached under his date's skirt.

"That's it, that's it," she gasped.

"It can't be," the fellow retorted. "I part mine on the side."

"I have a friend who thinks he may have a venereal disease," said
the embarrassed young man to his doctor.

"Well," replied the physician, "take him out and let's have a look
at him."

A leading musicologist asserts that J. S. Bach had twenty children
because there were no stops on his organ.

The silly teen-age girl had long been infatuated with a popular
local disc jockey and finally got to meet him when the station held an
open house. When she seductively suggested they get better acquainted, he took her into a vacant studio and unzipped his slacks. "I
suppose you know what this is?" he whispered.

"I sure do," she said, grasping it in her hand. "I'd like to say hello to Ricky, Bobby, Tina and the whole gang down at Danny's Pizzeria."

Do you enjoy cocktails?" the young chap asked the pretty blonde.

"I certainly do," she cooed. "Heard any good ones?"

While searching for an old Army buddy's apartment in a small town, a uniformed Vietnam veteran spotted two spinster ladies through a living-room window and stepped up onto their porch to ask for directions. When one answered the door, the other inquired who their visitor was.

"It's a young soldier and he's got a Purple Heart on," said the old lady at the door, looking the soldier up and down.

"I don't care what color it is," came the voice inside. "Let him in."

Impressed by the impeccable cleanliness of the restaurant, the customer summoned his waiter over to the table to compliment him.

"We take pride in our sanitary precautions," the waiter explained. "For example, the manager makes us carry a spoon, so we don't have to touch the food we serve, and we even have a string attached to our pants fly, so that we don't touch the zipper."

"But how do you get it back into your trousers?" the customer whispered.

"Don't know about the others," the waiter replied, "but I use my spoon."

Seeing her brother undressed for the first time, the little girl questioned her mother: "Why haven't I got one of those?"

"Be patient, dear," the mother answered knowingly. "If you're good, you'll get one when you grow up. And if you're *very* good, you'll get quite a few."

While swimming in the nude at a deserted California beach, the young chap sustained a painful sunburn over his entire body; and later that night, while in bed with his date, he found the agony almost unbearable. Stepping into the kitchen, he poured a tall glass of cold milk and submerged the object of his greatest discomfort.

"My God!" the girl gasped, watching him from the doorway. "I've always wondered how men load that thing!"

A man returned from a convention and proudly showed his wife a gallon of bourbon he'd won for having the largest sex organ of all present. "What!" she exclaimed. "Do you mean to tell me you exhibited yourself in front of all those people?"

"Only enough to win, darling," he replied. "Only enough to win."

Shortly after arriving at their honeymoon destination, the still-nervous groom became worried about the state of his bride's innocence. Deciding on a direct confrontation, he quickly undressed, pointed at his exposed manhood and asked his mate, "Do you know what that is?"

Without hesitating, she blushingly answered, "That's a wee-wee."

Delighted at the idea of instructing his naïve wife in the ways of love, the husband whispered, "From now on, dearest, this will be called a prick."

"Oh, come now," the girl chided. "I've seen lots of pricks and I assure you, that's a wee-wee."

Stopping to pay a call on some of his suburban constituents, the Congressman found that they were having a party and volunteered to return at a more convenient time. "Don't go," the host begged. "We're playing a game that you might enjoy. We blindfold the women and then they try to guess the identity of the men by feeling their genitals."

"How dare you suggest such a thing to a man of my dignity and stature?" the politician roared.

"You might as well play," the host urged. "Your name's already been guessed three times."

Two American tourists in France stopped a gendarme on the street and complained about the behavior of the druggist down the block. "We went there to buy some prophylactics," one admitted, "but the druggist didn't speak English and we couldn't make him understand what we wanted."

"Please continue," the officer urged.

"I tried to communicate by example," the tourist explained. "I exposed myself to him, put some money on the counter and pointed to my organ. He still didn't get the point, so my friend did the same."

"Did he understand then?" the gendarme asked.

"He smiled as if he did," the American grumbled. "But then he just opened his fly, took out the largest penis I've ever seen and scooped up the money."

The sexy redhead was telling her roommate about an unusual experience she'd had on a date the night before.

"George asked me to pose for him," she said, "in the nude."

"And of course you told him you're not a model," countered the roommate.

"Of course," said the redhead, "but he said that didn't matter, because he's not an artist."

Then there was the amorous actor who tried out for a part in the latest nude play only to find that the position he wanted had already been taken.

The abundantly endowed starlet had just stepped out of the bathtub in her hotel suite and was about to reach for a towel when she caught sight of a window washer taking in all of her charms. The starlet, too stunned to move, stood staring at the man.

"Whatcha lookin' at, lady?" he finally asked. "Aintcha never seen a window washer before?"

We are scholars. Yes we are. We recently traced the origin of the expression, "Hurrah for our side!" back to the crowds lining the streets when Lady Godiva made her famous ride sidesaddle through the streets of Coventry.

A svelte redhead was driving her Jag cross-country last summer. The trip was a hot and dusty one and when she spotted a small pool in a little glade not far off the road, she decided to stop for a swim. She slipped out of her clothes and plunged in, and had been enjoying the cool water a few minutes when she became aware of two farmers watching her from behind some bushes. Her clothes were at the other side of the pool, but there was an old washtub stuck in the sand near her, and holding that in front of her, she marched out of the water towards them.

"Don't you two old fools have anything better to do?" she snapped. "Do you know what I think?!"

"Yes, ma'm," drawled the taller of the two men, "you think that there washtub has a bottom in it."

We know a real friendly hatcheck girl who thinks that strip poker is a swell game because the fellows always give back her clothes.

"Love of my life," said the enraptured husband, "your beauty is such that it should be captured in the nude by the finest sculptor in the world."

Two gentlemen passing by the hotel room happened to overhear the conversation, paused for a moment, then rapped on the door.

"Who's there?" asked the husband.
"Two sculptors from New York," came the answer.

A girl with a well-developed sense of fashion realizes that bare skin never clashes with anything she's wearing.

"I know a place," said the sharp college coed to her sorority sister, "where men don't wear anything, except maybe a watch once in a while."
"Where is that?" the second campus cutie asked eagerly.
"Around the wrist, silly."

Don't ask us where we've been, but we just heard about the two nudists who decided to stop dating because they felt they were seeing too much of each other.

We know a girl who was chased out of a nudist colony because she had something on her mind.

An artist's model is nearly always unsuited for her work.

Vacation time was suntan time as far as Joan, an admirably proportioned secretary, was concerned, and she spent almost all of her day on the roof of her hotel sopping up the warm sun's rays. She wore a bathing suit the first day, but on the second, she decided that no one could see her way up there and she slipped out of it for an overall tan. She'd hardly begun when she heard someone running up the stairs; she was lying on her stomach, so pulling a towel over her derrière, she continued to recline as before.
"Excuse me, miss," said the flustered little assistant manager of the hotel, out of breath from running up the stairs. "The Hotel Plaza doesn't mind your sunning on the roof, but we would very much appreciate your wearing your bathing suit as you did yesterday."
"What difference does it make?" Joan asked rather coolly. "No one can see me up here and besides, I'm covered with a towel."
"Not exactly," said the embarrassed little man. "You're lying on the dining room skylight."

It's easy to admire a good loser at a strip-poker party.

Then there was the little old lady with varicose veins who won first prize at a costume ball. She went nude, as a road map.

She had just finished her shower when the doorbell rang. Tiptoeing to the front door, shivering in plump, pink nudity, she called, "Who is it?"

"The blind man," came a mournful voice, so she shrugged and opened the door with one hand while reaching for her purse with the other. When she turned to face the man, he was grinning from ear to ear, and she saw that he was holding a large package in his arms.

"You can see!" she exclaimed.

"Yeah," he nodded happily. "And mighty pretty, too. Now, where do you want I should put these blinds?"

A couple was strolling hand in hand across the nudist camp when the young male suddenly lowered his head and confessed: "Don't look now, Sally, but I think I'm falling in love with you."

Did you hear about the fellow who took a girl to a nudist camp and discovered that nothing looked good on her?

"That was the dullest party I've ever been to," complained the striking bachelor girl to her roommate. "God, was I bored."

"But you stayed quite a while, didn't you?" asked her roommate.

"Yes—but only because I couldn't find my clothes."

"How did you like your stay at the nudist camp?" asked one bachelor of another.

"Well," responded the neophyte, "the first three days were the hardest."

"Why do you lower your eyes when I say 'I love you'?" the young man asked the attractive girl in the nudist camp.

"To see if it's true," she replied.

A friend of ours, just came back from a nudist wedding, reports that he came within an inch of being best man.

Then there was the neophyte nudist who, despite his efforts to appear inconspicuous, stuck out like a sore thumb.

The popularity of TV Westerns is even influencing milady's dainty underthings: There's a new brassiere on the market that is patterned after television's "*Rawhide*"—it rounds 'em up and heads 'em out.

The history of women's fashions is a movement from skirts that barely covered the instep to skirts that barely cover the step-ins.

A heartening note in women's fashions, of late, is that they're running truer to form.

A sophisticated friend claims that nothing can replace the modern swimsuit—and it practically has.

Girls' dresses have gotten so short we wonder what the designers will be up to next.

The girl who stoops to conquer usually wears a low-cut dress.

Every man likes to see a girl stick to her knitting—especially when she's in a wet bathing suit.

We've always been partial to absent-minded professor jokes. Like the one about the guy who walked into the men's room, unbuttoned his vest and pulled out his necktie.

A fashion expert of our acquaintance predicts that if stretch pants get any tighter, they'll be replaced by spray paint.

The reason the modern girl's bathing suit is real cool is that most of it is real gone.

There's nothing like a girl with a plunging neckline to keep a man on his toes.

An old roué of our acquaintance recently pointed out that about the only thing you can look down on and approve of at the same time is a plunging neckline.

"Don't you know, young lady," said the irate policeman, "that two-piece bathing suits are not allowed on this beach?"
"All right, officer," replied the well-built miss, "which piece would you like me to remove?"

We find ourselves in complete accord with the etiquette expert who says that only well-reared girls should wear slacks.

Some girls get a lot out of a dress, and leave it out.

You're playing strip poker for high stakes when you get to panty-ante.

Strip poker is one game in which the more you lose, the more you have to show for it.

Sign at the entrance of a nudists' colony: "Please bare with us."

A New York fashion designer warns that if hemlines get any shorter, women won't dare sit down and men won't dare stand up.

Our grandmothers believed there was a destiny that shaped their ends, but modern girls put their faith in girdles.

And then there was the retired brassiere manufacturer who still liked to keep his hand in the business.

A women's wear manufacturer has announced a new brassiere called *Embargo*. Doesn't make much sense until you give it the old Serutan twist and spell it backward.

17
WOMEN

One of the oldest, yet most perfect, examples of a redundant expression is the phrase "foolish virgins."

"Do you know what virgins eat for breakfast?" he asked in his most seductive tone.

"No, what?" she replied coyly.

"Hmmm," he said, "just as I thought."

"I never slept with a man until I married your father," declared the stern mother to her wild young daughter. "Will you be able to say the same thing to *your* daughter?"

"Yes," replied the girl, "but not with such a straight face."

A beautiful girl appeared at the gates of Paradise and asked to be admitted. Saint Peter asked her the routine question: "Are you a virgin?"

"Of course," she replied.

To be sure, Saint Peter instructed an angel doctor to examine her. When he was finished, the doctor reported, "I think we can let her in, but I must report that there were seven slight dents in her maiden-head."

Saint Peter decided that he couldn't deny her admittance for such a trifle, so he sent her along to the registration clerk. "Your name?" asked the clerk.

"Snow White," she answered.

At his Sunday sermon, the local preacher lectured his congregation on the evils of sex and now planned to dramatically demonstrate the laxness of their morals. "Brothers and sisters," he exhorted, "upon pain of providential wrath, I want you all to consider your sinfulness. If there be any female virgins among this gathering, let them stand up now, so that we may honor them."

At first, not a single female arose, but then a young woman, holding her small child, stood up in the back row.

"*You?*" shouted the incredulous cleric. "Isn't it true that you're an unwed mother?"

"Right, preacher," the young woman replied. "But did you expect my six-month-old daughter to stand up all by *herself?*"

The very proper spinster didn't go out very often, but she'd had some important shopping to do that morning and so decided to have her lunch in what appeared to be a nice and quite respectable restaurant. With the noontime crowd, many customers shared their tables with strangers: the spinster selected a seat next to an attractive young office girl. The girl finished her sandwich and coffee, then settled back and lit up a cigarette. The older woman controlled herself for a few moments and then snapped, "I'd rather commit adultery than smoke in public."

"So would I," said the girl, "but I only have half an hour for lunch."

We've just heard about the old maid who sued a Miami Beach hotel for cruelty. Seems they gave her a room between two honeymooning couples.

The old maid rushed up to the policeman. "I've been raped, I've been attacked," she cried. "He ripped off my clothing. He smothered me with burning kisses, then he made mad, passionate love to me!"

"Calm yourself, calm yourself, madam," said the officer. "Just when did all this take place?"

"Twenty-three years ago this September," said the woman.

"*Twenty-three years ago!*" he exclaimed. "How do you expect me to arrest anyone for something he did twenty-three years ago?"

"Oh, I don't want you to arrest anyone, officer," said the woman. "I just like to talk about it, that's all."

The guy who first said, "You can't take it with you," had probably never met an old maid.

Said an old maid one fondly remembers,
"Now my days are quite clearly Septembers.
"All my fires have burned low,
"I'll admit that it's so,
"But you still might have fun in the embers."

Then there were the two old maids who went on a drunk—and nearly killed him.

The elderly spinster hired a young lawyer to prepare her will. "I have ten thousand dollars set aside," she explained, "and I want to spend it on *myself*. Nobody in this town has ever paid any attention to me, but they'll sit up and take notice when I die." Warming to the subject, she cackled, "I want to spend all of eight thousand dollars on the biggest, fanciest funeral this town has ever seen!"

"Well," said the lawyer, "that's a lot to pay for burying in these parts, but it's your money, madam, and you're entitled to spend it any way you like. Now what about the other two thousand?"

"I'll take care of that!" the old woman replied with a broad smile. "I've never been to bed with a man, and I aim to try *that* at least once before I'm through. As you can see, I'm not much to look at, but I figure for two thousand dollars I can get me a man that's young enough and handsome enough to please me."

That night, the lawyer reported the conversation to his wife. As they discussed the situation, the wife casually mentioned how nice it would be to have the two thousand dollars.

Minutes later, they were on their way to the spinster's house, the wife driving. As the lawyer stepped from the car, he instructed his wife: "Pick me up in two hours."

Returning at the prescribed hour, the wife tooted the horn. No response from the house. She then blew a prolonged blast. An upstairs window was raised and the lawyer thrust out his head. "Come back in four days," he shouted. "She's decided to let the county bury her."

A much-traveled playboy we know says that in various stages of her life, a woman resembles the continents of the world: From 13 to 18, for example, she's like Africa—virgin territory, unexplored. From 18 to 30, she's like Asia—hot and exotic. From 30 to 45, she's like America—fully explored and free with her resources. From 45 to 55, she's like Europe—exhausted, but not without points of interest. After 55, concludes the playboy, she's like Australia—everybody knows it's down there, but nobody cares much.

Women who insist on wearing the pants frequently discover that it is other women who are wearing the chinchilla.

It is written that a woman doesn't mind if a man is a cad—as long as his convertible is, too.

A gallivanting friend of ours has confided to us that women don't really look for too much in a husband: just someone to spend with the rest of their lives.

Our Research Department has come up with some interesting statistics that prove that four out of five women-haters are women.

All it really takes to separate the men from the boys is girls.

Generally speaking, women are.

A word to the weight-conscious: If you want to get a youthful figure, ask a woman her age.

The reason today's girls will do things their mothers wouldn't think of doing is that their mothers didn't think of doing them.

Some women, like prizefighters, won't go into action until they see a ring.

Women are the kind of problem most men like to wrestle with.

Give some girls an inch and they've got a new bathing suit.

Whoever it was who first called women the fair sex didn't know much about justice.

Women are to blame for most of the lying men do. They insist on asking questions.

If a girl expects to win a man she has to exhibit a generous nature —or else how generous nature has been to her.

Some men don't give women a second thought. The first one covers everything.

If exercise eliminates fat, how come women get double chins?

Too often, when you tell a secret to a girl, it goes in one ear and in another.

The best years of a woman's life are usually counted in man-hours.

Year in and year out, although other colors may make a momentary bid on the fashion scene, the most popular among women remains long green.

The proof that women are all alike is that every one of them thinks she's different.

The difference between a beautiful girl and a female robot is that the robot *stops* making noise when it gets oiled.

Many women could add years to their life if they'd just tell the truth about their age.

"Do you believe in clubs for women?" the young thing asked her dinner companion.

"Yes," he responded, "if kindness fails."

Then there was the nymphomaniac who just hated to be stood up.

Have you heard what they call uncircumcised Jewish babies? Girls.

Two Miami Beach beauties in teeny bikinis were taking their afternoon sunning when one asked, "Did you hear that they're holding a beauty contest here tomorrow night?"

"Sure," replied the other beachnik, blushing. "I won it last night."

Since the sweet young thing was warned by her mother not to talk to strange men, she only speaks to those who act familiar.

Sign in a pharmacy window: FOR THE GIRL WHO HAS EVERY-THING—PENICILLIN.

First prize at a recent costume ball we attended went to a young woman who wore a maternity jacket over her dress, together with the sign: I SHOULD HAVE DANCED ALL NIGHT.

She was a calendar model—until she missed a couple of months.

Some girls go to such lengths to get a mink coat that when they finally get one, they have trouble buttoning it.

Then there was the comely girl who got her birth-control pills mixed up with her saccharin tablets, and now she has the sweetest little baby in town!

A sexy blonde with a stunning figure boarded a bus and, finding no vacant seats, asked a gentleman for his, explaining that she was pregnant. The man stood up at once and gave her his seat, but couldn't help commenting that she didn't look pregnant. "Well," she replied with a smile, "it's only been about half an hour."

Some girls go out every Saturday night and sow wild oats, then go to church on Sunday and pray for a crop failure.

"Blessed are the pure," a waggish friend of ours misquotes, "for they shall inhibit the earth."

Heard tell about the widow who wears black garters in remembrance of those who have passed beyond.

When a girl can read the handwriting on the wall, she's in the wrong rest room.

A do-it-yourselfer named Alice
Used a dynamite stick for a phallus.
They found her vagina
In South Carolina
And part of her anus in Dallas.

He asked her for a burning kiss;
She said in accents cruel,
"I may be quite a red hot gal,
But I'm nobody's fuel."

Girls who think they will hate themselves in the morning should learn to sleep till noon.

A girl's conscience doesn't really keep her from doing anything wrong—it merely keeps her from enjoying it.

The shapely bachelorette was entertaining guests at a cocktail party with an account of the time she had miraculously escaped injury in an elevator whose cable had snapped.

"After you realized you were falling," interrupted one intrigued gentleman, "did the sins of your entire life pass before your eyes?"

"Hardly," she purred. "I only fell eleven floors."

The crowded elevator had just begun to rise when a well-stacked miss screamed and said, "I've been geesed!"

"You mean you've been goosed," corrected the proper fellow standing next to her.

"I can count," came her sarcastic reply.

"Gee," exclaimed the breathless coed, telling her wide-eyed companion all about last night's big panty raid. "This bruiser from the football team got me cornered, so I had to fork over my panties. What else could I do? Later," the miss went on, "I gave him the slip."

The modest maiden had just purchased some lingerie and asked if she might have the sentence "If you can read this, you are too damn close" embroidered on her panties.

"Yes, madam," said the clerk. "I'm quite certain that can be done. Would you prefer block or script letters?"

"Braille," said she.

So seldom is she in her cups, Margie's forgotten what size she takes.

We heard of a club for nymphomaniacs whose meetings consist entirely of examining prospective members.

A fashion expert we know tells us that miniskirts are really quite functional, because they enable girls to run faster—and when they wear them, they have to.

> *Once bedded, your militant miss*
> *Is likely to say with a hiss,*
> *"By God, all us sisters*
> *Would kick out you misters,*
> *If we didn't need* that *to do* this.*"*

The pert young stenographer came bouncing home one evening wearing a gorgeous mink stole. Swirling before her wide-eyed roommate, she asked, "How do I look?"

"Guilty!" came the reply.

A sweet young thing of our acquaintance decided that she would rather be a young man's slave than an old man's darling, because she couldn't stand the idea of old age creeping up on her.

You can't judge the modern girl by her clothes. There isn't enough evidence.

What some young ladies refer to as a diary might be more aptly described as a whodunit.

Rules are the means of a girl's assessing which man she likes well enough to break them for.

Rationing, we're told, is pretty much a thing of the past in Great Britain now. But when the austerity program was in full swing, eggs were very hard to get. One store received its allotment and put a sign in the window, announcing: SALE OF EGGS RESTRICTED TO EXPECTANT MOTHERS.

"Put a dozen eggs under the counter for me," requested one young lady. "I'll call for them in the morning."

Over morning coffee the three shop girls were considering what kind of man they'd prefer being shipwrecked with on a desert island.

"I'd want a fellow who was a wonderful conversationalist," said the first.

"That would be nice," said the second, "but I'd rather have a guy who knew how to hunt and could cook the things he caught."

The third smiled and said, "I'd settle for a good obstetrician."

18
WITS
& HALFWITS

"**I** believe you have the wrong number," said the old gentleman into the phone. "You'll have to call the weather bureau for that information."

"Who was that?" his young wife asked.

"Some guy wanting to know if the coast was clear."

The wife was bent over the breakfast table in pain. "My head aches," she moaned, "I've a terrible pain in my stomach and my left breast burns as if it's on fire."

"Don't fret, sweetheart," soothed hubby. "Here's an aspirin for your head, Alka-Seltzer for your stomach and if you'll lift your breast out of the hot coffee, I'm sure it won't burn so much."

The passionate young thing was having a very difficult time getting across what she wanted from her rather dense boyfriend. Finally, she asked, "Would you like to see where I was operated on for appendicitis?"

"Gosh, no!" he replied. "I hate hospitals."

An old favorite which might bear one more telling is the one about the lady who visited a furniture store and asked to see a "sexual couch."

The salesman, masking his amusement, politely asked, "Don't you perhaps mean a sectional couch, madam?"

"No, no," she replied emphatically. "I'm sure my interior decorator told me I should have a sexual couch for an occasional piece in the living room."

Alfred had been married to lovely Arlene for less than a year and already he was beginning to suspect she was untrue to him.

Forced to leave town for the weekend on a business trip, Alfred explained the problem to his close friend, Wendell, and asked him to keep an eye on his wife while he was away.

Upon his return, Alfred demanded a complete account of Arlene's activities.

"Well," Wendell said, "the night you left a good-looking guy came over to the house. Arlene got all dressed up and they went out to a night club. I followed them and saw them drinking together and dancing very closely. Finally around three in the morning, they got into a cab and I could see them hugging and kissing in the back seat. I followed them back to your house and watched through the living-room window while they mixed more drinks and hugged and kissed each other some more. Then they went into the bedroom and they switched out the lights, so I couldn't see anymore."

"That's the trouble," exclaimed Alfred. "Always that element of doubt!"

The husband wired home that he had been able to wind up his business trip a day early and would be home on Thursday. When he walked into his apartment, however, he found his wife in bed with another man. Furious, he picked up his bag and stormed out; he met his mother-in-law on the street, told her what had happened and announced that he was filing suit for divorce in the morning.

"Give my daughter a chance to explain before you take any action," the older woman pleaded. Reluctantly, he agreed.

An hour later, his mother-in-law phoned the husband at his club.

"I knew my daughter would have an explanation," she said, a note of triumph in her voice. "She didn't receive your telegram!"

An attractive, but not too bright, girl of our acquaintance nearly ruined herself before discovering that what the doctor ordered was not, as she misunderstood, "three hearty males a day."

The two office workers were complaining about the short lunch hours.

"The boss takes an hour-and-a-half every day and expects us to get by on thirty minutes," said Tom.

"If I had an extra fifteen, I could go home for lunch," agreed Bill.

"The boss is never around at noon. Why don't we just *take* the extra fifteen minutes," Tom suggested.

Bill agreed and that very day he went home for lunch. Naturally his wife wasn't expecting him and when he didn't find her in the front part of the house, Bill looked in the bedroom. When he opened the door, he discovered his wife in bed with his boss. Bill backed out of the room quietly, slipped out of the house without being noticed and hurried back to the office.

The following morning Tom asked him if he was going to take the extra fifteen minutes again that day.

"Hell, no," said Bill. "I almost got caught yesterday."

We've just received this tidbit from a usually reliable source concerning a certain Senator who, it seems, had to visit Chicago recently for a Committee Hearing and wanted to take a female acquaintance along.

"I have senatorial immunity," he assured her, "so you needn't be afraid of the Mann Act."

"Afraid of it?" she giggled. "Why, Senator, I just adore it!"

The naïve miss was seated in her doctor's office.

"Our tests indicate that you are pregnant," said the M.D., "and there is every indication that you are going to have twins."

"But how can that be, doctor?" the girl protested. "I've never been out on a double-date in my life."

The high-priced lawyer was sitting in his office when his secretary announced the arrival of a new client: a very sexy dish.

"I wish to divorce my husband," said the dish.

"On what grounds?" the lawyer asked.

"Infidelity," came the reply. "I don't think my husband has been faithful to me."

"What makes you think that?"

"Well," said the dame, "I don't think he's the father of my child."

Janice, the cute upstairs maid in the Johnson household, came to her mistress with a sad story to tell. Janice, it seemed, was going to have a baby—out of wedlock—and she would have to quit. Mrs. Johnson, though stunned, came back with a game offer, for good servants are hard to find, and Janice was good.

"You'll do no such thing, my dear," she said. "You'll have your child here and we'll adopt it and raise it as our own." And so it was arranged, and everybody was happy.

But the following year, it was the same story. Once again Mrs.

Johnson insisted that the family adopt the child and Janice stay on. The third year was a repeat performance.

When Janice came to her for the fourth time, Mrs. Johnson shook her head from side to side. "Janice, Janice," she said, "whatever are we to do with you?"

"There's nothing to be done, madam," said Janice. "This time I'm truly leaving. I refuse to work for such a large family."

The distraught father hurried down the beach to the spot where his lovely daughter lay. A bronzed lifeguard stood over her.

"I've just resuscitated her, sir," he said.

"Then, by God," exclaimed the father, "you'll *marry* the girl!"

A bookseller of our acquaintance admits to having been momentarily flustered when a dewy-eyed damsel asked for a volume she titled *How to Make Friends and Influential People.*

She stood at the teller's window in the bank, a vision of desirable femininity marred only slightly by the fact that the light in her baby-blue eyes was more than somewhat vacant. The teller examined her and the check she wished to cash with equal concentration. Then he asked her if she could identify herself.

For a moment, her lovely brow was corrugated by puzzlement; then, her expression brightening, she pulled a small mirror from her handbag, glanced in it, and, with relief, said, "Yes. It's me all right."

Before you allow yourself to fall in love with a pair of bright eyes, make sure it's not just the sun shining through the back of her head.

We recently met a beautiful creature who is so dumb she believes that the English Channel is the one on TV on which you watch British movies.

Her name was Clarissa and she was curved, Harry decided, in a manner that could only be called awesome. She was also, alas, virtually brainless, but luckily this lack was not a hindrance to the type of entertainment Harry had in mind for the evening. He was, therefore, delighted when she agreed to accompany him to his apartment.

As he mixed the drinks with fingers nervously nimble with anticipation, Clarissa wandered aimlessly around his apartment, pausing here and there to cast a perplexed eye over a book title or painting that eluded her. Finally, she stopped stock-still before his fireplace.

"What in the world is that thing?" she asked, pointing to a carved wooden object resting on the mantel.

"Oh, that's African," he responded. "It was used in fertility rites. Actually, it's a phallic symbol."

"Well," Clarissa said, demurely patting her hair into place, "I'd hate to tell you what it looks like."

Flustered and flushed, Carol sat in the witness chair. The beautiful but empty-headed blonde had gotten herself named corespondent in a divorce case, and was presently being questioned in court.

"So, Miss Jones," the lawyer intoned, "you admit that you went to a hotel with this man?"

"Yes, I do, but I couldn't help it."

"Couldn't help it? Why not?"

"He deceived me."

"And how did he do that?"

"Well," Carol said earnestly, "he told the clerk at the reception desk that I was his wife."

An engaging but somewhat vacant young lady we met recently thought "vice versa" meant dirty poems.

Grace and Martha were from a very prim and proper Eastern finishing school, and they were spending their vacation together in New York; on this particular afternoon, they had accepted an invitation from a bohemian artist, whom they had met a few weeks before on a visit to the Village, to attend an exhibition of his paintings. As they approached an extremely provocative nude, Grace couldn't help noticing that the canvas bore a striking resemblance to her girlfriend.

"Martha," she gasped, "that painting looks exactly like you. Don't tell me you've been posing in the *nude!*"

"Certainly not!" Martha stammered, blushing furiously. "H-he must have painted it from memory."

A number of showgirls were entertaining the troops at a remote Army camp. They had been at it all afternoon and were not only tired but very hungry. Finally at the close of their performance the major asked, "Would you girls like to mess with the enlisted men or the officers this evening?"

"It really doesn't make any difference," spoke up a shapely blonde. "But we've just got to have something to eat first."

Some months ago a rape case was being tried in a Hollywood court. The victim, a movie starlet, was on the stand. "Now then, young lady," the prosecutor began, "please tell the court, in your own words, just what happened. First of all, can you identify the man?"

"That's the one," said the girl, pointing.

"And can you tell the court when this occurred?"

"Yes, sir," she replied thoughtfully. "As I remember, it was last June, July, August and September."

Simple George was no great catch, so when he met a remarkably beautiful girl who seemed to be wildly in love with him, he immediately proposed marriage.

"Poor dear boy," she said, "don't you realize that I'm a nymphomaniac?"

"Darling," replied ardent George, "I don't care if you steal, as long as you're faithful to me."

Strolling into the admitting office of a large hospital, a well-developed lass told the nurse on duty that she wanted to see an upturn.

"You mean an *intern*, don't you, dear?" asked the kindly nurse.

"Well, whatever you call it, I want a contamination," replied the girl.

"You mean *examination*," corrected the nurse.

"Maybe so," allowed the girl. "I want to go to the fraternity ward."

"*Maternity* ward," said the nurse, with a slight smile.

"Look," insisted the girl, "I don't know much about big words but I do know that I haven't demonstrated for two months and I think I'm stagnant."

The cute young trick thought she had a sure winner the other day at the track. The tote board listed her horse as starting at 25 to 1, and she knew the race didn't begin until 1:00 P.M.

On the last night of his first buying trip to Paris, a young furniture importer from America met an attractive French girl in the hotel elevator. She spoke no English, however, and neither could understand a word the other was saying until the resourceful merchant devised a means of communication for the occasion. Taking out a pencil and notebook, he drew a sketch of a taxi. She nodded approvingly, and off they went for a ride in the Bois de Boulogne. A little later, he drew a picture of a table laden with food and wine bottles, and when she nodded her assent, they headed for a sumptuous repast at Maxim's. After dinner, she was delighted with a sketch he made of a dancing couple, so they danced the evening away at a popular Left Bank boîte. Finally the girl picked up the pencil and, with a knowing glance at her clever escort, she proceeded to make a crude drawing of what was clearly intended to be a four-poster bed. He stared at his charming companion in amazement; and when he took her home, while he was kissing her good night on her doorstep, during the long ride back to his hotel, and even on his flight back home the following afternoon, he still couldn't figure out how she had known he was in the furniture business.

An experienced steward on a plush cruise ship was giving a young apprentice advice on how to handle unexpected situations: "If you enter a cabin at an embarrassing moment, pretend not to notice and try to say something to put the passenger at ease. For instance, yesterday I entered a cabin just as a lovely young lady was about to step into the shower. Without a moment's hesitation, I turned away, saying, 'Excuse me, sir,' and went out."

That afternoon, while serving tea to the passengers, the young steward walked in on a honeymoon couple making love in a lower berth. Remembering what he had been told, he promptly turned away and, fumbling with the cups, politely inquired: "Either of you gentlemen take sugar?"

The new bride complained to her doctor about the birth-control pills he had given her.

"What seems to be the problem?" he asked.

"They must not be the right size, doctor," she said. "They keep falling out."

Coming home early from work one afternoon, the exec found his wife lying naked in bed, breathing heavily and clearly distracted.

"Alice, what's the matter?" he asked.

"I think I'm having a heart attack," she gasped.

Quickly, he rushed downstairs to the phone and was dialing a doctor when his son hurried in and exclaimed: "Daddy! There's a naked man in the front closet."

Going over to the closet, the exec opened the door and found his best friend cowering there. "For God's sake, Frank," blustered the husband, "my wife is upstairs having a heart attack and here you are sneaking around scaring the children."

The perky bride returned home with an ultra-Mod, clear-plastic minidress and held it up for her stodgy husband's approval.

"Why, you can see right through it," the astonished husband gasped.

"No you can't, silly," she answered. "Not when I'm in it."

Then there was the secretary who was so dumb she thought a penal colony was an all-male nudist camp.

A business acquaintance informs us that he once hired a not-too-bright stenographer who thought her typewriter was pregnant because it skipped two periods.

A gangster wished to move into the higher levels of society but was afraid his favorite blonde would embarrass him with her unpolished language. He decided to send her away for a very expensive crash course in grammar. She returned three months later, burst into his office and exclaimed, "Were you blue while I was gone?"

"All that money," the mobster moaned, "and she *still* has her tenses wrong."

"I hope you're not planning to be alone in that bachelor's apartment tonight," the worried mother cautioned her daughter.

"Don't be silly," the young thing answered. "He'll be there with me."

A movie-studio president who was not exactly noted for his knowledge of the English language received a well-written story titled *The Optimist.* After reading the manuscript, he called a meeting of the company's most creative minds and announced, "Gentlemen, we got us a great story here, but I want all of you to think of something simpler for a title. There ain't many people will know that an optimist is an eye doctor."

The young reporter was interviewing a woman who had just reached her hundredth birthday.

"To what do you attribute your remarkable good health?" he asked.

"Well," she said, thoughtfully, "I've always eaten moderately, worked hard, I don't smoke or drink and I keep good hours."

"Have you ever been bedridden?" the reporter asked.

"Well, sure," said the elderly lady, "but don't put that in your paper."

An acquaintance of ours thinks the Playboy Foundation is some kind of undergarment the Bunnies wear.

"I think my wife must be going crazy," said the worried little man to his insurance agent. "She's terribly afraid that someone's going to sneak into our house and steal her clothes."

"Would she want me to cover them in a policy?" asked the agent.

"She thinks she's got a better idea," replied the man. "She's hired a guy to stand in the closet and guard them."

Drawn by the crowd, we stopped in at a bookstore recently that had a huge sign in the window reading: NEWLY TRANSLATED FROM THE ORIGINAL FRENCH: 27 MATING POSITIONS.

Inside, copies of the book—pre-wrapped—were selling like hot cakes.

It was only by accident that we heard one harried clerk say to another, after ringing up his 423rd sale of the volume for the day, "This is really the most extraordinary sale I've ever seen for a chess book."

When the announcer on the Armed Forces radio network finished the newscast, he closed with the correct time. "For you Navy men," he said, "it's now eight bells. For you men in the Army, it's now 0800. And for all you officers," he concluded, "the little hand's on eight and the big hand's on twelve."

The cute and efficient young maid seemed to enjoy her work until one day, without warning, she gave notice.

"Why do you wish to leave?" the lady of the house asked her. "Is there anything wrong?"

"I just can't stand the suspense in this house a minute more," the maid replied.

"Suspense?" said the confused mistress. "What do you mean?"

"It's the sign over my bed," the girl explained. "You know, the one that says: WATCH YE, FOR YE KNOW NOT WHEN THE MASTER COMETH."

A colonel was chatting with a young second lieutenant in the officer's club when a major approached, coughed discreetly and said he'd like to speak to the colonel about a matter of some importance. "Go ahead," said the colonel.

"I'd rather not in front of the lieutenant, sir," murmured the major.

"Well," observed the colonel, "spell it, then."

19
DEFINITIONS

ACUTE ALCOHOLIC:	an attractive drunk.
ADOLESCENCE:	the age between puberty and adultery.
ADULTERY:	when a husband is too good to be true.
ADULT WESTERN:	one in which the hero still loves his horse, only now he's worried about it.
ALCATRAZ:	pen with a lifetime guarantee.
ALCOHOLIC:	a guy you don't like who drinks as much as you do.
ALCOHOLIC ACTOR:	a ham on rye.
ALIMONY:	bounty on the mutiny.
	a system by which, when two people make a mistake, one of them has to pay for it.
	the billing without the cooing.
	having an ex-husband you can bank on.
	disinterest, compounded annually.

a splitting headache.

the high cost of leaving.

ANATOMY: something that everybody has, but it looks better on a girl.

APPETIZERS: little things you eat until you lose your appetite.

ARTIFICIAL INSEMINATION: copulation without representation.

inoculate conception.

ARTIST'S MODEL: attireless worker.

ASPHYXIATION: a fanny fetish.

ASSAULT: what every woman likes to be taken with a grain of.

AUTOEROTICISM: doing your own thing.

AUTOMATED: a couple making love in a car.

AVALANCHE: a mountain getting its rocks off.

BACHELOR: a man who believes in life, liberty and the happiness of pursuit.

a man who has no children to speak of.

a fellow who is crazy to get married— and knows it.

a man who never makes the same mistake once.

one who's foot-loose and fiancée free.

a fellow who can take women or leave them and prefers to do both.

a man who thinks seriously about marriage.

a rolling stone who gathers no boss.

a man who never has a bride idea.

a man who believes in wine, women and s'long.

a callous cad who is cheating some good woman out of her alimony.

a guy with a strong will looking for a girl with a weak won't.

a fellow who prefers to ball without the chain.

BACHELOR APARTMENT: a wildlife sanctuary.

BAD TRIP: acid indigestion.

BAR BELLE: something to be picked up.

BAR STOOL: what Daniel Boone stepped in.

BATHING BEAUTY: a girl worth wading for.

BEATNIK: Santa Claus the day after Christmas.

a man who's dropped the job but kept the coffee break.

BEATNIK CANNIBAL: one who eats three squares a day.

BEDBUG: a nymphomaniac.

BEER BARON: malty millionaire.

BELLY-DANCER'S AGENT: abdominal showman.

BIGAMIST:	a fog over Italy.
	a man who has loved not wisely but two well.
BIGAMY and MARRIAGE:	having one wife too many.
BIGOTRY:	an Italian redwood.
BIKINI:	a bare trap.
BISEXUAL:	a man who likes girls as well as the next fellow.
BITCH:	an underdog.
BORE:	a guy with a cocktail glass in one hand and your lapel in the other.
BOW-WOW:	a TV performer's low-cut dress.
BRAGGART:	a man who enters all conversation feat first.
BRAGGING:	the patter of little feats.
BRITISH ATHEIST:	one who doesn't believe in John Lennon.
BROTHEL:	Home Is Where the Tart Is.
BUCCANEER:	a hell of a price to pay for corn.
BUDDHIST:	one who practices yoga bare.
BUFFALO:	a greeting between two nudists.
BULLDOZER:	a chap who sleeps through political speeches.
BURLESQUE:	a broad take-off.

BURLESQUE THEATER: a place where belles peel.

CAD: a man who refuses to help his date with the breakfast dishes.

CALCULATED RISK: a computer date with a girl who doesn't take the pill.

CALL GIRL: a negotiable blonde.

CASTRATION: a eunuch experience.

CAT-O'-NINE-TAILS: a hipster with a busy social life.

CENSOR: a person who sticks his No's into other people's business.

CENTAUR: the world's cheapest hooker.

CHAFING DISH: a girl who has been stood up on a date.

a girl in a tight leotard.

CHAPERONE: one who could never make the team but is still in there intercepting passes.

an elderly woman who accompanies young women to see that they do not indulge in any of the things she would have indulged in if she hadn't been chaperoned when she was a young woman.

CHASTITY BELT: an antithrust suit.

CHASTITY BELT and
UNCHIVALROUS KNIGHT: an antitrust suit, and the unchivalrous knight is the one who files it.

CHERRY COBBLER   a virgin shoemaker.

CHERRY TART   a contradiction in terms.

CHESTNUT: a man who is crazy about well-developed females.

CHEST PROTECTOR: a bouncer at a topless restaurant.

CHIMPANZEE: a gay monkey.

CHINESE VOYEUR: Peking Tom.

CHISELER: a man who goes stag to a wife-swapping party.

CHIVALRY: a man's inclination to help a woman from everyone but himself.

CLEAR CONSCIENCE: poor memory.

CLOTHES LINE: "How would you like a new gown by Givenchy and a cocktail dress by Oleg Cassini?"

COBRA: the kind worn by Siamese twins.

COCKTAIL PARTY: a gathering at which you meet people who drink so much you can't even remember their names.

COCKTAILS: sips that passion the night.

COLLEGE: a fountain of knowledge where all go to drink.

COMIC STRIP: a burlesque queen who tells jokes while she peels.

COMPULSIVE GAMBLER: a guy who'd rather lay a bet than anything.

CONDOMINIUM: a prophylactic for midgets.

CONFIDENCE: picking up a girl who's already walking home from a ride.

CONFIRMED BACHELOR: a man who goes through life without a hitch.

CONNOISSEUR: a man who collects old masters and young mistresses.

CONTINENCE: mind over what matters.

CONTRACEPTIVE: a labor-saving device.

                                 an article to be worn on every conceivable occasion.

CONVERSATION PIECE: a girl men like to talk about.

                                 a gal who likes to talk in bed.

COOKIE: a virgin doughnut.

COOPERATION: an exchange between a man and woman in which she coos while he operates.

COOPERATIVE GIRL: a miss who reclines to answer a question.

COUNTERFEIT MONEY: homemade bread.

COURTSHIP: an entertaining introduction to a dull book.

CROTCH: the place where Lawrence Welk parks his car.

DEATH: nature's way of telling us to slow down.

DEBATE: what lures de fish.

DIFFERENCE BETWEEN FRUSTRATION and PANIC: Frustration is the first time you discover you can't do it the second time. Panic is the second time you discover you can't do it the first time.

DIFFICULT AGE: when she's too old to be a Brownie and too young to be a Bunny.

DIVORCE COURT: a hall of blame.

DOUBLE JOINT: tea for two.

DRIP-DRY: an ignorant teetotaler.

DRIVE-IN: place where a guy parks his car to try out his clutch.

DRIVE-IN MOVIE: wall-to-wall car-petting.

DRY DOCK: a nondrinking member of the medical profession.

ECSTASY: something that happens between the Scotch and soda and the bacon and eggs.

EFFICIENT NURSE: one who can make a patient without disturbing the bed.

EGOTIST: a guy who suffers from I strain.

ELOQUENCE: the ability to describe Raquel Welch
                              without using one's hands.

ENTRANCE EXAM: a premarital checkup.

EROGENOUS ZONE: the skin you love to touch.

EUNUCH: a man cut off from temptation.

EUNUCH KING: an impotentate.

EXECUTIVE SUITE: a sugar daddy.

EXHIBITIONIST: a person who discards three aces in a
                              strip-poker game.

EXOTIC DANCER: a girl who brings home the bacon a strip
                              at a time.

EXPERIENCE: the wonderful knowledge that enables
                              you to recognize a mistake when you
                              make it again.

FAIRY: one who'd rather switch than fight.

FALSE PREGNANCY: laboring under a misconception.

FALSIES: hidden persuaders.

                              extra padded attractions.

                              absentease.

FALSIE SALESMAN: a fuller bust man.

FEAST OF THE VESTAL
VIRGINS: cherries' jubilee.

FLAG-WAVING SPEECH: star-spangled banter.

FOOTBALL GAME: a contest where a spectator takes four
                              quarters to finish a fifth.

FORNICATION:	adultery without benefit of clergy.
FRUSTRATION:	a transvestite in a nudist colony.
	nixed emotions.
FUN-LOVING:	the only kind there is.
G-STRING:	a gownless evening strap.
GAY BLADE:	the Fire Island fencing champion.
GENIUS:	a nudist with a memory for faces.
GIGOLO:	a fee-male.
GIRLS' SCHOOL:	an institution of higher yearning.
GLASS:	Chinese marijuana.
GOLD-DIGGER:	a girl who breaks dates by going out with them.
	a human gimme pig.
	a girl who's got what it takes to take what you've got.
	a gal who believes in sinner take all.
	fund-loving girl.
GOOD CLEAN FUN:	a couple taking a bath together.
GOOD SCOUT:	someone who knows the lay of the land and will take you to her.
GOSSIP:	someone who puts one and one together—even if they're not.

GOURMET:	a man who is invited for an evening of wine, women and song—and asks what kind of wine.
GRIMACE:	a World War I pilot with one wing shot away.
HANGOVER:	wrath of grapes.
HAPPINESS:	finding the owner of a lost bikini.
HAPPY MARRIED COUPLE:	husband out with another man's wife.
HARLOT:	a place that sells used hars.
HARP:	a nude Steinway.
HENPECKED HUSBAND:	one who is afraid to tell his pregnant wife that he is sterile.
HERMAPHRODITE:	bisexual built for two.
HIGH-FIDELITY:	a drunk who goes home regularly to his wife.
HIGH NOON:	a four-Martini lunch.
HISTORICAL NOVEL:	one with a shapely wench on the jacket, and no jacket on the shapely wench.
HOLLYWOOD:	a city where they put beautiful frames in pictures.
	a place where you can lie on the sand and look at the stars. Or vice-versa.
HOME COOKING:	the place many a man thinks his wife is.
HOMOGENEOUS:	a wise old queer.
HOMOSEXUAL:	a man's man.

HOMOSEXUALITY: a mutual aberration society.

HORIZON: a call girl hopping out of the sack.

HULA: a shake in the grass.

HUNGARIAN: a physically well-endowed man from Gary, Indiana.

HUSBAND: an unfortunate who began by handing out a line and ended by walking it.

HYMEN: a greeting to male companions.

HYPOCHONDRIAC: one who can't leave being well enough alone.

ILLEGITIMATE CHILD: a bungle of joy.

IMMATURITY: knowing where it's at—but not what it's for.

IMPOTENCE: emission impossible.

INCEST: sibling revelry or a sport the whole
                               family can enjoy.

                               rolling your own.

                               sibling ribaldry.

                               having the kin you love to touch.

INDIVIDUALIST: a man who lives in the city and com-
                               mutes to the suburbs.

INHIBITIONS: being tied up in nots.

INTELLECTUAL GIRL: one who can think up excuses that her
                               boyfriend's wife will believe.

INTOXICATION: a physical state in which one feels so-
                               phisticated without being able to pro-
                               nounce it.

IRONY: a windy day when, just as a beautiful
                               girl with a short skirt approaches, dust
                               blows in your eyes.

IVY LEAGUE DRINKER: one who buckles from the back.

JAMAICA: what's usually asked of a fraternity man
                               when he comes back from a date.

JURY: a group of twelve people selected to
                               decide who has the better lawyer.

KISS: an application for a better position.

KOOL-AID: charity for hippies.

LAS VEGAS: a great place to get tanned and faded at
                               the same time.

LATE DATE IN PARIS: keeping a girl up until the *oui* hours of
                               the morning.

LATENT HOMOSEXUALITY: swishful thinking.

TO LAY: the object of a proposition.

LEGAL SECRETARY: any girl over eighteen.

LESBIAN: a mannish depressive with delusions of gender.

LESBIAN COCKTAIL LOUNGE: a her-she bar.

LESBIANS: bosom buddies.

LIBERTINE: a swinging adolescent.

LIQUOR STORE: a stupor market.

LOCOMOTIVE: a crazy reason for doing it.

LOGARITHM: a Catholic birth-control record.

LOUSY BASTARD: a fellow who sits in church and scratches while his parents get married.

LOVE LETTER: something that often turns out to be a noose paper.

LOVER'S LEAP: the distance between twin beds.

LOW-CLASS BROTHEL: humpty-dumpty.

THE LSD SET: high society.

LUCK: what a man has when he meets a girl who's at the age when her voice is changing from "No" to "Yes."

MADAM: someone for whom the belles toil.

one who offers vice to the love-lorn.

MADISON AVENUE EXECU-
TIVE: one who takes the padding out of his
                                    shoulders and puts it on his expense ac-
                                    count.

MAD-MONEY: psychiatrist's fee.

MAIDEN AUNT: a girl who never had sense enough to
                                    say uncle.

MAIDENHEAD: a virgin who trips out regularly.

MAN HATER: a girl who makes love with her eyes
                                    closed—because she can't stand to see a
                                    guy having a good time.

MANIC DEPRESSIVE: a person whose philosophy is: easy
                                    glum, easy glow.

MARIJUANA: the only kind of grass capable of mow-
                                    ing down the gardener.

MARRIAGE: like taking a bath—not so hot once you
                                    get accustomed to it.

                                    the evil aye.

                                    wall-to-wall carping.

                                    an expensive way to have a woman for
                                    nothing.

MASOCHISM: the agony of the ecstasy.

MASOCHIST: one who would rather be switched than
                                    fight.

                                    a person who gets his kicks getting his
                                    kicks.

MASSEURS: people who knead people.

MATERNITY DRESSMAKER: a mother frocker.

MATE SWAPPING: intermarital extracourse.

MERMAID: a bottomless girl in a topless suit.

METALLURGIST: a man who can look at a platinum blonde and tell whether she is virgin metal or a common ore.

METEOR: what most girls are than Twiggy.

METEOROLOGIST: a man who can look into a girl's eyes and predict whether.

MINIMUM: a tiny British mother.

MINUTE-MAN: a fellow who double-parks in front of a house of ill repute.

MISTRESS: a cutie on the q.t.

halfway between a mister and a mattress.

MONASTERY: a home for unwed fathers.

MONEY: the poor man's credit card.

MONKEY WRENCH: injury sustained at a discothèque.

MONOTONY: marriage to one woman at a time.

MORALITY: that instinctive sense of right and wrong that tells some people how everyone else should behave.

MOTEL: a love-inn.

MOTHER'S DAY: nine months after Father's Day.

MOURNER: the same as "nooner"—only sooner.

MUSIC LOVER:	a girl who'll do it for a song.
NAÏVE FATHER:	one who thinks his daughter has been a good girl because she returns from a date with a Gideon Bible in her purse.
NATURALIST (Las Vegas edition):	a fellow who throws sevens.
NAVAHO ERECTION:	a scrotum pole.
NEUROTIC:	a person who worries about things that didn't happen in the past, instead of worrying about something that won't happen in the future, like normal people.
	a woman who likes a psychiatrist's couch better than a double bed.
NICE GIRL:	one who whispers sweet nothing-doings in your ear.
NIGHT CLUB:	a place where the tables are reserved but the patrons aren't.
NOEL COWARD:	a guy who's afraid to go home to his wife after the office Christmas party.
NUDISM:	a different way of looking at things.
	exposure with composure.
NUDIST:	one who suffers from clothestrophobia.
	a buff buff.
NUDIST CAMP:	a place where the peeling is mutual.
	a place where nothing goes on.
NUDIST COLONY:	a place where men and women air their differences.

NUDISTS: people who go in for altogetherness.

NYMPHOMANIA: aye trouble.

a disease in which the patient enjoys being bedridden.

NYMPHOMANIAC: a go-go-go-go girl.

a girl who belives that it's every man for herself.

OFFICE CHRISTMAS PARTY: best way for a secretary to get a raise while lying down on the job.

OLD AGE: a time when a man sees a pretty girl and it arouses his memory instead of his hopes.

OLD-FASHIONED GIRL: the one who gets kissed good-night instead of good morning.

OLD MAID: a girl of twenty-four—where she should be about thirty-six.

a confirmed hope addict.

OPTIMIST: a husband who goes down to the marriage bureau to see if his license has expired.

a man who sits in the last row of a theater and winks at the showgirls.

a pregnant showgirl who rubs vanishing cream on her stomach.

a man who makes a motel reservation before a blind date.

a man who, after coming home unexpectedly and finding cigar butts in the

ashtrays, decides his wife must have
given up cigarettes.

ORAL CONTRACEPTIVE: the word "no."

ORGASM: the gland finale.

ORGY: group therapy.

                             a screw ball.

ORIENTAL GROCERY
CLERK: a Chinese checker.

PAJAMAS: item of clothing usually placed next to
                             the bed in case of fire.

PANSY: one who likes his vice versa.

PAPOOSE: a consolation prize for a chance on an
                             Indian blanket.

PARANOID: a couple interrupted by a cop in lovers'
                             lane.

PARLAY: one that is just average.

PATIENCE: the difference between rape and seduc-
                             tion.

PEEPING TOM: a window fan.

PEER GROUP: a voyeurs' club.

PENICILLIN: what you give the man who has every-
                             thing.

PERAMBULATOR: last year's fun on wheels.

PESSIMIST: one who has faith in future degenera-
                             tions.

PESSIMIST—OPTIMIST: A pessimist is a man who thinks women are bad, and an optimist is one who hopes they are.

PETTING PARTY: an affair that lasts until someone gives in, gives up or gives out.

PEYOTE: a trance plant.

PHILANDERER: a man with a perfect sense of two-timing.

PICNIC and PANIC
(Difference BETWEEN): twenty-eight days.

PIÉCE DE RÉSISTANCE: A French virgin.

PILLAGE: about sixteen for most girls.

PIMP: a snatch purser.

a fornicaterer

PLATONIC FRIENDSHIP: what develops when two people grow tired of making love to each other.

PLATONIC RELATIONSHIP: mind over mattress.

PLAYBOY: a man with an eye for an aye.

POISE: raising only your eyebrows on your first trip to a nudist camp.

POLITICAL MODERATE: a guy who makes enemies left and right.

POLYUNSATURATED: a dry parrot.

POPULAR GIRL: one who has been weighed in the balance and found wanton.

POPULATION EXPLOSION: the result of so many overbearing
                                women.

                                when people take leave of their census.

POTHOLDER: what you don't want to be when the
                                fuzz arrives.

POT ROAST: cookout for grassheads.

POWDER: what a guy takes if his girl forgets her
                                pill.

PRACTICAL NURSE: one who falls in love with a wealthy old
                                patient.

PREGNANCY: taking seriously something that was
                                poked in fun.

PRIMATE: a sultan's favorite wife.

PROPOSAL: a proposition that lost its nerve.

PROSTITUTE: a member of the fare sex.

                                a busy body.

PROSTITUTE, OFFSPRING
OF A: brothel sprouts.

PROSTITUTION: fee love.

                                the only business in which profits go up
                                when the assets go down.

PROTEIN: a call girl too young to vote.

                                an adolescent call girl.

PRUDERY: meddle-class morality.

PSYCHIATRIST: someone who doesn't have to worry as long as other people do.

PSYCHOLOGIST: a man who watches everybody else when a beautiful girl enters the room.

PUBERTY: that time in every girl's life when she's fit to be tried.

PURITAN: a man who no's what he likes.

PUSHOVER: a girl who is dedicated to the proposition.

PYLON: what a nymphomaniac might say at a nude beach party.

RACEHORSE: an animal that can take several thousand people for a ride at the same time.

RACE RIOT: a din of inequity.

RACE TRACK: a place where windows clean people.

RAMIFICATION: what made Mary have a little lamb.

RAPE: an assault with a friendly weapon.

unnegotiated piece.

RELAY: the second time around.

REMARRIAGE: the triumph of hope over experience.

REPEAL: a stripteaser's encore.

SADIST: one who is kind to masochists.

that little old whine-maker.

a man who gives a paralytic friend a self-winding wrist watch.

SAFETY BELT:	the one you don't drink before driving home.
SAINT VALENTINE'S DAY MASSACRE:	a gang-bang.
SALESMAN:	a guy who can make his girlfriend feel sorry for the chick who lost her bra in his car.
SALESMANSHIP:	the difference between rape and rapture.
SCABBARD:	a non-union poet.
SCORE PAD:	a bachelor apartment.
SCRATCH PAD:	a Greenwich Village bank.
SEDUCTION:	genital persuasion.
SEX:	the most fun you can have without laughing.
SEX DRIVE:	a trip to a motel.
	trying to find a motel that has a vacancy.
SEX LECTURE:	a sermon on the mount.
SEX SURVEY:	a pubic-opinion poll.
SEXUAL REVOLUTION:	copulation explosion.
SHEBANG:	a girl who can't say no.
SHORT AFFAIR:	leer today, yawn tomorrow.
SHOTGUN WEDDING:	a case of wife or death.
SHRUNKEN HEAD:	a pot-smoking midget.

SINGING STRIPTEASER: a skin diva.

SLEEP: that which if you don't get enough of, you wake up half a.

SLIPCOVER: a maternity dress.

SNAKE DANCER: woman who can writhe to the occasion.

SNOW JOB: something a man uses to defrost a woman.

SPECIMEN: an Italian astronaut.

SPICE: the plural of spouse.

SPINSTER: a girl aged in the wouldn't.

an unlusted number.

SPORT OF KINGS: queens.

STAGNATION: a country of fun-loving males.

STALEMATE:	last season's girlfriend.
	a moldy spouse.
STICK SHIFT:	one of Twiggy's dresses.
STOIC:	de boid what brings de babies.
STRAPLESS EVENING GOWN:	a bust-truster.
STRIP POKER:	a card game that begins according to Hoyle and ends according to Kinsey.
SUBURB:	a community in which a man will lend you his wife but not his golf clubs.
SUBURBAN HUSBAND:	a gardener with sex privileges.
SUCCESS:	making money to pay the taxes you wouldn't be paying if you hadn't made so much money in the first place.
SUGAR DADDY:	a man who can afford to raise Cain.
SUICIDE:	the sincerest form of self-criticism.
SUMMERTIME:	the season when there's nothing much on radio, TV or most girls at the beach.
SUN BATHING:	a fry in the ointment.
SYCOPHANT:	a mentally disturbed pachyderm.
SYMPATHY:	that which one woman offers another in exchange for the details.
SYNONYM:	a word you use when you can't spell the other one.
TATTLETALE:	a girl who talks about her affairs.
TAX OFFICE:	a den of inequity.

TAXPAYERS:	people who don't have to pass a civil-service exam in order to work for the government.
TEASE:	a girl who is always thinking of a man's happiness—and how to prevent it.
TITILLATE:	a tardy meal for a breast-fed baby.
TOLL-HOUSE COOKIE:	a cute prostitute.
TRADE RELATIONS:	what incestuous couples do at a wife-swapping party.
TRANSISTOR:	a girl who used to be your brother.
TRANSVESTITE:	a fellow who likes to eat, drink and be Mary.
	a drag addict.
TRIPLETS:	what you might get from small doses of LSD.
TWIST EXPERT:	the torque of the town.
TWO, THREE, FOUR:	TWO is company, THREE is a crowd and FOUR is a wife-swapping party.
UNDERCOVER AGENT:	a girl spy.
UNICORN:	a horse with a horn on.
URINATION:	what Israel was told in 1948.
VAN DYKE:	a truck-driving Lesbian.
VICIOUS CIRCLE:	a wedding ring.
VIRGIN:	a chick who no's everybody.
	a girl who hasn't met her maker.

VIRGIN BRIDE:	a right-ring extremist.
VOLUPTUOUS WOMAN:	one who has curves in places where some girls don't even have places.
VOYEURISM:	looking at the world through roué's-colored glasses.
WEDDING RING:	a one-man band.
WELL-BALANCED GIRL:	one with an empty head and a full sweater.
WELL-PROPORTIONED GIRL:	one with a narrow waist and a broad mind.
WHIPPED CREAM:	masochistic milk.
WHIPPERSNAPPER:	the photographer at a flagellation party.
WIENER:	the first to cross the line in a Mexican horse race.
WIFE:	the woman who stands by her husband through all the trouble he wouldn't have had if he'd stayed single.
WIFE-SWAPPING:	a type of sexual fourplay.
WILL:	a dead giveaway.
WINDOW DRESSER:	a girl who doesn't pull down the shades.
WINTER:	the season of the year when gentlemen befur blondes.
WOLF:	a man who has a retirement plan for girls.
	a man with a little black book of cancelled chicks.

a man who treats all women as sequels.

WOMEN'S COURT: a place where many girls are tried and found wanton.

YES MAN: one who stoops to concur.

ZEBRA: the largest size a woman can buy.

ZOMBIE: something some men drink and other men marry.

20
PLAYS
ON WORDS

Our Research Department tells us that in the days of Queen Elizabeth I, some ladies-in-waiting liked to curl up with a good book, while others were satisfied with one of the pages.

Imagine the girl's surprise when she walked into the playboy's apartment and discovered he had no chairs, no tables, no bed, no furniture at all. She was floored!

For her first week's salary, the gorgeous new secretary was given an exquisite nightgown of imported lace. The next week her salary was raised.

We just overheard a couple of our pretty stenographers discussing one of the more dashing members of our staff. "He dresses so well," said one.
"And so quickly," replied the other.

The best dressed woman at a recent society ball was the lovely Miss Agnes S. Stevens, whose gown was cut so low in back it revealed her initials.

From London comes the story of the three professors of literature who, while returning from luncheon, encountered several ladies of pleasure who were patrolling the street *en masse.* "What might one call such a congregation?" mused the first professor, a Shakespearean specialist: "A flourish of strumpets?"
The second professor, being an authority on the novels of Anthony Trollope, naturally contributed "A chapter of trollops."

But the best description, we think, came from the youngest and least specialized of the professors. He called the ladies "An anthology of pro's."

The svelte young secretary was dissatisfied with her job and so walked into her boss' office one morning and announced that she had found a new position.

"Excellent," the boss exclaimed. "We must try it at once!"

Canned and frozen juices are becoming more and more popular, but most men still prefer to squeeze their own tomatoes.

We just heard about the street cleaner who got fired because he couldn't keep his mind in the gutter.

"To me," said one, "he's a pain in the neck."

"Strange," said the other, "I had a much lower opinion of him."

The husband who knows where his wife keeps her nickels and dimes has nothing on the husband who knows where to find the maid's quarters.

The movie producer traveled all the way to Europe, but had to return to Hollywood disappointed. He contacted the beautiful Italian actress he'd been seeking, all right, but, unfortunately, she refused to come across.

"Darling," he breathed, "after making love I doubt if I'll ever be able to get over you—so would you mind answering the phone?"

The sophisticated lady was approached on the dance floor by a gentleman slightly her junior.

"I'm sorry," she said in a superior tone, "but I couldn't dance with a child."

"Oh, I'm sorry," he said. "I didn't know your condition."

A world-traveling friend who has just returned from Tibet, informs us that a "coolie" is a quickie in the snow.

In a recent discussion on world affairs, a friend observed the difference between war and peace is there has never been a good war.

"My mother," said the sweet young steno, "says there are some things a girl should not do before twenty."

"Your mother is right," said the junior exec. "I don't like a large audience either."

Verily, a man never knows whether he likes bathing beauties until he has bathed one.

Our Research Department has come up with the significant statistic that the average number of times a girl says no to temptation is once weakly.

Girls who look good in the best places usually get taken there.

"Hey, wise guy," complained the delightful dish, "what's the big idea? You promised you'd take me to Florida!"

"I said nothing of the sort," insisted her gentleman friend. "I merely commented that I was going to Tampa with you."

A yachtsman we know told us that he bought his bountiful girl a bikini and anticipates seeing her beam with delight.

The new bank employee in the finance department was dictating to his comely secretary. He paused, uncertain about the proper use of a word in his next sentence.

"Do you 'retire a loan'?" he asked the girl.

"Not when I can help it," she replied with a demure smile.

Word is in from the Middle East about the sultan who left a call for seven in the morning.

The coed cutie returned to the sorority house after her first breakfast date at a neighboring fraternity with her steady boyfriend. Asked what she had, she replied dreamily, "Him and eggs."

"Why, hello, there," said the sultry brunette to the young exec as he entered the elevator. "How's tall, dark and hands?"

"May I be of help, sir?" asked the impeccably attired, haughty salesman in the foreign-car showroom.

"Yep," said the casually dressed and obviously self-made man of means. "My girlfriend isn't feeling well. Wha'cha got in the way of a get-well car?"

"Don't you think he dresses nattily?" asked one secretary of another regarding the young executive walking past the water cooler.

"Natalie who?" her co-worker demanded.

A switch on the oldest Party Joke in the world goes like so: Who was that lady I saw you outwit last night?

An ornithologist of our acquaintance is troubled by the fact that the stork is too often held responsible for circumstances that might better be attributed to a lark.

A woman with a past attracts men who hope history will repeat itself.

Passionate picnickers should bear in mind that some girls are like flowers—they grow wild in the woods.

The curvy redhead was wearing something she called an Atomic Bikini—50 percent fallout. "If anybody tries to criticize this bathing suit," she declared, "I'll just laugh it off."

In the traditional ocean-liner interview, the reporter said to the glamorous movie queen, "I understand you were courted by many European noblemen during your four weeks abroad."

"That's right, honey," she replied, hiking her skirt still higher and smiling into the flashing cameras. "I managed to make every second count."

Cynthia's fine figure had been poured into a beautiful form-fitting gown and she made a point of calling her date's attention to it over and over again throughout the evening. Finally over a nightcap in his apartment he said, "You've been talking about that dress all evening long. You called my attention to it first when we met for cocktails, mentioned it again at dinner and still again at the theater. Now that we're here alone in my penthouse, what do you say we drop the subject?"

Next to a beautiful girl, sleep is the most wonderful thing in the world.

Almost as pitiable as the fellow who was tried and found wanting is the guy who wanted and was found trying.

History credits Adam and Eve with being the first bookkeepers, because they invented the loose-leaf system.

You never know how a girl will turn out until her folks turn in.

A girl should use what Mother Nature gave her before Father Time takes it away.

Some men like big girls, other like little lasses.

Latest word we have from Hollywood concerns a young producer moving into lavish new offices who had his interior decorator on the carpet because she'd forgotten to include a studio couch.

Pierre, the passionate masseur, was recently fired when he rubbed a lady customer the wrong way.

Sometimes a girl can attract a man by her mind, but more often she can attract him by what she doesn't mind.

A good resolution is like many a pretty modern girl—easy to make but hard to keep.

After a pleasant picnic in the woods, Mark described his girlfriend as the down-to-earth type.

Girls who don't repulse men's advances advance men's pulses.

Whether or not a girl in a rented bathing suit attracts a lot of attention depends primarily on where the rent is.

The man who can read women like a book usually likes to read in bed.

Some girls make friends quickly. With strangers it takes a little longer.

The wife of a pal of ours is suing for divorce. She claims he was spending his nights sitting up with a chic friend.

When a boy is young he thinks girls are made with sugar and spice and everything nice. When he gets older, he discovers that it only takes sugar.

Gently massaging the trick knee of his curvacious young patient, the doctor inquired:

"What's a joint like this doing in a nice girl like you?"

Americans are people who insist on living in the present, tense.

Two models were conversing chicly on a street corner when a third went riding by in a brand-new compact car, waving to them gaily.

"I understand," meowed one, patting her hair into place, "that she did it for a Lark."

Many a girl owes the fact that she's a prominent figure to a prominent figure.

Some women take a man to the cleaners as soon as they spot him.

A wag-about-town we know told us recently that his current girlfriend is truly electric. "In fact," he added, "everything she owns is charged."

"But Robert," she gasped, "why did you park here when there are so many nicer spots farther down the road?"

He stopped what he was doing just long enough to mutter, "Because I believe in love at first site."

The John Birch Society is reportedly organizing a youth auxiliary —the Sons of Birches.

Many a man has been slapped because his hand was quicker than the aye.

We know a girl who thinks she's a robot just because she was made by a scientist.

"Daughter," said the suspicious father, "that young man who's been walking you through the park strikes me as being exceedingly unpolished."

"Well," she answered coyly, "he *is* a little rough around the hedges."

"What are you reading?" asked the prison librarian.

"Nothing much," replied the prisoner. "Just the usual escape literature."

We've just heard that the Italian government is installing a clock in the Leaning Tower of Pisa. Reason? What good is it if you have the inclination, but don't have the time?

A chorus cutie who always slept in the buff awoke one morning to find herself completely dressed. "My God," she cried, "I've been draped!"

Then there was the movie actress who climbed the ladder of success, wrong by wrong.

Who says the dieting craze is wearing thin? We know a guy whose girlfriend told him that if it wasn't for Metrecal she wouldn't be able to get into her pants. So he's been drinking the stuff ever since.

Overheard at El Morocco: "She's the kind of girl you could fall madly in bed with."

Then there was the coffee bean who, though she could be made instantly, still preferred the old grind.

Then there was the college girl who was expelled from school for having a record player in her room—the local disc jockey.

She was only the telegrapher's daughter, but she didit, didit, didit. . . .

We suppose you've heard about the farmer's daughter who got sent home from the country fair because she couldn't keep her calves together.

Why a man would want a wife is a big mystery to some people. Why a man would want *two* wives is a bigamystery.

The next phase in the space race is sure to make headlines: Scientists are planning to put three hundred head of cattle into orbit. It'll be the herd shot round the world.

When the sultan entered his harem unexpectedly, his wives let out a terrified sheik.

The man who likes to lie in bed can usually find a girl willing to listen to him.

The manufacturer of a well-known tonic for people with "tired" blood received this testimonial from a little old lady who lived on a farm in Tennessee: "Before taking your tonic," the woman wrote, "I was too tired to hoe the fields or pick the cotton. But after only two bottles of your delicious mixture, I've become the best cotton-picking hoer in the county."

And, of course, you've also heard about the village smithy who made his living selling iron chastity belts at forty dollars a crack.

We know a hundred-dollar-a-night call girl working the Minneapolis–St. Paul area. Customers nicknamed her the tail of two cities.

When her gardener suddenly took ill, the wealthy matron decided to visit him in the hospital. Approaching the visitors' desk, she announced, "I've come to see Mr. Johnston in room six-thirteen."

"Are you his wife?" asked the nurse on duty.

"Certainly not!" retorted the haughty dowager. "I'm his mistress."

One nice thing about the battle of the sexes—it will never be a cold war.

The British anthropologist was doing some research in an isolated African village, and the local tribal leader asked if he would like to attend a trial his people were conducting that afternoon. "I think you'll be surprised," said the chief, "at how well we've copied your country's legal procedures. You see, we have read the accounts of many English trials in your newspapers."

When the scientist arrived at the crudely constructed courthouse, he was indeed amazed at how closely the African court officials resembled those of his native land. Both counsels were suitably attired in long black robes and the traditional white powdered wigs worn by all British jurists, each arguing his case with eloquence and proper judicial propriety. But he couldn't help being puzzled by the occasional appearance of a bare-breasted tribal maiden who ran through the crowd waving her arms frantically. After the trial, the anthropologist congratulated his host on what he had seen and then asked, "What was the purpose of having a seminude woman run through the courtroom during the trial?"

"No purpose," replied the tribal chieftain, "but all the accounts we read in your papers about British trials invariably mention something about 'an excited titter' running through the gallery."

We were not particularly surprised to learn recently that Democrats generally have more children than Republicans. After all, who ever heard of anyone enjoying a good piece of elephant?

The battle of the sexes will never be won by either side, because there's too much fraternizing with the enemy.

During his examination of a newly arrived Viennese film starlet, a Hollywood gynecologist inquired, "Have you had a checkup within the past year, miss?"

"I don't believe so, darlink," she purred. "Just an occasional Hungarian or two."

Many a girl with a big wardrobe started out with just a little slip.

An English friend reports that during a recent trip to Africa he was a luncheon guest at a monastery and was served such delicious fish and chips that he asked the good brothers if he might be allowed to meet the cook, in order to thank him personally for the delicious meal. There were several men working in the kitchen and our friend asked which of them had prepared the fish and chips.

"Well, I'm the fish friar," one man replied, "and that's the chip monk over there."

A wedding ring may not be as tight as a tourniquet, but it does an equally good job of stopping circulation.

A friend of ours says that an ounce of suggestion is sometimes worth a pound of lure.

The prof was telling his eight A.M. class, "I've found that the best way to start the day is to exercise for five minutes, take a deep breath of air and then finish with a cold shower. Then I feel rosy all over."

A sleepy voice from the back of the room responded: "Tell us more about Rosy."

And then there was the eager young miss who, after a young man grabbed her knee, exclaimed, "Heaven's above!"

A young man walked into a drugstore that was being tended by the owner's somewhat prudish wife. "May I have six contraceptives, miss?" he asked.

"Don't 'miss' me," she replied.

"OK," the eager fellow said, "better make it seven."

We've heard about a girl who wanted a divorce because her husband was getting indifferent.

A knowledgeable friend of ours informs us that when a girl tells her boyfriend she's a perfect thirty-eight, she should expect him to grasp what she's talking about.

Some coeds have a faculty for making love, while others just have a student body.

The striking but rather plump coed visited the kindly campus psychiatrist to report despondently that she thought she was losing her boyfriend.

"Why don't you diet?" asked the good doctor.

"That's a groovy idea," said the coed. "What color do you think he'd like?"

"I'm sorry, miss," said the county clerk, "I can't issue your marriage license until you've filled out your form."

Almost in tears, the girl replied, "Well, if my boyfriend doesn't care, I don't see why you should."

Walking up to the hardware-store clerk, the attractive female asked: "Can you give me a screw for a doorknob?"

"Sure," replied the clerk, "and if you're good, I'll buy you dinner besides."

"What would you like for Christmas?" the sophisticated parents asked their young son.

"I wanna watch," he answered, so they let him.

During a visit to the zoo, the inquisitive child asked: "Mommy, how do lions make love?"

"I don't know, dear," replied the mother. "Most of your father's friends are Rotarians."

Then there were the two Burmese girls looking for a Mandalay.

"My wife's an angel," observed the little man to the chap sitting next to him at the bar.

"You're lucky," answered the other. "Mine's still alive."

The sexy coed was being driven back to college by her wealthy father's chauffeur when a tire blew out. Seeing that the chauffeur couldn't remove the hubcap, the girl reached for the toolbox and asked, "Do you want a screwdriver?"

"Might as well," he muttered. "I sure can't get this damn hubcap off."

According to a waggish pundit we know, the trouble with political jokes is that they sometimes get elected.

Then there was the sweet young nymph who hated to be laughed at but didn't mind being satyrized.

Then there was the bachelor who continually felt the need to insert his masculinity.

A muscle-bound beach bum was showing off by lifting two bikinied beauties high in the air, one on each arm. "Wow," said a nearby girlwatcher to his crony, "look at the dolls on that boob!"

Then there was the lusty swan who left his pond during the mating season, stopped the first human he saw and demanded, "Take me to your Leda."

The shapely topless dancer went to Mass dressed in her working clothes, but was stopped at the door by the priest. "Miss," he said, "you can't go in like that."

"But, Father," protested the churchgoer, "I have a divine right."

"And your left isn't bad, either," the man of the cloth responded, "but you still can't enter the church without covering your head."

A handsome advertising executive attended a party given by a female co-worker and left with an extremely attractive guest. In the office the next morning, he thanked the hostess and explained that he really liked her friend. "Oh, she's not really a friend of mine," the girl responded, "only an acquaintance."

"Well, in that case," the exec chuckled, "I'm happy to have made your acquaintance."

Convicted of murder and sentenced to death, the shapely young lady asked, as a last request, that she be hanged in the nude. Although the warden thought this unusual, he felt a last request was not something to be denied. When the condemned prisoner arrived at the gallows, the hangman gasped, "My God, you have the most beautiful body I've ever seen."

Came the whispered reply, "It's all yours if you keep your trap shut."